VOCA

突破英文词汇10000

刘 毅 编著

（美）Laura E. Stewart 校阅

外语教学与研究出版社
FOREIGN LANGUAGE TEACHING AND RESEARCH PRESS
北京 BEIJING

京权图字：01-2003-5141

图书在版编目（CIP）数据

突破英文词汇10000 / 刘毅编著. — 北京 ：外语教学与研究出版社，2009.6（2019.1 重印）
ISBN 978-7-5600-8650-7

I. ①突… II. ①刘… III. ①英语－词汇 IV. ①H313

中国版本图书馆CIP数据核字(2009)第089420号

出版人　蔡剑峰
责任编辑　于晓皖
封面设计　彭　山
版式设计　张　峰
出版发行　外语教学与研究出版社
社　址　北京市西三环北路19号（100089）
网　址　http://www.fltrp.com
印　刷　北京京科印刷有限公司
开　本　889×1194　1/32
印　张　14.375
版　次　2009年7月第1版　2019年1月第19次印刷
书　号　ISBN 978-7-5600-8650-7
定　价　27.90元（含MP3光盘一张）

购书咨询：（010）88819926　电子邮箱：club@fltrp.com
外研书店：https://waiyants.tmall.com
凡印刷、装订质量问题，请联系我社印制部
联系电话：（010）61207896　电子邮箱：zhijian@fltrp.com
凡侵权、盗版书籍线索，请联系我社法律事务部
举报电话：（010）88817519　电子邮箱：banquan@fltrp.com
物料号：186500001

序 言

学习英文最常遇到的一个问题，便是词汇量不足。一个词汇量不足的人，在英文听、写、说各方面的能力都会受到严重的限制，因此往往无法适当地与英美人士沟通；在参加考试时，更经常因为看不懂题目，而不知如何作答。

有鉴于此，我们特别为广大读者编写了一系列的词汇丛书。从最基本的Vocabulary Fundamental，到足以应付留学考试之需的Vocabulary 22000，循序渐进，为您扎实地打好词汇基础。无论您正在学校求学或已步入社会，都会发现本系列书籍就是您苦寻已久、增强英文实力的最佳利器。学校老师也可采用本系列书籍作为辅助教材，以弥补平日上课内容之不足。

一般均认为背单词是件既吃力、又往往不见成效的苦差事，因而总是望之却步。本系列书籍的问世恰可打破以上观念。以下列出词汇系列丛书的各项特点：

1. 以“课”为单元，容易安排学习进度，也避免了背词典式学习方法的冗长与杂乱无章。

2. 每个单词均附有国际音标、词性说明及中文解释。

3. 适当列出各单词的衍生词、同义词或反义词，以达到举一反三、事半功倍的效果。

4. 以例句说明单词的用法，各例句附有汉语译文，以便于参考。

5. 每一部分后均有习题，以加深对所学单词的印象；每一课后面附有效果检测，以检验对所学单词的理解程度，并增强活用单词的能力。

词汇量的增加绝非一蹴而就的，但是若能采用系统的方法，依旧可缩短增加词汇量所需的时间。因此，本系列丛书的读者，只要按部就班，循序渐进，必可在最短的时间内，获得最大的成效。请切记随时要活用所学的单词，唯有如此，这些词汇才真正成为您自己的词汇。

Vocabulary 10000

1. 本书所列单词共计 1,300 个，加上各词的衍生词、同义词及反义词，则实际收录约 2,500 词，均属于难度较高的词，经常在书籍及报刊杂志上出现。读完本书，您的词汇量应当在 10,000 词以上。

2. 详细列出各词的国际音标、词性说明及中文解释，省却查词典的麻烦，另附有英文解释，以培养直接用英文思考、判断的能力。中英文解释均是以该词最常用的意义为主，一词若有若干常用解释或词性，则一并列出。单词后面附有例句，以说明该词的用法；例句附有中文翻译，可对照参考。

3. 每一课分为五个部分，有助于分段记忆。课前有预备测验，每一部分之后有习题，课后有效果检测，可借助于重复测验来加深对单词的印象，并学会如何活用单词。

4. 本书共分为 24 课。其中，第 1 课至第 5 课列出了各单词的同义词，第 6 课至第 10 课列出了反义词，第 11 课至第 15 课则列出衍生词，借以迅速扩大读者的词汇范围。在第 20 课至第 24 课中则列举出许多词形、词义比较接近的单词，直接加以比较分析，以达到正确使用单词的目的。

编者

目录

LESSON 1

预备测验

选出最恰当的答案：

1. A monument was built to *commemorate* the ______.
   (A) caution (B) victory (C) building
2. The children *huddled* together for ______.
   (A) warmth (B) travel (C) expenditure
3. *Censure* is sometimes harder to bear than ______.
   (A) fortitude (B) praise (C) punishment
4. The new vaccine *eradicated* all traces of the ______ within three months.
   (A) wealth (B) disease (C) crime
5. The barbarians *defiled* the church by using it as a ______.
   (A) stable (B) temple (C) shrine

解答 1. B 2. A 3. C 4. B 5. A

第一部分

WORD	MEANING	TYPICAL USE
abdomen /ˈæbdəmen, æbˈdəʊ-/ *n.* (人体的)腹部 同 belly	the middle part of the body containing the stomach and bowels	The pregnant woman has an enlarged ***abdomen***. 那位孕妇大腹便便。

WORD	MEANING	TYPICAL USE
bereave /bɪˈriːv/ *v.* 1. 剥夺；使丧失	1. deprive ruthlessly; rob; take away	The lost hikers were ***bereft*** of hope when the rescue plane did not see them. 救援的飞机没有看到他们，那些迷路的远足者丧失了希望。
2. 使丧失(亲属等)而孤独 同 deprive	2. leave desolate and alone	The children are ***bereaved*** by the death of their parents. 那些死了父母亲的孩子是孤独可怜的。
consecrate /ˈkɒnsɪkreɪt/ *v.* 奉为神圣；尊崇 同 devote	devote to some special use; make holy or sacred	This battlefield is ***consecrated*** to the memory of the soldiers who died here. 这个战场被视为圣地以纪念死在这里的战士。
evoke /ɪˈvəʊk/ *v.* 唤起；引起 同 invoke	bring out; call forth; cause to appear	A good joke does not necessarily ***evoke*** a hearty laugh. 好笑话并不一定逗人大笑。
groove /ɡruːv/ *n.* 沟；槽；凹线 同 furrow	a long narrow channel or furrow; corrugation; rut	Wheels left ***grooves*** in a muddy dirt road. 车轮在泥泞的路上留下了凹痕。

WORD	MEANING	TYPICAL USE
jolt /dʒəʊlt/ *v.* 摇动;使颠簸 同 joggle	shake roughly; shake with sudden jerks	The old car ***jolted*** its passengers badly as it went over the rough road. 那辆旧车子驶过崎岖不平的道路时,把乘客颠得很厉害。
obsolete /ˈɒbsəliːt/ *adj.* 作废的;过时的 同 antiquated	no longer in use; out of date	Bowing to greet a lady is now an ***obsolete*** custom. 如今,见面时向女士行鞠躬礼已是过时的习俗。
prowl /praʊl/ *v.* (为寻觅、偷窃等)潜行 同 rove	wander about quietly and secretly in search of something; stroll	Many wild animals ***prowl*** at night looking for something to eat. 许多野兽夜出潜行觅食。
scoop /skuːp/ *v.* 掘;挖 同 shovel	dig out; hollow out	The children ***scooped*** holes in the sand. 孩子们挖沙坑。
status /ˈstætəs/ *n.* 状况;地位 同 situation	state or condition of affairs; position; standing; stage	Diplomats are interested in the ***status*** of world affairs. 外交家关心世界局势。

WORD	MEANING	TYPICAL USE
sue /sjuː, suː/ v. 起诉;控告 同 indict	start a law case against; appeal to; charge; impeach	The farmer ***sued*** the railroad station because his cow was killed by the train. 那位农夫控告火车站,因为他的牛被火车轧死了。

EXERCISE 1.1 从第一部分中选出最恰当的单词,填入空格内:

1. The counter of the sink has many ______ along which the water will run off.
2. The cat ______ around the cellar looking for mice.
3. We all sympathized with the husband who was ______ of his beloved wife.
4. Her singing ______ admiration from the public.
5. We still use this machine though it is ______.

解答 1. grooves 2. prowled 3. bereaved
4. evoked 5. obsolete

第二部分

WORD	MEANING	TYPICAL USE
bandit /ˈbændɪt/ *n.* 强盗;土匪 同 brigand	a highway man or robber, especially one of a gang; outlaw	The ***bandit*** in a typical Western movie rides a horse and goes armed, either alone or in a group. 在典型的西部片中,土匪不管是独自一人还是成群结队,都骑着马且全副武装。
commemorate /kəˈmeməreɪt/ *v.* 纪念;庆祝 同 celebrate	honor the memory of; observe	Christmas ***commemorates*** the birth of Jesus Christ. 圣诞节是庆祝耶稣基督诞生的节日。
defile /dɪˈfaɪl/ *v.* 弄脏;弄污 同 infect	make dirty or impure; pollute; sully	The children's muddy shoes ***defiled*** all the rugs in the hotel. 孩子们沾满烂泥的鞋子弄脏了旅馆所有的地毯。
deviation /ˌdiːvɪˈeɪʃən/ *n.* 离题;偏差 同 delegate	turning aside; divergence; detour	Running in the hall is a ***deviation*** from the school rules and will not be allowed. 在走廊里奔跑是违反校规的行为,因而是不允许的。

1127

WORD	MEANING	TYPICAL USE
fortitude /ˈfɔːtɪtjuːd/ *n.* 坚韧;刚毅 同 endurance	courage in facing pain, danger or trouble; firmness of spirit	She could bear the disappointments of other people with tolerable ***fortitude***. 她能够毅然忍受他人带给她的失望。
inconsolable /ˌɪnkənˈsəʊləbl/ *adj.* 伤心的 同 depressed	not to be comforted; brokenhearted	The little girl was ***inconsolable*** at the loss of her kitten. 那个小女孩因失去了她的小猫而伤心不已。
nibble /ˈnɪbl/ *v.* 啃;细咬 同 bite	eat away with quick, small bites as a rabbit or a mouse does	Aren't you hungry? You are only ***nibbling*** your food. 你不饿吗? 你只是一点一点啃着吃东西。
pageant /ˈpædʒənt/ *n.* 壮观;虚饰 同 exhibition	an elaborate spectacle; exposition	The coronation of the new king was a splendid ***pageant***. 新国王的加冕典礼非常壮观。
scourge /skɜːdʒ/ *n.* 引起灾害的事物或人 同 disaster	something or someone which causes great trouble or misfortune	After the ***scourge*** of flood usually comes the ***scourge*** of disease. 洪水过后往往会有瘟疫发生。

WORD	MEANING	TYPICAL USE
tumble /ˈtʌmbl/ *v.* 跌落;跌倒 同 fall	fall to the ground; fall suddenly and violently	The crippled child ***tumbled*** down the stairs and was badly hurt. 那跛脚的小孩从楼梯上跌下来,受伤很重。

EXERCISE 1.2 从第二部分中选出最恰当的单词,填入空格内:

1. The iron in the ship caused a(n) ______ of the magnetic needle of the compass.
2. A marathon runner must have great ______ to run such a long distance.
3. The pretty girl's reputation was ______ by malicious gossips.
4. The boy is just learning to walk; he is always ______ over the floor.
5. The inauguration ceremony of the new President was a splendid ______.

答案 1. deviation 2. fortitude 3. defiled 4. tumbling 5. pageant

第三部分

1.27

WORD	MEANING	TYPICAL USE
afflict /əˈflɪkt/ *v.* 使痛苦 同 distress	cause pain to; trouble very much; sicken; ail	There are many illnesses which ***afflict*** old people. 老人承受许多疾病带来的痛苦。

WORD	MEANING	TYPICAL USE
censure /ˈsenʃə(r)/ *v.* 责难 同 blame	express an unfavorable opinion; reprove; reproach	His employer ***censured*** him for neglecting his work. 他的老板责备他工作玩忽大意。
dissimulation /dɪˌsɪmjʊˈleɪʃən/ *n.* 假装;掩饰 同 deception	the act of deceit; hypocrisy; pretention; make believe	The thief intruded into the house with caution and ***dissimulation***. 窃贼小心掩饰着闯入屋内。
flog /flɒg/ *v.* 重打;鞭笞 同 spank	beat or whip hard; paddle; cane	Nowadays, it is an inhumane punishment to ***flog*** the disobedient soldiers or sailors. 现今,鞭笞不服从的士兵或水手是不人道的惩罚。
inscription /ɪnˈskrɪpʃən/ *n.* 题字;碑铭 同 caption	something written on a monument, coin, etc.; heading; epigraph	According to the ***inscription*** on its cornerstone, this building was erected in 1919. 根据基石上的碑铭,这栋建筑建于1919年。
meddle /ˈmedl/ *v.* 干预或扰乱他人之事 同 intervene	touch unnecessarily; interfere; butt in	The gifts of charity ***meddled*** with a gentleman's private affair. 慈善捐赠扰乱了一位绅士的私事。

WORD	MEANING	TYPICAL USE
posture /ˈpɒstʃə(r)/ *n.* 人体的姿势 同 attitude	the position of the body; way of holding the body; demeanor	He doesn't sit straight; his ***posture*** is very bad. 他坐得不正;他的姿势很糟糕。
rummage /ˈrʌmɪdʒ/ *v.* 翻寻;寻找 同 ransack	search thoroughly by moving things about; search	John ***rummaged*** all the drawers to find his gloves. 约翰为了寻找他的手套,翻遍了所有的抽屉。
spout /spaʊt/ *v.* 喷出;涌出 同 pour	come or send out suddenly in a stream; eject; exude	The water ***spouted*** out when the pipe was broken. 当水管破裂时,水喷涌而出。
traverse /trəˈvɜːs/ *v.* 走过;横过 同 intersect	pass across, over or through; cut across; bisect	The climber ***traversed*** a long horizontal crack in the face of the mountain slope. 登山者横越山坡表面的水平裂缝。
wistful /ˈwɪstfʊl/ *adj.* 渴望的 同 yearning	wishful; longing; desirous; wantful	A child stood looking with ***wistful*** eyes at the toys in the shop window. 小孩站在橱窗前看着里面的玩具,眼中流露出渴求的神情。

EXERCISE 1.3 从第三部分中选出最恰当的单词，填入空格内：

1. He was ______ his horse in a very cruel way.
2. She ______ for change from the bottom of her purse.
3. The law does not ______ unduly with a person's private life.
4. The lights ______ the sky searching for enemy planes.
5. The ______ on the ancient monument was very hard to read.

解答 1. flogging 2. rummaged 3. meddle 4. traversed 5. inscription

第四部分

WORD	MEANING	TYPICAL USE
amicable /ˈæmɪkəbl/ *adj.* 友善的 同 amiable	having or showing a friendly attitude; affable; agreeable	The ***amicable*** flash of her white teeth was very impressive. 她友善地一笑，露出雪白的牙齿，给人留下很深刻的印象。
blizzard /ˈblɪzəd/ *n.* 大风雪；暴风雪 同 snowstorm	a long severe snowfall	The soldiers are very exhausted for they have advanced forward without rest in a ***blizzard***. 士兵们筋疲力尽，因为他们在暴风雪中不间断地持续行军。

WORD	MEANING	TYPICAL USE
cruise /kruːz/ v. 往返航行;海上巡弋 同 voyage	sail or travel about from place to place for pleasure or on business	If I were rich, I would like to ***cruise*** in the Southern Pacific for six months in a private yacht. 假如我有钱的话,我要乘私人游艇在南太平洋上航行六个月。
eradicate /ɪˈrædɪkeɪt/ v. 根除;歼灭 同 extirpate	get rid of entirely; destroy completely; annihilate; uproot	Yellow fever has been ***eradicated*** in the United States but it still exists in some countries. 黄热病在美国已经绝迹,但在一些国家却依然存在。
glimmer /ˈglɪmə(r)/ n. 微光 同 gleam	a faint, unsteady light; glow; flicker	The doctor's report gave us only a ***glimmer*** of hope. 医生的报告仅仅给了我们一丝希望。
lump /lʌmp/ n. 堆;团;大量 同 block	a mass of something solid without a special size or shape; bump	On his desk, many articles and documents are always piled in a great ***lump***. 他的桌上总是堆着一大堆东西和文件。
ransack /ˈrænsæk/ v. 细细搜索 同 rummage	search thoroughly through; scour	The woman ***ransacked*** the house for her lost jewelry. 那女人仔细搜查房屋,寻找丢失的珠宝。

WORD	MEANING	TYPICAL USE
slash /slæʃ/ *v.* (以剑、刀等)砍 同 gash	make long, quick cuts with something sharp	He ***slashed*** a path through the high grass with a long knife. 他用一把长刀在高高的草丛中开辟出一条小径。
slump /slʌmp/ *v.* 陷;猛然落下 同 depress	drop or fall heavily or suddenly	Our feet ***slumped*** repeatedly through the melting ice. 经过正在融化的冰时,我们的脚一再地陷下去。
vogue /vəʊg/ *n.* 时尚;流行 同 fashion	popularity or acceptance; mode	That pop-song had a great ***vogue*** at one time. 那首通俗歌曲有一阵子非常流行。

EXERCISE 1.4 从第四部分中选出最适当的单词,填入空格内:

1. Enemy soldiers ______ the city and carried off its treasures.
2. Tired from his long walk, he ______ into a chair.
3. We saw the ______ of a distant light through the trees.
4. He used to have a great ______ as a film actor, but no one goes to the cinema to see him now.
5. What the Ice Age did was to ______ the abundant mammalian life in the northern hemisphere.

答案 1. ransacked 2. slumped 3. glimmer
4. vogue 5. eradicate

第五部分

WORD	MEANING	TYPICAL USE
ascribe (**to**) /əsˈkraɪb/ *v.* 将……归因于…… 同 attribute	think as caused or coming from; assign (to)	He ***ascribes*** his success to skill and hard work. 他把他的成功归因于技巧和辛勤的工作。
bulwark /ˈbʊlwək/ *n.* 壁垒；堡垒 同 safeguard	a person, thing or idea that is a defense or a protection; support	The soldiers kept their heads down behind the ***bulwark***. 士兵们低着头，躲在堡垒的后面。
dubious /ˈdjuːbɪəs/ *adj.* 惊疑的；暧昧的 同 doubtful	uncertain; ambiguous; not very good or reliable	She looked around this way and that in a ***dubious*** manner. 她用一种怀疑的态度审视四周。
facet /ˈfæsɪt/ *n.* (事情的)一面 同 aspect	any of the many parts of subject to be considered; phase	Selfishness was a ***facet*** of his character that we seldom saw before. 我们以前很少看到他个性中自私的一面。

WORD	MEANING	TYPICAL USE
heed /hiːd/ *n.* 注意 同 attention	give careful attention to; take notice of; mind	For the first time he had to pay ***heed*** to his appearance, and in fact he became very well-dressed from then on. 那是他第一次不得不去注意自己的外表，而事实上从那时起他的穿着就考究起来了。
huddle /ˈhʌdl/ *v.* 挤成一团 同 gather	crowd close; press in a mass or heap	The boys ***huddled*** together under the rock to keep warm. 男孩们在岩石下缩成一团相互取暖。
mumble /ˈmʌmbl/ *v.* 喃喃而言；咕哝 同 murmur	speak unclearly; speak in a low tone; mutter; whisper	The old man ***mumbled*** something to me, but I could not understand him. 那老人向我咕哝了一些事，但是我听不懂他在说什么。
relic /ˈrelɪk/ *n.* 遗迹；遗物；遗俗 同 remainder	a thing, custom, or the remains left from the past	This ruined bridge is a ***relic*** of the Gulf War. 这座破败不堪的桥是海湾战争遗留下来的。

WORD	MEANING	TYPICAL USE
smog /smɒg/ *n.* 烟雾 同 fume	a combination of smoke and fog in the air	Automobile exhaust fumes are one of the major causes of ***smog***. 汽车排出的废气是造成烟雾的主要原因之一。
wayfarer /ˈweɪˌfɛərə(r)/ *n.* 旅人；徒步旅行者 同 traveller	a tourist, especially one who travels on foot; journeyer	The thirsty ***wayfarer*** was glad to find a fresh spring near the road. 口干舌燥的旅行者发现了路边的清泉，非常高兴。
wont /wəʊnt, wɒnt/ *n.* 习惯 同 habit	habitude; rule; practice; custom	He always speaks with his mouth full of food; it is his ***wont***. 他总是满嘴塞满食物就说话；这是他的习惯。

EXERCISE 1.5 从第五部分中选出最恰当的单词，填入空格内：

1. Four people were ______ under one umbrella to avoid the sudden shower.
2. I'm feeling better than yesterday, but it is ______ that I can go to school tomorrow.
3. No one knows who wrote that play, but it is usually ______ to Cyril Tourneur.
4. The Americans believe that a free press and free speech are ______ of democracy.

5. Take ______ of what I say, or you will fail in the final examination.

解答 1. huddled 2. dubious 3. ascribed
4. bulwarks 5. heed

效果检测

EXERCISE 1.6 找出与其他三个不相关的词：

______ 1. (A) abdomen (B) intuition
(C) belly (D) paunch

______ 2. (A) contaminate (B) defile
(C) inflect (D) pollute

______ 3. (A) torment (B) distress
(C) afflict (D) cheat

______ 4. (A) hurricane (B) blizzard
(C) draught (D) tempest

______ 5. (A) out-of-date (B) antiquated
(C) obsolete (D) impolite

______ 6. (A) burglar (B) outlaw
(C) bandit (D) chisel

______ 7. (A) bereave (B) deprive
(C) nibble (D) rob

______ 8. (A) discharge (B) blame
(C) reprove (D) censure

______ 9. (A) endurance (B) resolution
(C) fortitude (D) emphasis

______ 10. (A) rummage (B) explore
(C) ransack (D) search

解答 1. B 2. C 3. D 4. C 5. D
6. D 7. C 8. A 9. D 10. B

EXERCISE 1.7 读下面的句子,选出句中斜体词所代表的意义:

______ 1. At one time, criminals were *flogged* as a punishment.
(A) confined (B) killed
(C) buried (D) whipped

______ 2. The value of the jewelry was very *dubious*.
(A) uncertain (B) tremendous
(C) trifling (D) various

______ 3. Roman emperors built arches to *commemorate* their victories.
(A) encourage (B) record in history
(C) celebrate (D) publicize widely

______ 4. A doctor's life is *consecrated* to curing poor and sick people.
(A) limited (B) dedicated
(C) subjected (D) depended

______ 5. You must not *censure* him until you know the whole story about his mistakes.
(A) reprove (B) insult
(C) doubt (D) despise

______ 6. The police *ascribed* the automobile accident to fast driving.
(A) supposed (B) attributed
(C) described (D) illustrated

______ 7. Instead of fighting, the two nations settled the quarrel in an *amicable* way.
(A) natural (B) negotiative
(C) peaceable (D) reasonable

______ 8. Most science books written 20 years ago are now *obsolete*.

(A) antiquated (B) more useful

(C) studied again (D) very expensive

______ 9. There seems to be a *vogue* for sailing small boats this summer.

(A) difficulty (B) utility

(C) fashion (D) request

______ 10. Rain runs down a *spout* from the roof to the ground.

(A) flow (B) dust

(C) seed (D) filth

解答 1. D 2. A 3. C 4. B 5. A
6. B 7. C 8. A 9. C 10. A

EXERCISE 1.8 找出与斜体词意义最接近的单词:

______ 1. good *posture*

(A) attitude (B) personality

(C) placard (D) profession

______ 2. insect's *abdomen*

(A) harm (B) instinct

(C) characteristic (D) belly

______ 3. *bulwark* of freedom

(A) definition (B) tyranny

(C) protection (D) disturbance

______ 4. the mounted *bandit*

(A) knight (B) robber

(C) instrument (D) urn

______ 5. the *scourge* of Heaven

(A) bliss (B) delusion

(C) expectation　　(D) punishment

解答　1. A　2. D　3. C　4. B　5. D

EXERCISE 1.9 从下列生词中选出最恰当的词,填入空格内:

VOCABULARY LIST

censure	consecrated	defiled	inconsolable
obsolete	rummaged	huddle	spout
eradicate	groove	meddle	heed

1. One country should not ______ with the internal affairs of another.
2. The police officers ______ the ship in search of drugs.
3. He ______ his whole life to the service of his country's welfare.
4. No tyrant can hope to ______ the love of liberty, which is strongly embedded in men's hearts.
5. The death penalty for theft has long been ______.
6. No one will defend them if they incur public ______.
7. The river was ______ by the wastes poured out of many factories.
8. He cut a(n) ______ in the wood with a chisel to make the water run off along it.
9. They were warned repeatedly, but they were careless and did not give ______.
10. The mother cat was ______ because her kitten died a few days ago.

解答

1. meddle　2. rummaged　3. consecrated
4. eradicate　5. obsolete　6. censure
7. defiled　8. groove　9. heed
10. inconsolable

LESSON 2

预备测验

选出最恰当的答案：

1. The cross-road in front of the school is a *menace* to the ______.

   (A) children's safety　(B) traffic rules

   (C) construction of buildings

2. The girl's dresses showed most of the *hues* of the ______.

   (A) admiration　(B) rainbow　(C) fashion

3. My brother was *absolved* of ______ for the automobile accident.

   (A) cause　(B) prediction　(C) blame

4. The ______ was standing in the *pulpit* to give a sermon.

   (A) pastor　(B) shadow　(C) pillar

5. He ______ numerous *fractures* in his fox hunting days.

   (A) captured　(B) suffered　(C) wished

解答 1. A 2. B 3. C 4. A 5. B

第一部分

WORD	MEANING	TYPICAL USE
absolve /əbˈzɒlv/ *v.* 赦免 同 exonerate	free from sin, guilt, responsibility; exculpate; clear	The judge ***absolved*** the man of the crime. 法官赦免了那个人的罪。

WORD	MEANING	TYPICAL USE
bias /ˈbaɪəs/ *n.* 偏见 同 prejudice	leaning of the mind; inclination; preconception	The umpire should have no ***bias*** in favor of either side. 裁判员对双方应不偏不倚。
contend /kənˈtend/ *v.* 竞争；辩论 同 compete	struggle against; fight; argue; contest	Our baseball team is ***contending*** for the championship. 我们棒球队在争夺冠军。
deplore /dɪˈplɔː(r)/ *v.* 悲痛；深悔 同 lament	be very sorry about; regret deeply; mourn; grieve	We ***deplore*** the terrible traffic accident, in which 30 persons were killed and 50 injured. 这次可怕的车祸造成30人死亡，50人受伤，对此我们感到悲痛不已。
fracture /ˈfræktʃə(r)/ *n.* 骨折；断裂 同 shatter	a break or crack, especially of a bone; split; splinter	The boy fell from a tree and suffered ***fractures*** of his right arm and leg. 男孩从树上摔下来，造成右胳膊和右腿骨折。
magnitude /ˈmægnɪtjuːd/ *n.* 大小；量，长(度) 同 bulk	greatness of size or importance; extent; mass	A crowd of great ***magnitude*** attended the President's inauguration. 大批民众参加了总统的就职典礼。

WORD	MEANING	TYPICAL USE
pith /pɪθ/ *n.* 精华部分 同 essence	the important or essential part; point; marrow	The ***pith*** of his speech was focused on the importance of education. 强调教育的重要性是他演讲的精华部分。
relish /ˈrelɪʃ/ *n.* 胃口;喜好 同 zest	a good favor; pleasure; taste; appetite; savor; flavor	I have no ***relish*** for seeing people being whipped. 我不喜欢看到别人被鞭笞。
sneak /sniːk/ *v.* 潜行;行为鬼祟 同 lurk	move silently and secretly, usually for a bad purpose; go stealthily	Trying not to be seen, they quietly ***sneaked*** into the room. 为了不被人瞧见,他们鬼鬼祟祟地进入房间。
tidings /ˈtaɪdɪŋz/ *n.* 消息 同 information	a message; news; intelligence	The messenger brought ***tidings*** from the battle-field. 报信者带来战场上的消息。

EXERCISE 2.1 从第一部分中选出最恰当的单词,填入空格内:

1. The first settlers in America had to ______ with unfriendly Indians, sickness, coldness, and lack of food.
2. A ______ of the leg can be very serious in old people.
3. Most newspapers try not to show ______ in their reporting.
4. They say that hunger is the best ______ for food.

5. The book was a work of such ______ that it took 10 years to write.

答案 1. contend 2. fracture 3. bias 4. relish 5. magnitude

第二部分

WORD	MEANING	TYPICAL USE
aghast /əˈgɑːst/ *adj.* 惊骇的；恐怖的 同 astonished	filled with surprise, horror, or terror; surprised	Many people would be ***aghast*** at the thought of another war. 许多人一想到再打仗就觉得很恐怖。
cumber /ˈkʌmbə(r)/ *v.* 阻碍；拖累 同 hinder	trouble or burden with something useless or unnecessary	We shall not ***cumber*** our thoughts with his reproaches. 他的谴责不会妨碍到我们的想法。
decree /dɪˈkriː/ *v.* 命令；决定 同 determine	give an order; to order or settle by authority; decide	The city government ***decreed*** that all dogs must be licensed. 市政府颁布法令，所有的狗都必须有牌照。
frolic /ˈfrɒlɪk/ *v.* 嬉戏；作乐 同 frisk	play in gay and lively manner; play about joyously	The children were ***frolicking*** with the puppy in the backyard. 小孩们和小狗在后院玩耍。

WORD	MEANING	TYPICAL USE
intercourse /ˈɪntə(ɜː)kɔːs/ *n.* 交往;交通 同 relations	connection; communication; transactions	There was much commercial ***intercourse*** between the two countries before World War Ⅱ. 第二次世界大战前,这两个国家之间有许多商业往来。
menace /ˈmenəs/ *n.* 威胁 同 intimidation	something that threatens; threat	In dry weather forest fires are a great ***menace***. 天气干燥时森林火灾是一大威胁。
precipice /ˈpresɪpɪs/ *n.* 悬崖 同 cliff	a very steep cliff or slope; crag or steep mountainside	I was standing on the very edge of a bank, a ***precipice*** not less than fifty feet deep. 我站在海岸的最边缘,那里是一个五十多英尺深的悬崖。
sanctuary /ˈsæŋktjʊərɪ/ *n.* 圣所;圣堂;神殿 同 shrine	a sacred place; a temple	The church is generally considered as a ***sanctuary***. 教堂通常被认为是神圣的地方。

WORD	MEANING	TYPICAL USE
sprout /spraʊt/ *v.* 长出;发芽 同 grow	begin to grow; shoot forth	After a light spring rain, leaves began to ***sprout*** from trees. 一场小小的春雨后,树木开始冒出新芽。
tread /tred/ *v.* 行走于;步行于 同 trample	set the foot down; walk or step on	She ***trod*** lightly in order not to wake the sleeping baby. 她轻手轻脚地走,以免吵醒睡梦中的婴儿。

EXERCISE 2.2 从第二部分中选出最恰当的单词,填入空格内:

1. They have ______ that all the conflicts between countries should end.
2. After a shower a meadow ______ with the yellow buds of dandelion.
3. The gunman ______ him with weapons and forced him to give up his money.
4. My friend's suggestion that we should run away from home left my sister ______.
5. Airplanes, good roads and telephones make ______ with different parts of the country far easier than it was 50 years ago.

解答 1. decreed 2. sprouts 3. menaced 4. aghast 5. intercourse

第三部分

WORD	MEANING	TYPICAL USE
ammunition /ˌæmjʊˈnɪʃən/ *n.* 弹药;军火 同 bullets	supplies of what is needed for firing guns; cartridge	The soldiers still had their guns but they were out of ***ammunition***. 士兵们枪炮还在,却没有弹药。
doting /ˈdəʊtɪŋ/ *adj.* 过于喜爱的;溺爱的 同 fond	foolishly fond; too fond; loving blindly	The ***doting*** mother alienates her husband by lavishing too much love on their child. 这个溺爱孩子的母亲给了孩子太多的爱,以至于疏远了丈夫。
engross /ɪnˈgrəʊs/ *v.* 全神贯注于 同 absorb	occupy wholly; fill up completely; take up attention of	The artist was so ***engrossed*** in his painting that he didn't notice the people watching him. 这位艺术家太专注于作画,以至于没注意到人们在看他。
gush /gʌʃ/ *n.* 涌出;倾流 同 flow	a rush of water or other liquid from an enclosed place; stream	If you got a deep cut in your arm, there's usually a ***gush*** of blood. 假使你的手臂上有很深的割伤,通常会有鲜血涌出。

WORD	MEANING	TYPICAL USE
insuperable /ɪnˈsjuːpərəbl/ *adj.* 不能超越的；不能克服的 同 unconquerable	too difficult to be conquered or passed; unbeatable	The deep river was an ***insuperable*** barrier to those who could not swim. 对不会游泳的人来说，这条深河是无法超越的障碍。
ordeal /ɔːˈdiːl/ *n.* 残酷的考验；痛苦的考验 同 trial	a severe test or experience; tribulation	Her life has been full of ***ordeals***: sickness, poverty and loss of her beloved son. 她生活坎坷：身患疾病、穷困潦倒，还失去了深爱的儿子。
pouch /paʊtʃ/ *n.* 小袋；囊 同 sack	a bag; a small bag attached in the pocket; poke	He kept his tobacco in a leather ***pouch*** fastened to the belt. 他把烟草放在腰带上的皮囊中。
screech /skriːtʃ/ *v.* 尖叫；发出尖锐刺耳的声音 同 shriek	give a sharp, high scream; cry; shrill	The brakes ***screeched*** and the car suddenly stopped with a jerk. 随着刺耳的刹车声，那辆车猛地停住了。
stature /ˈstætʃə(r)/ *n.* 身材；身长 同 height	the height of a person or thing; elevation; altitude	A man who is six feet tall is above the average ***stature*** in China. 在中国，一个人身高六英尺是超过平均身高的。

WORD	MEANING	TYPICAL USE
undermine /ˌʌndəˈmaɪn/ v. 1. 用危险手段伤害;暗中破坏	1. weaken by secret or deceitful means; corrodSe	The President's enemies are spreading ill rumors to ***undermine*** his authority. 总统的对手散布谣言来暗中破坏他的威信。
2. 在……之下挖掘;逐渐损毁 同 erode, dig	2. dig beneath; wear away the earth beneath to remove support	The house is unsafe since the foundations were ***undermined*** by floods. 自从地基被洪水损毁后,房子很不安全。

EXERCISE 2.3 从第三部分中选出最恰当的单词,填入空格内:

1. Some people tried to ______ the chairman's influence by spreading ill rumors about him.
2. He heard a(n) ______ of anger from the old woman's room.
3. He was so ______ in his work that he completely forget the time.
4. The boy was so courageous that he overcame every ______ difficulty and became the leader of his tribe.
5. After the War, the people passed through terrible ______.

解答 1. undermine 2. screech 3. engrossed 4. insuperable 5. ordeals

第四部分

WORD	MEANING	TYPICAL USE
assess /əˈses/ *v.* 评估;估定 同 appraise	estimate the value of property; value(at)	Damages from last week's flood have been ***assessed*** at $50,000. 上星期的洪水所造成的损失估计为 50,000 美元。
chamber /ˈtʃeɪmbə(r)/ *n.* 1. 房间;寝室 同 room	1. a room (in a house); a bedroom	The children searched each and every ***chamber*** of the house for the cat. 孩子们为了找到小猫查遍了每间房子。
2. 立法或司法团体	2. a group of lawmakers	The Congress of the United States has two ***chambers***: the Senate and the House of Representatives. 美国国会分为参议院和众议院。
disdain /dɪsˈdeɪn/ *v.* 鄙视;轻视 同 despise	treat with contempt; look down on; scorn; contempt	Now that she is rich, she ***disdains*** to speak to her old friends. 现在她有钱了,不屑于跟她的老朋友讲话了。

WORD	MEANING	TYPICAL USE
espy /ɪsˈpaɪ/ *v.* 看出;看到(尤其从远处) 同 perceive	catch sight of; see at a distance	One day Robinson Crusoe ***espied*** a footprint on the sand. 有一天鲁滨逊·克鲁索远远地看到沙子上有一个脚印。
glossy /ˈglɒsɪ/ *adj.* 平滑的;有光泽的 同 sleek	smooth and shiny; polished; slick; burnished; sheeny	The beautiful ***glossy*** coat of the cat shone as it lay in the sunlight. 当小猫躺在太阳光下时,它那美丽光滑的毛闪闪发亮。
janitor /ˈdʒænɪtə(r)/ *n.* 看门者 同 doorman	a doorkeeper or porter; caretaker; gatekeeper	The ***janitor*** swept the floors and locked up the building every night. 看门人每晚都扫地和锁门。
packet /ˈpækɪt/ *n.* 包裹;(邮件等)一捆 同 parcel	a small bundle; package	She bought a ***packet*** of envelops at the stationery store. 她在文具店买了一捆信封。
pulpit /ˈpʊlpɪt/ *n.* (教堂的)讲坛;布教台 同 lectern	a platform or raised structure in a church from which the minister preaches; desk	The eloquent and ornate carving on a church ***pulpit*** was done by Indian hands. 教堂讲坛上生动而华丽的雕刻是印第安人的手笔。

WORD	MEANING	TYPICAL USE
scorch /skɔːtʃ/ *v.* 1. 把……烤焦；把……烧焦	1. burn the surface of; parch	The meat was black and ***scorched*** outside but still raw inside. 那块肉外表焦黑，但里面仍然是生的。
2. 使干焦；使枯萎 同 singe	2. dry up; wither	The grass is ***scorched*** by so much hot sunshine in summer. 夏天强烈的阳光把草都晒枯萎了。
surge /sɜːdʒ/ *v.* (波浪)起伏；汹涌 同 rise	rise and fall as a ship does on the waves	The ship ***surged*** in the stormy seas, rolling and pitching with each wave. 大船在暴风雨的海上随波起伏。
utensil /jʊ(uː)ˈtensl/ *n.* 器皿；用具 同 implement	an instrument; anything useful for a particular purpose; tool	Pots, pans and kettles are useful kitchen ***utensils***. 罐子、盘子和水壶是有用的厨房用具。

EXERCISE 2.4 从第四部分中选出最恰当的单词，填入空格内：

1. It is wrong to ______ a man merely because he has no money.
2. This is the death ______ where murderers wait to be put to death.
3. The committee met to ______ the idea of establishing a new college school.
4. She ______ my shirt by setting the iron too high for the fabric.
5. She turned around just in time to ______ an old friend disappear in the crowd.

解答 1. disdain 2. chamber 3. assess 4. scorched 5. espy

第五部分

WORD	MEANING	TYPICAL USE
bayonet /ˈbeɪənɪt/ *n.* 刺刀 同 dagger	a knife or dagger that may be fixed to the end of a rifle; dirk	When the soldiers ran out of ammunition, they fixed ***bayonets*** to their rifles. 弹药用完了，士兵们就把刺刀上膛。
compassion /kəmˈpæʃən/ *n.* 怜悯；同情 同 sympathy	sorrow for the suffering of others; pity; mercy; clemency	***Compassion*** for the orphans caused him to give money for their support. 因同情孤儿，他便拿出钱来资助他们。
detain /dɪˈteɪn/ *v.* 1. 使迟缓；阻止 同 retard	1. prevent a person from going away; delay	Lazy boys sometimes are ***detained*** at school to do extra work after ordinary lessons are finished. 懒惰的孩子有时在正课结束后被留在学校做额外的作业。
2. 拘留；扣押	2. hold as a prisoner; confine	The police ***detained*** the suspected thief for more questioning. 警察将窃贼拘留作进一步的讯问。

WORD	MEANING	TYPICAL USE
faction /ˈfækʃən/ *n.* 小派；小党派 同 clique	a group or party within a large group; part; side	A ***faction*** in our club tried to make the president resign. 我们俱乐部中有一个小派别，千方百计要使主席辞职。
hue /hjuː/ *n.* 色彩；色度 同 color	tone; tint; a shade of color	The diamond shone with every ***hue*** under the bright sun. 钻石在阳光下闪烁着各种色彩。
luster /ˈlʌstə(r)/ *n.* 1. 光彩；光辉 同 shimmer	1. a bright shine on the surface	He polished the metal until it had a fine ***luster.*** 他磨着那块金属，直到它发出美丽的光泽。
2. 荣誉；光荣 同 honor	2. glory; fame; splendor	The deeds of heroes add ***luster*** to a nation's history. 英雄的事迹使国家的历史增辉。
persevere /ˌpɜːsɪˈvɪə(r)/ *v.* 坚持不懈 同 persist	continue steadily in doing something hard; be stubborn; hold on	He ***persevered*** in his study until he succeeded. 他孜孜不倦地坚持学习直到成功。
rave /reɪv/ *v.* 发狂语 同 effervesce	talk wildly; speak in a confused manner	Because of his high fever, the sick man ***raved*** all night. 那个病人因高烧而整夜说胡话。

WORD	MEANING	TYPICAL USE
slay /sleɪ/ *v.* 杀戮;杀害 同 kill	kill violently; put to death	He intended to ***slay*** his father's murderer. 他意欲杀死谋害他父亲的凶手。
tablet /ˈtæblɪt/ *n.* 药片 同 pill	a small piece of medicine pressed into a flat, round cake; capsule	The doctor told her to take three ***tablets*** a day. 医生告诉她每天吃三片。
voluptuous /vəˈlʌptjʊəs/ *adj.* 肉感的 同 sensuous	delighting in sensual pleasure; fleshly; carnal	Nowadays an actress with ***voluptuous*** beauty seems to be very popular. 现今，有肉感美的女演员似乎很吃香。

EXERCISE 2.5 从第五部分中选出最恰当的单词，填入空格内：

1. I was ______, partly by the rain, and partly by company that I liked very much.
2. After all the ammunition ran out, the soldiers fought with their ______.
3. He belongs to the liberal ______ of the political party.
4. The dancer's movements were slow and ______.
5. The world's main religions all teach us to have ______ for the poor, and those in need.

解答 1. detained 2. bayonets 3. faction 4. voluptuous 5. compassion

效果检测

EXERCISE 2.6 找出与其他三个不相关的词：

_______ 1. (A) preoccupied (B) engrossed
(C) absorbed (D) supplemented

_______ 2. (A) bereave (B) deplore
(C) lament (D) bemoan

_______ 3. (A) instrument (B) utensil
(C) facility (D) implement

_______ 4. (A) trial (B) rebuke
(C) ordeal (D) tribulation

_______ 5. (A) bias (B) torment
(C) prejudice (D) inclination

_______ 6. (A) estimate (B) compensate
(C) appraise (D) assess

_______ 7. (A) tablet (B) lump
(C) pill (D) capsule

_______ 8. (A) despise (B) reprove
(C) disdain (D) scorn

_______ 9. (A) escarpment (B) cliff
(C) crack (D) precipice

_______ 10. (A) glory (B) luster
(C) desire (D) splendor

解答 1. D 2. A 3. C 4. B 5. B
6. B 7. B 8. B 9. C 10. C

EXERCISE 2.7 读下面的句子,选出句中斜体词所代表的意义:

______1. When the soldiers had used all their *ammunition*, they went on fighting with their swords.

(A) ration (B) weapons

(C) strength (D) bullets

______2. Public tranquility was disturbed by a discontented *faction*.

(A) reality (B) throng

(C) accident (D) clique

______3. Her heart was filled with *compassion* for the motherless children.

(A) sympathy (B) regret

(C) wistfulness (D) sorrow

______4. The priest *absolved* the boy when he confessed he had stolen some money from his father's desk drawer.

(A) exonerated (B) consoled

(C) reproved (D) blamed

______5. The boy did not reach the *stature* of his father; he was always under his arm.

(A) feature (B) independence

(C) height (D) position

______6. This matter is not very important, and shouldn't *detain* us a long time.

(A) retard (B) embarrass

(C) disdain (D) deplore

______7. Farmers in the 1930's had to *contend* against drought and dust.

(A) prevent (B) conquer

(C) struggle (D) censure

______8. In 1845 Daewonkoon *decreed* the expulsion of the Jesuits.

(A) prohibited (B) practised

(C) prescribed (D) proclaimed

______ 9. Cut a piece of lead or zinc and observe the *luster* of its fresh surface.

(A) brilliance (B) fraction

(C) pureness (D) groove

解答 1. D 2. D 3. A 4. A 5. C 6. A 7. C 8. D 9. A

EXERCISE 2.8 找出与斜体词意义最接近的单词：

______ 1. *glossy* fur (A) heavy (B) shaggy (C) lustrous (D) comfortable

______ 2. firm *tread* (A) body (B) footstep (C) position (D) resolution

______ 3. gorgeous *hue* (A) color (B) costume (C) implement (D) appearance

______ 4. *pith* of speech (A) essence (B) manner (C) necessity (D) divergence

______ 5. *insuperable* difficulties

(A) not extreme (B) ordinary

(C) unconquerable (D) imaginary

解答 1. C 2. B 3. A 4. A 5. C

EXERCISE 2.9 从下列单词中选出最恰当的词,填入空格内:

VOCABULARY LIST

surged	deploring	gush	undermine
packet	persevered	bias	hues
sneaked	disdained	detained	faction

1. The honest official ______ the offer of a bribe from the citizen.
2. She ______ in typing the assignment despite her exhaustion and her loss of accuracy.
3. He liked old-fashioned ways and had a ______ against progress.
4. The room was decorated in various ______ of blue ranging from light to dark.
5. She tied a ribbon around the ______ of letters.
6. The man ______ about the barn watching for a chance to steal the cow.
7. He got home two hours late and said he had been ______ in the office by some special business.
8. There was a ______ of blood as the wound reopened.
9. The little girl was ______ the loss of her doll.
10. A big crowd ______ out of the baseball stadium.

解答 1. disdained 2. persevered 3. bias 4. hues 5. packet 6. sneaked 7. detained 8. gush 9. deploring 10. surged

LESSON 3

预备测验

选出最恰当的答案：

1. Too strong a sense of ______ *hampered* him from enjoying life.

   (A) pleasure (B) humor (C) duty

2. They *denounced* him to the police as a(n) ______.

   (A) observer (B) criminal (C) witness

3. A strange ______ *pervaded* the garden, like the hush before a storm.

   (A) stillness (B) odor (C) feeling

4. They *despoiled* the villagers of their ______.

   (A) diseases (B) visitors (C) belongings

5. A(n) ______ provided the only *access* to the attic.

   (A) bandit (B) ladder (C) soldier

答案 1. C 2. B 3. A 4. C 5. B

第一部分

WORD	MEANING	TYPICAL USE
access /ˈækses/ *n.* 1. 进入	1. a way of getting to a place	The only ***access*** to the farm house is across the rice fields. 进入那农舍的唯一通道是穿越稻田。
2. 接近 同 approach	2. the right or privilege to approach	Only high officials had ***access*** to the emperor. 只有地位显赫的官员才能接近皇帝。
beckon /ˈbekən/ *v.* 招手或点头示意 同 signal	sign by a motion of the head or hand	The guide for visitors ***beckoned*** us to follow him. 导游招手叫我们跟着他。
concur /kənˈkɜː(r)/ *v.* 1. 同意;意见一致 同 agree	1. agree; be of the same opinion	I ***concur*** with the speaker in condemning every criminal. 我和那个演说家一致同意谴责每一个犯罪分子。
2. 同时发生	2. happen at the same time; come together	This summer two weeks of rain ***concurred*** with our vacation. 今年夏天,我们两个星期的假期里一直都下着雨。

WORD	MEANING	TYPICAL USE
denounce /dɪˈnaʊns/ *v.* 当众指责 同 accuse	speak against in public; accuse; denunciate; damn	He was ***denounced*** as a coward and traitor. 他被当众指责为懦夫和卖国贼。
fray /freɪ/ 1. *n.* 争吵;斗争 同 combat	1. noisy quarrel; fight	The first blow makes the anger, but the second makes the ***fray***. 第一拳引起愤怒,第二拳则招致争吵。
2. *v.* 磨损;磨破 同 shred	2. make ragged or worn along the edge	Long wear had ***frayed*** the collar and cuffs of his old shirts. 他旧衬衫的领口和袖口因为穿得时间太长都磨破了。
hamper /ˈhæmpə(r)/ *v.* 妨碍;阻碍 同 hinder	get in the way of; hold back; impede; interfere with	Heavy clothing ***hampered*** the movements of the climbers. 笨重的衣服妨碍了登山者的行动。
malady /ˈmælədɪ/ *n.* 疾病 同 ailment	disease; sickness; illness; affliction; complaint	Cancer and tuberculosis are serious ***maladies*** in every country. 癌症和肺结核在每个国家都是严重的疾病。

WORD	MEANING	TYPICAL USE
plod /plɒd/ *v.* 缓步或重步在……走 同 trudge	walk heavily or slowly	The old man was ***plodding*** wearily along the bank of the river. 那位老人拖着疲惫的步子沿河岸走着。
remnant /ˈremnənt/ *n.* 残余;遗物 同 residue	a small part left; rest; remains	Since the factory moved, this town has only a ***remnant*** of its former population. 自从那家工厂迁走后,这个小镇只剩下了原先的居民。
snore /snɔː(r)/ *v.* 打鼾;(睡眠时)粗重地呼吸 同 wheeze	breathe noisily when sleeping	The child with a cold in his nose ***snored*** all night. 那个感冒鼻塞的孩子整夜呼吸粗重。
tinge /tɪndʒ/ *v.* 微染;染以轻淡的颜色 同 tincture	color something slightly; tint; stain	Blood ***tinged*** the water as he washed his wound. 当他清洗伤口时,血把水染成了红色。

EXERCISE 3.1 从第一部分中选出最恰当的单词,填入空格内:

1. The two scientists, working separately and unknown to each other, had reached conclusions that ______.
2. Poor health and lack of money ______ his efforts to get a college education.
3. ______ to the mountain towns is often difficult because of poor roads.

4. The preacher ______ war, calling it immoral destruction.

5. ______ of the meal lay on the table when he had finished eating.

答案 1. concurred 2. hampered 3. Access 4. denounced 5. Remnants

第二部分

WORD	MEANING	TYPICAL USE
ailment /ˈeɪlmənt/ *n.* 疾病 同 malady	pain or disease; trouble; distress	It was necessary for them to have remedies for their ***ailments***. 给他们吃特效药治疗疾病是必要的。
bicker /ˈbɪkə(r)/ *v.* 争吵;争论 同 wrangle	quarrel, especially about small matters; argue	The children are ***bickering*** with each other about who is the tallest among them. 小孩们在互相争论他们中间谁最高。
contrive /kənˈtraɪv/ *v.* 发明;设计 同 hatch	plan with cleverness or skill; invent; project	The inventor ***contrived*** a new kind of engine with fewer moving parts. 发明家设计了一种新的引擎，这种引擎的活动零件比以前少了。

WORD	MEANING	TYPICAL USE
dazzle /ˈdæzl/ *v.* 以强光使目眩 同 glare	hurt (the eyes) with too bright or quick moving lights; daze	The bright light of the motor car on the dark country road ***dazzled*** my eyes. 在黑暗的乡村道路上，汽车耀眼的灯光让我睁不开眼睛。
fumble /ˈfʌmbl/ *v.* 摸索；搜寻 同 grope	move fingers or hands awkwardly in search of something	She ***fumbled*** about in her handbag for a pen to write a memorandum. 她在手提包里摸索着找钢笔，想写个备忘录。
impair /ɪmˈpɛə(r)/ *v.* 损害 同 damage	make worse; weaken; harm	Poor food and hard work ***impaired*** her health and she became thin. 没有营养的食物和繁重的工作损害了她的健康，使她变瘦了。
mortify /ˈmɔːtɪfaɪ/ *v.* 使感到羞辱；使蒙屈辱 同 humiliate	wound (a person's feelings); degrade	The parents were ***mortified*** by their children's bad behavior before the guests. 孩子们在客人面前的不良行为使父母感到羞辱。
predominant /prɪˈdɒmɪnənt/ *adj.* 主要的；有势力的 同 outstanding	having more power, authority or influence than others; salient	The United States became the ***predominant*** nation in the Western Hemisphere. 美国成为西半球的主要国家。

WORD	MEANING	TYPICAL USE
sanitary /ˈsænɪtərɪ/ *adj.* 卫生的 同 hygienic	having to do with health; healthful	He worked to improve the ***sanitary*** conditions of slums. 他谋求改善贫民区的卫生状况。
wallet /ˈwɒlɪt/ *n.* 皮包；皮夹 同 purse	a folding pocketbook, usually of leather	He always keeps a lot of money in his ***wallet***. 他总是在钱夹内放许多钱。
warrant /ˈwɒrənt/ *n.* 正当的理由；权利 同 assurance	proper reason for action; guarantee; permit; authority; right	Do you consider the wild behavior of the crowd was enough of a ***warrant*** for the police to use force? 你认为人群野蛮的行为足以让警察动用武力吗?

EXERCISE 3.2 从第二部分中选出最适当的单词，填入空格内：

1. The outlaws ______ a robbery of the cargo train.
2. The doctor made sure that the injection needle was ______.
3. Two children ended their ______ and became friendly again.
4. A mother is ______ when her child behaves badly in the church.
5. Coming out of the dark theater, we were ______ by the bright sunlight.

解答 1. contrived 2. sanitary 3. bickering
4. mortified 5. dazzled

第三部分

WORD	MEANING	TYPICAL USE
allocate /ˈæləkeɪt/ *v.* 拨出;分配 同 apportion	divide and give as shares; assign	The Ford Foundation ***allocated*** millions of dollars for cancer research. 福特基金会拨出几百万美元用于癌症的研究。
brawl /brɔːl/ *n.* 争吵;打架 同 fight	a noisy and disorderly quarrel; bicker; wrangle	The ***brawl*** in the street could be heard in the house nearby. 在附近的房子里都可以听到街上的争吵声。
cynical /ˈsɪnɪkəl/ *adj.* 怀疑人生价值的;讽刺的 同 sarcastic	contemptuous; sneering; unbelieving; suspicious	The boys made several ***cynical*** remarks to cover up their disappointment at being left out of the play. 男孩子们冷嘲热讽地来掩盖他们不被允许参加游戏的失望。
embellish /ɪmˈbelɪʃ/ *v.* 装置;布置 同 adorn	add beauty to; decorate; ornament; beautify	She ***embellished*** the simple dress with colorful laces and ribbons. 她用花边和缎带来装饰那条素净的连衣裙。

WORD	MEANING	TYPICAL USE
gallant /ˈgælənt/ *adj.* 英勇的 同 splendid	brave and high-spirited; courageous; grand	The defence of the Alamo was a heroic action of ***gallant*** men. 阿拉莫防御战是勇者的英雄行为。
immerse /ɪˈmɜːs/ *v.* 浸入 同 plunge	dip or lower into a liquid until covered by it; merge; immerge	He ***immersed*** his aching feet in a bucket of cold water. 他把疼痛的双脚浸入一桶凉水中。
ostentatious /ˌɒstenˈteɪʃəs/ *adj.* 夸张的；虚饰的 同 showy	done for display; intended to attract notice; pretentious	He rode his new bicycle up and down in front of our house in an ***ostentatious*** way. 他骑了一辆新自行车，在我家门前炫耀地骑来骑去。
presentiment /prɪˈzentɪmənt/ *n.* 预感 同 foreboding	a feeling that something is about to happen	Soapy followed the man with a ***presentiment*** that luck would again run against him. 索皮跟随着那个人，预感到幸运将再次与他背道而驰。
satiate /ˈseɪʃɪeɪt/ *v.* 使饱；使满足 同 surfeit	feed fully; satisfy fully; supply with too much; saturate	She was so ***satiated*** with bananas that she would not even look at one. 她吃香蕉都吃腻了，连看都不想看。

WORD	MEANING	TYPICAL USE
undulate /ˈʌndjʊleɪt/ *v.* 波动;起伏;震动 同 wave	move in waves; rise and fall with a wavelike motion; billow; swing	The field of wheat was ***undulating*** in the breeze. 麦田在微风中起伏。

EXERCISE 3.3 从第三部分中选出最恰当的单词,填入空格内:

1. It is difficult to make friends with a person who is ______ about friendship.
2. He welcomed his friend in a(n)______ manner, though he didn't like his visting him.
3. I felt a strong ______ that my belief would finally give way.
4. That space has already been ______ for building a new hospital.
5. The grass was ______ like waves in the field.

答案 1. cynical 2. ostentatious 3. presentiment 4. allocated 5. undulating

第四部分

WORD	MEANING	TYPICAL USE
apparel /əˈpærəl/ *n.* 衣服;服装 同 garment	a person's outer clothing; suit; dress	A shop selling woman's ***apparel*** is at the corner of the street. 拐角处有一家女士服装店。

WORD	MEANING	TYPICAL USE
cajole /kəˈdʒəʊl/ *v.* 用甜言蜜语诱惑 同 coax	persuade by pleasant words or flattery; urge	He ***cajoled*** his friends into deciding in his favor. 他诱惑朋友做有益于自己的决定。
discard /dɪsˈkɑːd/ *v.* 抛弃 同 reject	give up as useless or worn; throw aside	You can ***discard*** your old coat but not your old friends. 你可以抛弃旧衣服，但不可抛弃老朋友。
effete /ɪˈfiːt/ *adj.* 疲惫的；枯竭的 同 exhausted	no longer able to produce; worn out	During the middle ages, Greek civilization declined and became ***effete***. 希腊文明在中世纪时逐渐衰亡了。
grudge /ɡrʌdʒ/ *n.* 怨恨 同 resentment	ill will, sullen feeling (against)	She has had a ***grudge*** against me ever since I disagreed with her. 自从我不赞成她之后，她就对我怀恨在心。
kidnap /ˈkɪdnæp/ *v.* 绑架；劫持 同 abduct	steal or carry off a person (child) by force; take away; ravish	Four men ***kidnapped*** the little girl, but the police soon caught them and rescued the girl. 四个人绑架了一个小女孩，但是警方很快抓到他们，解救了那个小女孩。

WORD	MEANING	TYPICAL USE
pact /pækt/ *n.* 协定;公约 同 treaty	a solemn agreement; compact; contract; bargain	There is some hope that a peace ***pact*** will be signed between the two countries. 这两国之间有签订和平公约的希望。
pry /praɪ/ *v.* 细查;探问 同 peep	examine closely and curiously; spy; investigate; snoop	She ***pries*** too closely into the private life of her friends. 她太爱刺探朋友的私生活了。
scour /ˈskaʊə(r)/ *v.* 1. 搜索 同 ransack	1. move quickly over in order to search something	Men ***scoured*** the whole country looking for the lost child. 人们在全城搜索,寻找那个迷路的孩子。
2. 磨亮;擦净	2. clean or polish by hard robbing; scrub	The servant ***scoured*** the frying pan until it shone like silver. 佣人擦洗平底锅,直到它像银子一样闪闪发光为止。
swagger /ˈswæɡə(r)/ *v.* 昂首阔步 同 strut	walk with a swinging movement as if proud	He ***swaggered*** down the street after winning the fight. 打赢之后,他昂首阔步地沿街而去。

WORD	MEANING	TYPICAL USE
vagary /ˈveɪɡərɪ, vəˈɡɛərɪ/ *n.* 奇异的幻想；妄想 同 fancy	an unusual, purposeless or unexpected idea, act or thought, humor	The building of this house in the shape of the temple was a rich man's ***vagary***. 这栋房屋庙宇式的外型是一位富人的奇想。

EXERCISE 3.4 从第四部分中选出最恰当的一个单词，填入空格内：

1. My father repaired the toy that I had ______ as a useless thing.
2. She was always ______ into other people's affairs.
3. He ______ the town looking for the lost child, but he couldn't find him.
4. My outgoing friends were able to ______ the shy newcomer into attending the party.
5. I always feel she has a(n) ______ against me, although I do not know what wrong I've done to her.

解答 1. discarded 2. prying 3. scoured 4. cajole 5. grudge

第五部分

WORD	MEANING	TYPICAL USE
asset /ˈæset/ *n.* 有价值或有用的东西 同 property	something that has value; possession; belongings	Ability to get along with people is an ***asset*** in business. 在商业界，与人相处的能力是可贵的。
chasm /ˈkæzəm/ *n.* 深坑或裂缝；利害冲突 同 gap	a deep opening or crack in the earth; yawn; crater	There was a deep political ***chasm*** between the two countries which nearly led to a war. 两国间严重的政治冲突几乎导致了一场战争。
despoil /dɪsˈpɔɪl/ *v.* 夺取；抢劫 同 depredate	rob; steal from; spoil	The cities of Greece and Asia were ***despoiled*** of their most valuable ornaments. 希腊与亚洲城市中最宝贵的装饰品被洗劫一空。
facetious /fəˈsiːʃəs/ *adj.* 好开玩笑的 同 humorous	sly; joking; said in fun; jocular	I became angry with the little boy at his ***facetious*** remarks. 我对那小男孩的玩笑话感到生气。

WORD	MEANING	TYPICAL USE
hurtle /ˈhɜːtl/ *v.* 碰撞；动手 同 dash	move or rush with great speed; lunge; crash	The wing of the airplane came off and the machine ***hurtled*** to the ground. 机翼脱落，于是飞机撞到了地面上。
larceny /ˈlɑːsnɪ/ *n.* 盗窃；盗窃罪 同 robbery	theft; stealing; the unlawful take or carrying away of the property	He wanted to be accused of ***larceny***, because he felt comfortable in prison. 他想以盗窃罪被起诉，因为他感觉监狱里很舒服。
pervade /pə(ɜː)ˈveɪd/ *v.* 遍布；弥漫 同 spread	go or spread throughout; diffuse; impregnate	He worked so hard that the weariness ***pervaded*** his whole body. 他努力工作，以致身心疲惫。
recant /rɪˈkænt/ *v.* 公然撤回或取消 同 retract	take back formally or publicly; withdraw	Though he was tortured to make him change his religion, the prisoner would not ***recant***. 虽然受了酷刑，但那个囚犯绝不改变自己的宗教信仰。
shambles /ˈʃæmblz/ *n.* 混乱；迷惑 同 confusion	general disorder; babel; bedlam	He left his affairs in a complete ***shambles*** when he died. 他死后，留下的事务一片混乱。

WORD	MEANING	TYPICAL USE
taboo /tæˈbuː/ *n.* 禁忌;禁止 同 prohibition	prohibition; interdiction; restriction	Eating human flesh is a ***taboo*** in civilized countries. 在文明的国度里,吃人肉是被禁止的。
trappings /ˈtræpɪŋz/ *n.* 马的装饰物;装饰 同 decorations	ornamental coverings for a horse; fittings	He wore all the ***trappings*** of high office. 他佩戴上高官的所有装饰物。

EXERCISE 3.5 从第五部分中选出最恰当的单词,填入空格内:

1. The enemy troops ______ the villages of their belongings.
2. The violent wind caused chimney-pots and roof-tiles to ______ down to the ground.
3. The radio voice was a ______ of several different operators' speaking at once.
4. Many questions and problems that were once ______ are now discussed openly.
5. The subversive ideas that ______ all these periodicals may do great harm.

解答 1. despoiled 2. hurtle 3. shamble 4. taboos 5. pervade

效果检测

EXERCISE 3.6 找出与其他三个不相关的词：

_______ 1. (A) impair (B) weaken
(C) invalid (D) injure

_______ 2. (A) cynical (B) contemptuous
(C) effete (D) sneering

_______ 3. (A) infirmity (B) ailment
(C) malady (D) scourge

_______ 4. (A) healthful (B) consecrated
(C) hygienic (D) sanitary

_______ 5. (A) submerge (B) plunge
(C) absolve (D) immerse

_______ 6. (A) hinder (B) impede
(C) slash (D) hamper

_______ 7. (A) humorous (B) facetious
(C) obstinate (D) waggish

_______ 8. (A) assign (B) allocate
(C) apportion (D) allay

_______ 9. (A) contrive (B) scheme
(C) implore (D) hatch

_______ 10. (A) ostentatious (B) gaudy
(C) pretentious (D) prominent

解答 1. C 2. C 3. D 4. B 5. C
6. C 7. C 8. D 9. C 10. D

EXERCISE 3.7 读下面的句子,选出句中斜体词所代表的意义:

______ 1. The teacher was *mortified* by his own inability to answer such a simple question.

(A) distressed (B) humiliated
(C) surprised (D) satisfied

______ 2. He has been suffering from a strange *malady* for a long time.

(A) screech (B) pageant
(C) sound (D) ailment

______ 3. I am not about to *cajole* you into the reception of my opinion.

(A) beseech (B) coax
(C) imply (D) request

______ 4. She was *cynical* about her husband's vow to quit smoking.

(A) distrustful (B) commenting
(C) complaining (D) critical

______ 5. Whoever violates the *taboo* will be stricken to death by unseen beings.

(A) regulation (B) ceremony
(C) feast (D) prohibition

______ 6. The electric wire is *fraying* and could be dangerous to handle.

(A) worn (B) burning
(C) watering (D) magnetic

______ 7. He had all the *trappings* of a cowboy, but he couldn't even ride a horse.

(A) technics (B) conditions
(C) ornaments (D) qualities

______ 8. The storekeeper *warranted* the quality of the eggs.

(A) doubted (B) guaranteed
(C) examined (D) worried

______ 9. She *embellished* her white hat with a black belt and pink roses.

(A) filled (B) ornamented

(C) added (D) exchanged

______ 10. The *chasm* between England and the American colonies grew wider and wider until it finally resulted in the American Revolution.

(A) struggle (B) distance

(C) gap (D) difference

解答 1. B 2. D 3. B 4. A 5. D 6. A 7. C 8. B 9. B 10. C

EXERCISE 3.8 找出与斜体词意义最接近的单词：

1. *gallant* ship (A) splendid (B) floating (C) fast (D) heavy
2. a street *brawl* (A) quarrel (B) accident (C) passage (D) ornament
3. a trade *pact* (A) exchange (B) policy (C) relation (D) agreement
4. *sanitary* place (A) sacred (B) clean (C) lonesome (D) vacant
5. *pry* about the affairs (A) wander (B) creep (C) peep (D) trudge

解答 1. A 2. A 3. D 4. B 5. C

EXERCISE 3.9 从下列单词中选出最恰当的词,填入空格内:

VOCABULARY LIST

fray	dazzles	beckoned	effete
gallant	mortified	access	pervade
despoil	hurtle	plodded	predominant

1. The only ______ to that building is along that muddy track.
2. The fleet of warships, gaily decorated with flags for the review, made a (n) ______ show.
3. To look straight at the headlights ______ the eyes.
4. His old shirt was beginning to ______ at the cuffs.
5. In the eyes of priests, God seems to ______ all of creation in the world.
6. The teacher was ______ by his pupil's poor answer.
7. He stood waiting until the policeman ______ him on.
8. The Roman Empire was once strong, but it grew ______ when there were enough slaves to do all the work.
9. The ______ feature of his character is pride.
10. The old man ______ along the road, hardly able to lift each foot.

解答 1. access 2. gallant 3. dazzles 4. fray
5. pervade 6. mortified 7. beckoned
8. effete 9. predominant 10. plodded

LESSON 4

预备测验

选出最恰当的答案：

1. The fun of playing the game was a greater *incentive* than the ______.

   (A) fighting　(B) participation　(C) prize

2. The spy went in the *guise* of a ______ and was not recognized by the enemy.

   (A) monk　(B) sanitary　(C) pretention

3. He *dissipated* his large fortune in a few years of heavy ______.

   (A) working　(B) trial　(C) spending

4. You are always *badgering* me with such a(n) ______.

   (A) amicable greeting　(B) silly question

   (C) sincere praise

5. He got too near the ______ and *singed* his long beard.

   (A) door　(B) water　(C) fire

答案 1. C 2. A 3. C 4. B 5. C

第一部分

WORD	MEANING	TYPICAL USE
abdicate /ˈæbdɪkeɪt/ *v.* 放弃权力 同 relinquish	give up (office, power, or authority); surrender	When the king ***abdicated*** his throne, his brother succeeded him. 国王退位时,由其弟弟继承王位。
accrue /əˈkruː/ *v.* 自然增殖;自然增加;积累 同 accumulate	come as a natural product or result; add up; be received; amass	Ability to think clearly will ***accrue*** to you from good habits of study. 清晰的思维能力将因良好的学习习惯而自然增强。
badger /ˈbædʒə(r)/ *v.* 困扰 同 tease	keep on annoying or teasing; bother or question persistently	The salesman has been ***badgering*** my father for two weeks to buy a new car. 两个多星期以来,那推销员一直缠着我父亲买新车。
baffle /ˈbæfl/ *v.* 使困惑;使迷惑 同 bewilder	make effective action impossible by confusing; hinder; thwart	They succeeded in ***baffling*** the enemy's attack plans. 他们成功地扰乱了敌人的进攻计划。

WORD	MEANING	TYPICAL USE
conjecture /kənˈdʒektʃə(r)/ *v.* 推测;猜想 同 surmise	guess; speculate; suspect	He ***conjectured*** that his new stocks would rise on the stock market. 他推测自己的新股票价格将在股市中上涨。
derange /dɪˈreɪndʒ/ *v.* 使错乱;扰乱 同 upset	disturb the order or arrangement of; throw into confusion	The poor woman's mind has been ***deranged*** for many years. 那女人精神错乱已经好多年了。
fiend /fiːnd/ *n.* 恶魔;穷凶极恶的人 同 devil	an evil spirit; a very wicked person; witch	The natives thought the explorer was possessed by a ***fiend***. 当地人认为探险家被恶魔附身了。
pine /paɪn/ *v.* 渴望;苦思 同 yearn	long eagerly; waste away through sorrow or disease; wither	The mother was ***pining*** to see her son and daughter. 那位母亲渴望见到她的子女。
smother /ˈsmʌðə(r)/ *v.* 使窒息;闷死 同 choke	prevent from breathing freely; killed by depriving of air; throttle	The gas almost ***smothered*** the coal miners but they got out in time. 矿工们差点被瓦斯闷死,好在他们及时逃出。

WORD	MEANING	TYPICAL USE
throb /θrɒb/ *v.* 悸动;跳动 同 pulse	beat rapidly or strongly; flutter; palpitate	The long climb up the mountain made her heart ***throb*** rapidly. 长时间爬山让她心跳加速。

EXERCISE 4.1 从第一部分中选出最恰当的单词,填入空格内:

1. The dead man had been ______ by smoke from the chimney.
2. Your heart will ______ when you are excited with terror.
3. The thief ______ our pursuit by locking us in the house before escaping.
4. If you put your money in the bank, interest ______.
5. The origin of the human race is a matter of pure ______.

解答 1. smothered 2. throb 3. baffled 4. accrues 5. conjecture

第二部分

WORD	MEANING	TYPICAL USE
broth /brɒ(ɜː)θ/ *n.* 煮肉的清汤 同 soup	a thin soup made from water in which meat, fish or vegetable have been boiled	Many people usually drink hot ***broth*** when they are sick. 很多人在生病时喝热的肉汤。

WORD	MEANING	TYPICAL USE
crevice /ˈkrevɪs/ *n.* 裂缝；破口 同 crack	a narrow split or cut; cranny	Some tiny plants grow in the ***crevice*** of the stone wall. 有些小植物从石墙的裂缝中长出来。
demean /dɪˈmiːn/ *v.* 降低自己的身份；贬低自己 同 degrade	lower in the dignity or standing; humble; debase	The duke's son ***demeaned*** himself by doing manual labor with his servants. 公爵的儿子降低自己的身份，和用人一起做工。
foster /ˈfɒstə(r)/ *v.* 养育；看护 同 nurse	bring up; care for fondly; rear; cherish	We ***fostered*** the young girl while her mother was in hospital. 小女孩的母亲住院时，我们照顾她。
incentive /ɪnˈsentɪv/ *n.* 刺激；鼓励 同 stimulus	a thing that urges a person on; a cause of action or effort; motive	Our country has prospered by various ***incentive*** systems. 我们的国家因各种不同的奖励制度而繁荣起来。
maze /meɪz/ *n.* 迷宫 同 labyrinth	a network of paths through which it is hard to find one's way	A guide led us through the ***maze*** of tunnels in the cave. 向导带领我们穿过山洞里迷宫般的隧道。

WORD	MEANING	TYPICAL USE
pore /pɔː(r)/ 1. *v.* 专心阅读；深思	1. gaze earnestly or steadily; study or give close attention to; ponder	She ***pored*** over the picture book in silence enjoying the various colors. 她默默地专心致志地阅读那本图画书，欣赏着各种不同的颜色。
2. *n.* 毛孔	2. any of the very small openings in the surface of the skin through which moisture can pass	Like human skin, soil has holes that are called ***pores***. 和人类的皮肤一样，土壤也有许多洞，叫作毛细孔。
rubbish /ˈrʌbɪʃ/ *n.* 废物；垃圾 同 trash	waste material to be thrown away; garbage; junk	Pick up the ***rubbish*** and throw it in the garbage can. 把废物捡起来丢进垃圾桶。
speculate /ˈspekjʊleɪt/ *v.* 沉思；思索 同 meditate	think long and carefully about some subject; consider; reflect	We don't need to ***specu-late*** about the possible winner in the game. 我们不必去想谁可能是这场比赛的赢家。
transfix /trænsˈfɪks/ *v.* 刺穿 同 petrify	fasten of fix by piercing through with something pointed	Sweet music caught and held him ***transfixed*** against the iron fence. 甜美的音乐穿过铁墙，紧紧地扣住了他的心弦。

EXERCISE 4.2 从第二部分中选出最恰当的单词,填入空格内:

1. Many books and magazines are filled with cheap, sensational and vulgar ______.
2. After waiting a long time, I opened a little ______ in the door.
3. His interest in my scholastic records gave me a(n) ______ and I worked twice as hard.
4. They ______ about the author's hidden meaning.
5. She was lost in a(n) ______ of narrow winding streets.

解答 1. rubbish 2. crevice 3. incentive 4. speculated 5. maze

第三部分

WORD	MEANING	TYPICAL USE
anomaly /əˈnɒməlɪ/ *n.* 反常的事物 同 abnormality	something abnormal; unusual irregularity	A bird that cannot fly is an ***anomaly***. 鸟不会飞是不正常的。
converge /kənˈvɜːdʒ/ *v.* 集中于一点 同 focus	tend to meet at a point; be directed towards a single point	If you look at the end of your nose, your eyes ***converge***. 你如果看着自己的鼻尖,你的两眼就会向一点集中。

WORD	MEANING	TYPICAL USE
duplicate /ˈdjuːplɪkɪt/ *adj.* 完全相同的;副的 同 double	same; selfsame; alike; twofold	We have a ***duplicate*** key to the front door. 我们有一把复制的前门钥匙。
epoch /ˈiːpɒk;ˈepək/ *n.* 纪元;时代 同 age	a period of historical time; the starting point of such a period	The introduction of the computer will mark an ***epoch*** in language education. 电脑的使用将会为语言教学开创一个新纪元。
gaunt /gɔːnt/ *adj.* 憔悴的;骨瘦如柴的 同 haggard	very thin and bony; with hollow eyes and a starved look; lean	Hunger and suffering from cold has made the lost hikers ***gaunt***. 迷路的徒步旅行者因饥饿和寒冷而骨瘦如柴。
incessant /ɪnˈsesənt/ *adj.* 不断的 同 continuous	never stopping; unceasing; interminable; unending; timeless	The ***incessant*** barking of the dog kept him awake through the night. 一刻不停的狗叫声让他整夜未能入睡。

WORD	MEANING	TYPICAL USE
mute /mjuːt/ *adj.* 沉默的；无言的 同 silent	without speech; making no sound; dumb; unable to speak	Though the teacher asked a simple question about her parents, the little girl stood ***mute*** with embarrassment. 虽然老师只问了一个有关她父母亲的简单问题，但那小女孩无言地站着，似乎很困窘的样子。
partisan /ˌpɑːtɪˈzæn/ *n.* 帮伙；同党者 同 defender	a strong supporter of a person, party or cause; zealot	He was a passionate ***partisan*** of these people and had organized a Worker's Union. 他是这些人的热心伙伴，并组织了一个工会。
scan /skæn/ *v.* 1. 细察；审视 同 contemplate	1. examine carefully and closely; regard; pore over	The parents of the sick boy ***scanned*** the doctor's face for a sign of hope. 生病男孩的父母审视医生的脸，想从他的脸上看出男孩是否有康复的希望。
2. 匆匆一阅 同 overlook	2. glance at quickly; read hurriedly; skim	She ***scanned*** the newspaper in a few minutes. 她在几分钟之内把报纸大略翻阅了一下。

WORD	MEANING	TYPICAL USE
stab /stæb/ *v.* 刺;刺伤 同 pierce	pierce or wound with a pointed weapon	He ***stabbed*** a piece of meat from the plate with his fork. 他用叉子从盘中叉起一片肉来。

EXERCISE 4.3 从第三部分中选出最恰当的单词,填入空格内:

1. Railway lines seem to ______ when one looks at them from a distance.
2. A person's lungs are ______ but he has only one heart.
3. The ______ of his position is that he is very famous, but still doesn't make much money.
4. They ______ the mountainside for any sign of the climbers.
5. The invention of the steam engine marks a(n) ______ in the growth of history.

答案 1. converge 2. duplicate 3. anomaly
4. scanned 5. epoch

第四部分

WORD	MEANING	TYPICAL USE
botch /bɒtʃ/ *v.* (笨手笨脚地)弄坏 同 ruin	spoil something by poor work; do something badly	I tried to cook a nice dinner, but I'm afraid I've rather ***botched*** it. 我想做一顿美味的晚餐,但恐怕已经做砸了。

WORD	MEANING	TYPICAL USE
chafe /tʃeɪf/ v. 擦痛；擦热 同 abrade	make sore by rubbing or scraping; rub to make warm	Her new shoes ***chafed*** the skin on both her feet. 新皮鞋把她的两只脚磨疼了。
dissipate /ˈdɪsɪpeɪt/ v. 1. 使消散；驱散 同 scatter	1. spread in different directions	After a brisk morning wind ***dissipated*** the clouds, the sky was clear all day. 早上一阵强风把云吹散后，一整天天空万里无云。
2. 浪费 同 waste	2. spend foolishly; waste on things of little value	The foolish son ***dissipated*** his father's fortune by spending it on drinking and gambling. 愚蠢的儿子把父亲的财产乱花在喝酒和赌博上。
efface /ɪˈfeɪs/ v. 消除；抹杀 同 erase	rub out; do away with; wipe out; destroy	The inscriptions on the ancient monuments have been ***effaced*** by time. 古代石碑上的文字已经因时间长久而被磨蚀掉了。
glint /glɪnt/ n. 闪烁；闪光 同 flash	a gleam; sparkle; glitter	There was a ***glint*** in her eyes that showed she was angry. 她的眼神显示她在生气。

WORD	MEANING	TYPICAL USE
onerous /ˈɒnərəs/ *adj*. 繁重的；麻烦的 同 arduous	hard to take or carry; oppressive; troublesome; burdensome	Overtime work is often ***onerous***, though it is well paid. 加班通常很麻烦，虽然报酬不错。
iterate /ˈɪtəreɪt/ *v*. 重做；重述 同 repeat	say again or repeatedly; reiterate	The girl did not move though the policeman ***iterated*** his command that she go. 警察重述他的命令叫女孩走，但她没动。
propensity /prəˈpensɪtɪ/ *n*. 倾向；嗜好；习性 同 tendency	a natural inclination or bent; leaning	Most boys have a ***propensity*** for playing with machinery. 大多数男孩子都有摆弄机械的嗜好。
singe /sɪndʒ/ *v*. 微烧；烫焦 同 scorch	burn a little; sear; scald	Mother ***singed*** chicken to get rid of hairs. 母亲把鸡稍稍烫了一下，以便去毛。
strut /strʌt/ *v*. 昂首阔步 同 swagger	walk in a vain, important, or affected manner; parade; prance	The little boy put on his father's medals and ***strutted*** around the room. 那小男孩戴上他父亲的勋章，在房间内昂首阔步。

WORD	MEANING	TYPICAL USE
unravel /ʌnˈrævəl/ *v.* 解开;阐明 同 solve	solve; make clear	There are many kinds of diseases that medical science is yet to ***unravel***. 有许多种疾病医学尚无办法医治。

EXERCISE 4.4 从第四部分中选出最恰当的单词,填入空格内:

1. It takes many years to ______ the terrible memories of war.
2. He is engaged in the ______ job of correcting hundreds of themes a week.
3. The careless boy made so many mistakes making his model airplane that he completely ______ the job.
4. She ______ the meat over a high flame.
5. The candidate ______ about the room like a latter-day Napoleon.

答案 1. efface 2. onerous 3. botched
4. singed 5. strutted

第五部分

WORD	MEANING	TYPICAL USE
bellow /ˈbeləʊ/ *v.* 大声呼叫;怒吼 同 shout	shout loudly with anger, or with pain; roar	He ***bellowed*** in pain when the hammer came down on his finger. 当铁锤砸到手指时,他痛得大叫。

WORD	MEANING	TYPICAL USE
cloak /kləʊk/ *n.* 1. 宽大有袖或无袖的外衣 同 mantle 2. 掩饰;隐匿	1. a loose outer garment with or without sleeves 2. something which covers, hides or keeps secret	The horseback rider drew his ***cloak*** tightly around him in the rain. 在雨中,马背上的骑士把外衣拉紧。 His friendly behavior was a ***cloak*** for his evil intention. 他友善的行为掩饰了他的恶意。
devout /dɪˈvaʊt/ *adj.* 虔诚的 同 pious	paying attention to religious duties; devoted to religion	The minister was a very ***devout*** man and devoted his whole life to Christian mission work. 那位牧师是位虔诚的教徒。他把自己的一生都奉献给了基督教的传教工作。
guise /gaɪz/ *n.* 装束;外貌 同 appearance	style of dress; outward appearance	A man appeared at the castle gate in the ***guise*** of a woodcutter. 一个樵夫装束的人出现在城堡的大门口。
latent /ˈleɪtənt/ *adj.* 隐藏的;不易被察觉的 同 concealed	present but not active; hidden; covert	The power of a grain of wheat to grow into a plant remains ***latent*** if it is not planted. 如果不种植的话,一颗麦子仍然保存长成一株植物的力量。

WORD	MEANING	TYPICAL USE
pawn /pɔːn/ *v.* 典当;抵押 同 gage	leave something with another person as security for borrowed money that will be repaid; pledge	He ***pawned*** his watch to buy food until he could get a job. 他把表当了去买食物,等到他有了工作再赎回来。
quake /kweɪk/ *v.* 震动;战栗 同 shudder	shake or tremble; violate	When the cannon was fired, the earth ***quaked*** under his feet. 开炮时,大地在他脚下震动。
salvage /ˈsælvɪdʒ/ *n.* 对海上遇险的船舶、船员及货物的救护 同 rescue	the act of saving a ship or its cargo from wreck or capture	After the ship sank, ***salvage*** of its cargo was impossible. 船沉了之后,货物是不可能被打捞起来的。
sequel /ˈsiːkwəl/ *n.* 继续;结果 同 result	that which follows; continuation	Famine has often been the ***sequel*** of war. 饥饿常常是战争的结果。
virtual /ˈvəːtjʊəl/ *adj.* 实质上的;事实上的 同 actual	being something in effect though not in name; real	The battle was won with so great a loss of soldiers that it was a ***virtual*** defeat. 此役虽然获胜,但损失了大量的士兵,因此实际等于是一次败仗。

WORD	MEANING	TYPICAL USE
wizard /ˈwɪzəd/ *n.* 男巫 同 magician	a man supposed to have magical power; enchanter	He does things that are marvellous or apparently impossible; he is a ***wizard***. 他能做奇异的或显然不可能的事;他真是个巫师。

EXERCISE 4.5 从第五部分中选出最恰当的单词,填入空格内:

1. One of the most important aims of education is to develop students' ______ abilities to the utmost extent.
2. His television set was ______ to pay his room rent.
3. He ______ with pain when the tooth was pulled out.
4. She referred to the expected decease of her mother, and the gloomy ______ of funeral rites.
5. There is nothing new here; just the same old ideas in a different ______.

解答 1. latent 2. pawned 3. bellowed 4. sequel 5. guise

效果检测

EXERCISE 4.6 找出与其他三个不相关的词:

______ 1. (A) demon (B) witch
(C) fiend (D) devil

______ 2. (A) prediction (B) inclination
(C) propensity (D) tendency

______ 3. (A) stroll (B) strut
(C) swagger (D) stutter

______ 4. (A) relinquish (B) abdicate
(C) debase (D) surrender

______ 5. (A) virtual (B) righteous
(C) real (D) actual

______ 6. (A) surge (B) scorch
(C) singe (D) sear

______ 7. (A) baffle (B) dissemble
(C) mystify (D) perplex

______ 8. (A) quake (B) sting
(C) shiver (D) shudder

______ 9. (A) labyrinth (B) tyro
(C) maze (D) perplexity

______ 10. (A) temporary (B) covert
(C) latent (D) potential

解答 1. B 2. A 3. D 4. C 5. B
6. A 7. B 8. B 9. B 10. A

EXERCISE 4.7 读下面的句子,选出句中斜体词所代表的意义:

______ 1. Sudden illness *deranged* our plan for a trip.
(A) delayed (B) amended
(C) disturbed (D) influenced

______ 2. The boy *iterated* his assurance that he would be very careful with my bicycle.
(A) proclaimed (B) urged
(C) stressed (D) repeated

______ 3. Tom has been *badgering* his big brother to buy him a new bicycle.

(A) teasing (B) demanding

(C) suggesting (D) forcing

______ 4. *Salvage* of the furniture was hampered by the heat of the flames.

(A) protection (B) rescue

(C) alignment (D) concealment

______ 5. His mother *scanned* his face to see if he was telling the truth.

(A) indicated (B) scrutinized

(C) carassed (D) penetrated

______ 6. Among the *sequels* of the party were many stomach aches.

(A) diseases (B) expectations

(C) consequences (D) foods

______ 7. The odd noises and flashes of light in the empty house completely *baffled* him.

(A) horrified (B) surrounded

(C) perplexed (D) surprised

______ 8. A young woman of modest *guise* was standing before a shop window.

(A) appearance (B) height

(C) age (D) behavior

______ 9. The *incessant* noise from the factory kept me awake all night.

(A) irritating (B) shrill

(C) continuous (D) uncomfortable

______ 10. The male bird *strutted* in front of the female bird.

(A) swaggered (B) stopped

(C) crouched (D) screeched

解答 1. C 2. D 3. A 4. B 5. B
6. C 7. C 8. A 9. C 10. A

EXERCISE 4.8 找出与斜体词意义最接近的单词：

______ 1. *mute* letter (A) capital (B) last (C) silent (D) small

______ 2. *latent* period (A) sluggish (B) hidden (C) facetious (D) tardy

______ 3. *gaunt* face (A) lean (B) fat (C) large (D) bright

______ 4. *sequel* of a drama (A) development (B) performance (C) continuation (D) semblance

______ 5. *onerous* duty (A) unique (B) honorable (C) common (D) arduous

解答 1. C 2. B 3. A 4. C 5. D

EXERCISE 4.9 从下列单词中选出最恰当的词，填入空格内：

VOCABULARY LIST

conjecturing	pined	converged	demean
efface	baffled	sequel	propensity
cloak	dissipate	transfixed	scanned

1. The attention of all the audience ______ on the screen as soon as the motion picture started.
2. Day and night she ______ for her departed mother.
3. She would never ______ the memory of her dead child.
4. Don't ______ yourself by doing such a dishonorable thing.
5. Famine and disease are sometimes the ______ of floods or war.
6. The examination ______ me completely and I couldn't answer it.
7. She looks more attractive in ______ than in a coat.

8. He had a ______ to blame everything on his little brother.

9. I don't agree with his ______ that the government will lose the next election.

10. He was ______ to the spot when I told him the terrible news.

解答 1. converged 2. pined 3. efface 4. demean 5. sequel 6. baffled 7. cloak 8. propensity 9. conjecturing 10. transfixed

LESSON 5

预备测验

选出最恰当的答案：

1. The ______ man was *appeased* when they said they were sorry.

   (A) coward　　(B) angry　　(C) great

2. More than a thousand people were ______ in the *massacre*.

   (A) gathered　　(B) captured　　(C) killed

3. She worked herself up into a *frenzy* because she thought she'd miss her ____.

   (A) job　　(B) train　　(C) baby

4. At last she *surmised* from his ______ from school that there's something wrong with him.

   (A) friend　　(B) absence　　(C) compliment

5. A leader must take ______ unless he is *incapacitated*.

   (A) example　　(B) prestige　　(C) command

答案 1. B　2. C　3. B　4. B　5. C

第一部分

WORD	MEANING	TYPICAL USE
admonish /əd'mɒnɪʃ/ *v.* 警告 同 advise	warn of a fault; advise against doing something; forewarn	He ***admonished*** his friend not to be late for his work. 他警告他的朋友上班不可迟到。

WORD	MEANING	TYPICAL USE
bide /baɪd/ *v.* 等待 同 remain	wait for a long time until the right moment; wait	He seems to be doing nothing, but really he's just ***biding*** his time. 他好像无事可做,其实他是在等待良机。
condone /kən'dəʊn/ *v.* 宽恕;赦免 同 excuse	forgive (wrong action or behavior); overlook; pass over	A man who cheats on his income tax and on his expense account tends to ***condone*** these practices in his friends. 自己在所得税和费用账户上做手脚的人,对朋友的这类做法也会原谅。
designate /'dezɪgneɪt/ *v.* 指出;指示 同 appoint	mark out; point out; select for duty or other position	I ***designate*** you to act for me while I am away. 我指定你在我不在时代理我的事务。
fend /fend/ *v.* 抵挡;抵御 同 defend	defend oneself from; take care of; provide for	Most animals let their young ***fend*** for themselves at an early age. 大部分的动物让年轻的一代在年幼时就自己保护自己。

WORD	MEANING	TYPICAL USE
hardy /ˈhɑːdɪ/ *adj.* 强壮的 同 robust	able to bear hard treatment; strong	Only ***hardy*** plants will survive the severe cold in the Arctic area. 只有强壮的植物才能耐住北极地区的酷寒而生存下来。
limber /ˈlɪmbə(r)/ *v.* 使(自身)变柔软、灵活 同 supple	make flexible	Baseball players do exercises at the beginning of the season in order to ***limber*** themselves up. 棒球选手在赛季开始时做运动，以使身体灵活。
philanthropy /fɪˈlænθrəpɪ/ *n.* 慈善 同 charity	love of mankind; practical sympathy and benevolence	You must pay in humiliation of spirit for every benefit received at the hands of ***philanthropy***. 你必须以谦虚的精神去回报，因为每一既得的利益都来自慈善心。
recollect /ˌrekəˈlekt/ *v.* 记起；忆起 同 recall	remember (something past); call to mind again	Can you ***recollect*** the name of the author of ***Ivanhoe***? 你能想起《劫后英雄传》的作者的名字吗?

WORD	MEANING	TYPICAL USE
smite /smaɪt/ *v.* 打;击 同 affect	strike hard; have a powerful sudden effect on	He was ***smitten*** with the view that he stopped and took out his camera. 他被这一景象所震撼,所以停下来拿出照相机。
testimony /ˈtestɪmənɪ/ *n.* 证实;口供 同 proof	evidence; a solemn declaration, often one made by a witness in a lawcourt	According to the ***testimony*** of the medical profession, the health of the nation is improving. 据医学界宣称,该国人民的健康状况正在提高。

EXERCISE 5.1 从第一部分中选出最恰当的单词,填入空格内:

1. He is stiff when he begins to skate, but ______ up easily.
2. These x-marks on the drawing ______ all the possible entrances to the castle.
3. The teacher ______ the boys not to be late for the athletic meeting.
4. A few ______ men broke the ice on the pond and had a swim.
5. The sound of an explosion ______ our ears last night.

答案 1. limbers 2. designate 3. admonished 4. hardy 5. smote

第二部分

WORD	MEANING	TYPICAL USE
ale /eɪl/ *n.* 麦酒（一种啤酒）同 ginger	a kind of beer; an alcoholic drink similar to beer; lager; porter	He liked the bitter taste of the ***ale***; beer is his favorite drink. 他喜欢麦酒里的苦味；啤酒是他最喜爱的饮料。
blend /blend/ *v.* 混合；混杂 同 combine	mix together; mix thoroughly; mingle	***Blend*** the butter and the sugar before adding other ingredients of the cake. 在加入蛋糕的其他配料之前，先把奶油和糖混合一下。
carnivorous /kɑːˈnɪvərəs/ *adj.* 食肉的 同 cannibal	flesh-eating	The ***carnivorous*** animals are characterized especially by large, sharp canine teeth. 肉食动物的特征是牙齿大而尖。
denizen /ˈdenɪzən/ *n.* 居民；生活在特定地方的动物 同 inhabitant	a person or animal that lives in a place; occupant	The common English sparrow is a ***denizen*** of America; it was first brought from Europe to America about 1850. 美洲的英国种麻雀是外来的，大约在1850年第一次从欧洲被带到美洲。

WORD	MEANING	TYPICAL USE
frenzy /ˈfrenzɪ/ *n.* 暴怒；狂乱 同 ferment	near madness; mental derangement; very great excitement	She was in a ***frenzy*** of grief when she heard that her child was missing. 当她听说孩子走失时，伤心得快要发狂了。
incapacitate /ˌɪnkəˈpæsɪteɪt/ *v.* 使不能；使不适于 同 disable	limit in ability, power or fitness; paralyze	The player's injury ***incapacitated*** him for participating in the football match. 那名运动员的伤势使得他无法参加足球比赛。
massacre /ˈmæsəkə(r)/ *v.* 大屠杀 同 slaughter	slaughter of people or animals; pitilessly kill without mercy	The hunters came from the East to ***massacre*** the buffalo of the plains, killing several million in a short time. 来自东部的猎人屠杀平原上的水牛，在很短的时间内就杀了好几百万头。
ponder /ˈpɒndə(r)/ *v.* 考虑；沉思 同 meditate	think about deeply; consider seriously; muse	When I asked his advice he ***pondered*** the matter and then told me not to go. 当我征求他的意见时，他考虑了一下那件事，然后告诉我不要去。

WORD	MEANING	TYPICAL USE
riddle /ˈrɪdl/ *n.* 不可解之问题;谜 同 enigma	a puzzling question, statement or problem, usually as a game or pastime; puzzle; conundrum	To the ***riddle*** "What walks on four legs in the morning, two legs at noon, and three legs in the evening?" the answer is "man". 谜语:什么东西早上用四只脚走路,中午用两只脚,黄昏用三只脚? 答案是"人"。
spank /spæŋk/ *v.* 打 同 beat	strike with quick force; blow with the open hand; hit	The father ***spanked*** the naughty child for his bad manners. 父亲因那顽皮孩子的无礼行为而打他。
totter /ˈtɒtə(r)/ *v.* 蹒跚 同 stagger	stand or walk with shaky, unsteady steps; falter	The old man ***tottered*** across the room and sat down on the sofa. 那老人蹒跚地走过房间,然后坐在沙发上。

EXERCISE 5.2 从第二部分中选出最恰当的单词,填入空格内:

1. The crowd was in a(n) ______ after the home team scored the winning goal.
2. The king ordered all the infants in the country to be ______.
3. Before casting his vote, a responsible and mature citizen should ______ his

choice of candidates.

4. A bartender must know how to ______ different kinds of drinks.

5. The famous ______ of the Sphinx was an enigma that only Oedipus could interpret.

解答 1. frenzy 2. massacred 3. ponder 4. blend 5. riddle

第三部分

WORD	MEANING	TYPICAL USE
appease /ə'piːz/ v. 使平静，安静 同 placate	make calm or quiet; tranquilize	He tried to ***appease*** the crying child by giving him candy. 他试图用糖果来安抚哭泣的小孩。
catastrophe /kə'tæstrəfɪ/ n. 异常的大灾祸 同 calamity	a sudden, unexpected, and terrible event that causes great suffering; disaster	The war was a terrible ***catastrophe*** in which many people died and many buildings were destroyed. 战争是可怕的大灾祸，其间有许多人丧生，许多建筑物被摧毁。
daunt /dɔːnt/ v. 恐吓；使失去勇气或信心 同 dismay	frighten; cause to lose courage or the will to act; dishearten	He felt completely ***daunted*** by the difficulties that faced him. 他对面前的困难感到彻底气馁。

WORD	MEANING	TYPICAL USE
gape /geɪp/ v. 张嘴注视 同 stare, gawk	stare with the mouth open; yawn	The crowd ***gaped*** at the daring tricks performed by the tightrope walker. 观众们张大了嘴注视着走绳索人大胆的表演。
duration /djʊəˈreɪʃən/ n. 持续的时间 同 period	length of time; the time during which anything continues; term	He will be in the hospital for the ***duration*** of the school year. 整个学年他都会待在医院里。
implore /ɪmˈplɔː(r)/ v. 哀求;苦求 同 entreat	beg for; beseech	We ***implored*** him to act before it was too late. 我们苦苦哀求他及时行动。
muffle /ˈmʌfl/ v. 围住;将……蒙起以使声音低沉 同 wrap	wrap in something in order to soften or stop the sound; stifle	She ***muffled*** her throat in a warm scarf so as not to catch a cold. 她用一条保暖围巾围住脖子,以防感冒。
prank /præŋk/ n. 戏谑;恶作剧 同 trick	playful trick; a piece of mischief	On April Fool's Day people often play ***pranks*** on each other. 在愚人节人们彼此戏谑。

WORD	MEANING	TYPICAL USE
saunter /ˈsɔːntə(r)/ *v.* 闲逛;漫步 同 stroll	walk slowly and idly; amble	Soapy took the umbrella and ***sauntered*** off with it slowly. 索皮拿着雨伞闲逛。
trickle /ˈtrɪkl/ *n.* 细流 同 drip	a thin flow or stream; ooze	There was a ***trickle*** of blood from the wound on his face. 他脸上的伤口处有鲜血渗出。

EXERCISE 5.3 从第三部分中选出最恰当的单词,填入空格内:

1. A land reform program benefited the poor but it was a ______ for rich landowners.
2. She ______ the ball so that it would not awaken the family.
3. She ______ at the tall man, thinking that he might be her younger brother.
4. He served in the army for the ______ of World War Ⅰ.
5. To ______ my angry neighbor, I offered to make good the damage.

答案 1. catastrophe 2. muffled 3. gaped 4. duration 5. appease

第四部分

WORD	MEANING	TYPICAL USE
astound /əsˈtaʊnd/ *v.* 使惊异 同 amaze	shock with alarm or surprise; surprise very greatly	She was ***astounded*** by the news that she had won the speech contest. 她听到自己演讲比赛获胜的消息，感到十分惊讶。
clan /klæn/ *n.* 宗族；部落 同 tribe	a group of families with a common ancestor	The people living in that valley are all members of one ***clan***. 住在那座山谷里的都是同一部落的人。
distort /disˈtɔːt/ *v.* 歪曲；扭曲 同 falsify	change from the truth; turn from the true meaning; misrepresent	That man's speech ***distorted*** the truth. 那个人的讲话歪曲了事实真相。
entrust /ɪnˈtrʌst/ *v.* 信托；交托 同 commit	charge with a trust; trust	While travelling, they ***entrusted*** their children to the care of a baby sitter. 外出旅行时，他们把孩子交给保姆看管。
glutton /ˈglʌtn/ *n.* 贪吃的人；贪多者 同 gormandizer	a greedy eater; a person who eats too much; gorger	Sometimes he gets hungry and eats like a ***glutton***. 当他饥饿的时候，吃起东西来狼吞虎咽。

WORD	MEANING	TYPICAL USE
invalid 1. /ɪnˈvælɪd/ *adj.* 无效的 同 worthless 2. /ˈɪnvəliːd/ *adj.*, *n.* 有病的(人) 同 patient	1. not valid; without force or effect 2. not well; weak and sick	Unless a check is signed, it is ***invalid***. 支票除非签了名,否则是无效的。 He became an ***invalid*** as the result of ill health and lack of exercise. 他生病是健康状况不良又缺乏运动的结果。
overtone /ˌəʊvəˈtəʊn/ *n.* 寓意;弦外音 同 implication	things that are suggested but not shown or stated clearly	His words were polite but there was an ***overtone*** of anger in his voice. 他说话客气但是语气中带了一丝愤怒。
probe /prəʊb/ *v.* 探求;细察 同 investigate	search into; examine thoroughly	They ***probed*** his past career to judge his qualifications. 他们调查他过去的职业,以评判他的资格。
shrine /ʃraɪn/ *n.* 圣地 同 sanctuary	any sacred place, such as an altar, church, or temple; holy place	There are many sacred ***shrines*** in the Near East. 在近东有许多古迹圣地。
statute /ˈstætjuːt/ *n.* 成文法;法规 同 bill	a law, especially one passed by a lawmaking body; act; measure	The ***statute*** increased the taxes we must pay. 法律提高了我们必须缴的税额。

WORD	MEANING	TYPICAL USE
writhe /raɪð/ *v.* 扭动;转动 同 wriggle	twist and turn; twist about; squirm	The wounded soldier ***writhed*** uncomfortably in pain. 受伤的士兵痛得直打滚。

EXERCISE 5.4 从第四部分中选出最恰当的单词,填入空格内:

1. He ______ the mud, searching for the ring he dropped.
2. His loud voice includes a(n) ______ of anger.
3. He ______ the account of his experiences to make a better story.
4. The ______ of the United States are made by Congress.
5. You have eaten the whole pie; you are really a(n) ______.

答案 1. probed 2. overtone 3. distorted 4. statutes 5. glutton

第五部分

WORD	MEANING	TYPICAL USE
behold /bɪˈhəʊld/ *v.* 看 同 observe	look at; see; witness	Watching the first man land on the moon, we ***beheld*** a sight never seen before by man. 看着那第一个登上月球的人,我们看到了人类前所未见的景象。

WORD	MEANING	TYPICAL USE
condescend /ˌkɒndɪˈsend/ *v.* 屈尊;降格相从 同 deign	come down willingly or graciously to the level of one's inferiors in rank	They should change this bad habit and ***condescend*** to be pleased with the common people. 他们应该改变这种不好的习惯,放下架子和普通人一同欢笑。
dike /daɪk/ *n.* 1. 堤 同 bank	1. a bank of earth or a dam built as a defense against flooding	More than 5,000 years ago the Chinese were controlling the Yellow River floods with ***dikes***. 五千多年前,中国人用堤坝来控制黄河洪水的泛滥。
2. 沟 同 ditch	2. a narrow passage dug to carry water away.	The farmers dug a deep ***dike*** to carry water to the rice field. 农民们挖了一条深沟把水引到稻田里。
flip /flɪp/ *v.* (用指)轻弹 同 toss	toss or move with a snap of the finger	He ***flipped*** a coin on the counter to decide whether to go to the theater or not. 他在柜台上投币以决定要不要去看电影。

WORD	MEANING	TYPICAL USE
grisly /ˈɡrɪzlɪ/ *adj.* 可怕的；狰狞的 同 horrible	causing horror; frightful; ghastly; gruesome	My uncle who had travelled to many countries in the world told a ***grisly*** story about people who ate human flesh. 我那遍游世界各地的舅舅说了一个吃人肉的可怕故事。
knave /neɪv/ *n.* 骗子；诡计多端的人 同 rogue	a tricky or dishonest person; rascal; scoundrel	The ***knaves*** who set fire to the barn have been caught and sent to prison. 纵火烧谷仓的坏人被抓起来送到牢里去了。
parley /ˈpɑːlɪ/ *n.* 谈判；商议 同 negotiation	a talk held between leaders of opposing forces; talk; discussion	The general held a ***parley*** with the enemy's leader about exchanging prisoners. 将军和敌军的领袖商议交换俘虏的事。
shred /ʃred/ *n.* 碎片；细条；些许 同 fragment	a small piece either cut off or torn off; scrap; bit	There is not a ***shred*** of evidence that the missing money was stolen. 没有丝毫证据说明丢了的钱是被偷走的。

WORD	MEANING	TYPICAL USE
surmise /səˈmaɪz/ *v.* 臆测;猜测 同 guess	form an idea or opinion with few supporting facts; suppose	The judge ***surmised*** his guilt; there was no proof that he killed the man. 法官臆测他犯了罪;没有证据显示是他杀了那个人。
vicissitude /vɪˈsɪsɪtjuːd/ *n.* 变迁;变化 同 variety	regular change; a change of conditions or circumstances; a turn of fortune	The future is so uncertain that we cannot know all the ***vicissitudes*** of our fortunes. 未来是无法确知的,我们无法知道将来命运的所有变化。
warden /ˈwɔːdən/ *n.* 看守人;监护人 同 watchman	a person who looks after a place; a head keeper; warder	The fire ***warden*** told us not to light matches near the gas station. 消防队长告诉我们不要在靠近加油站的地方划火柴。

EXERCISE 5.5 从第五部分中选出最恰当的单词,填入空格内:

1. I ______ open the pages of the magazine to find an interesting article.
2. Her new dress was torn into ______ by herself.
3. The ______ of life may suddenly make a rich man very poor.
4. The future is so uncertain that no one can ______ the course of the rest of his life.

5. Mrs. Smith has no servant but her husband will never ______ to help her with the housework.

解答 1. flipped 2. shreds 3. vicissitudes 4. surmise 5. condescend

效果检测

EXERCISE 5.6 找出与其他三个不相关的词：

______ 1. (A) investigate (B) probe (C) testify (D) scan

______ 2. (A) scoundrel (B) bulwark (C) rascal (D) rogue

______ 3. (A) weigh (B) ponder (C) signify (D) contemplate

______ 4. (A) gruesome (B) ghastly (C) grisly (D) groove

______ 5. (A) clan (B) fiend (C) party (D) fraternity

______ 6. (A) reprove (B) reproach (C) admonish (D) advocate

______ 7. (A) derision (B) riddle (C) enigma (D) conundrum

______ 8. (A) pedlar (B) sentinel (C) warden (D) warder

______ 9. (A) implore (B) fumble (C) beseech (D) entreat

______ 10. (A) propensity (B) catastrophe (C) disaster (D) calamity

解答 1. C 2. B 3. C 4. D 5. B
6. D 7. A 8. A 9. B 10. A

EXERCISE 5.7 读下面的句子,选出句中斜体词所代表的意义:

______ 1. The driver *distorted* the account of the fact to escape blame.
(A) illustrated (B) reported
(C) falsified (D) explained

______ 2. The cat's happy expression bore *testimony* that it had eaten the cream.
(A) doubt (B) proof
(C) experience (D) revelation

______ 3. We shall seek no terms and we shall tolerate no *parley*.
(A) conference (B) rescue
(C) larceny (D) fray

______ 4. She *implored* her mother to give permission for her to go on the trip.
(A) persuaded (B) suggested
(C) beseeched (D) enforced

______ 5. The Red Cross appealed to *philanthropy* to save the life of a prisoner.
(A) public (B) charity
(C) justice (D) attorney

______ 6. The woman was *astounded* to learn that her dearest friend had been spreading bad gossip about her.
(A) surprised (B) irrigated
(C) disappointed (D) cumbered

______ 7. Jack devoted himself to the protection of the *denizens* of the forest.

(A) visitors (B) customers
(C) merchants (D) inhabitants

______ 8. We *surmised* that the traffic delay was caused by some accident on the highway.
(A) assessed (B) supposed
(C) decided (D) confessed

______ 9. She tried to *probe* my mind and discover what I was thinking.
(A) testify (B) approve
(C) investigate (D) flatter

______ 10. That man has been *designated* by the President as the next Secretary of State.
(A) appointed (B) decided
(C) admitted (D) recommended

解答 1. C 2. B 3. A 4. C 5. B
6. A 7. D 8. B 9. C 10. A

EXERCISE 5.8 找出与斜体词意义最接近的单词:

______ 1. a *vicissitude* of life (A) variation (B) condition
(C) shortness (D) process

______ 2. the *ale* house (A) gold (B) drug
(C) beer (D) log

______ 3. a *shred* of evidence (A) appearance (B) security
(C) division (D) bit

______ 4. *hardy* sports (A) difficult (B) robust
(C) important (D) dangerous

______ 5. the game *warden* (A) manager (B) observe
(C) participant (D) watchman

解答 1. A 2. C 3. D 4. B 5. D

EXERCISE 5.9 从下列单词中选出最恰当的词，填入空格内：

VOCABULARY LIST

carnivorous	designate	duration	admonished
distort	implore	daunted	muffled
condescended	fend	testimony	bide

1. The examination questions were rather difficult, but the students were not ______ by them.
2. He may get a good job if he can ______ his time.
3. We hope the war will be of short ______.
4. Now that his father is dead he must ______ for himself.
5. The colonel's wife finally ______ to visit the sergeant's sick wife.
6. Their guide ______ the mountain climbers to follow him carefully.
7. Sheep and cows are not ______ animals, but lions and tigers are.
8. The pupils presented their teacher with a gold watch as ______ of their respect and affection.
9. The sound of the bell was ______ by the curtains behind the door.
10. The committee will ______ him the winner of the contest tomorrow.

解答 1. daunted 2. bide 3. duration
4. fend 5. condescended 6. admonished
7. carnivorous 8. testimony 9. muffled
10. designate

LESSON 6

预备测验

选出最恰当的答案：

1. Some people gather books *haphazard* and without ______.
   (A) consideration　(B) hastiness　(C) random
2. She *rued* very bitterly when she ______ her mother.
   (A) lost　(B) insulted　(C) met
3. Let us be exact in what we say so as to *preclude* any possibility of ______.
   (A) failure　(B) anomaly　(C) misunderstanding
4. The doctor *reproved* the nurse who had been ______ her patient.
   (A) examining　(B) neglecting　(C) caring
5. It was definite that he was to be a passenger on the boat, though he would not be *explicit* about his ______.
   (A) destination　(B) ability　(C) ticket

解答 1.A 2.A 3.C 4.B 5.A

第一部分

WORD	MEANING	TYPICAL USE
abhor /əbˈhɔː(r)/ *v*. 憎恶；痛恨 反 adore	feel very great hatred and dislike for; hate very much; detest; loathe	Most people ***abhor*** the criminal for kidnapping the children. 大部分人憎恶那个绑架儿童的罪犯。

WORD	MEANING	TYPICAL USE
boost /buːst/ 1. *v.* 由后推;推上 反 lower	1. push up from below	If you ***boost*** me up, I can reach the window easily. 假使你把我往上推,我就能很容易够得着窗子。
2. *n.* 推动;激励	2. an act of promoting or uplifting; encouragement	His friend's willingness to help him was a big ***boost*** to his morale. 他的朋友自愿帮忙,这极大地鼓舞了他。
detention /dɪˈtenʃən/ *n.* 监禁;延迟 反 release	the act of holding back; detainment; delay	The jail is used for ***detention*** of persons who have been arrested. 监狱是用来监禁被逮捕的人的。
explicit /ɪksˈplɪsɪt/ *adj.* 明确的 反 implicit	clearly or fully expressed or stated, leaving nothing to be imagined; definite; precise	He gave such ***explicit*** directions that everyone understood them. 他给的指示很明确,每个人都能理解。
invidious /ɪnˈvɪdɪəs/ *adj.* 易招怨恨的 反 just	likely to cause ill will or resentment	Wise teachers avoid ***invidious*** rules against the students. 聪明的老师避免作出让学生厌恶的规定。

WORD	MEANING	TYPICAL USE
malign /mə'laɪn/ v. 诋毁;诽谤 反 praise	speak ill of; slander	You ***malign*** a generous person when you call him a stingy person. 当你说一个慷慨的人吝啬时,你就是在诋毁他。
potable /'pəʊtəbl/ adj. 适于饮用的 反 undrinkable	drinkable; fit for drinking	In places where the water is not ***potable***, they set up purifying systems. 在水无法饮用的地方,人们设立净化系统。
rue /ruː/ v. 后悔;悔恨 反 rejoice	be sorry for; regret; repent	I never went to school, and I've ***rued*** it bitterly all my life. 我终身懊悔没上过学。
subsist /səb'sɪst/ v. 存在 反 decease	keep alive; live; exist	People in the far north ***subsist*** chiefly on fish and meat. 住在北极地区的人主要以鱼和肉为生。
unruly /ʌn'ruːlɪ/ adj. 难控制的;不守法的 反 manageable	hard to rule or control; ungovernable	She was such an ***unruly*** child that nobody could get along with her. 她是一个不守规矩的孩子,没人能和她相处。

EXERCISE 6.1 从第一部分中选出最恰当的单词，填入空格内：

1. He was quite ______ about the matter, leaving no doubt about what he meant.
2. The mayor sued the television station because it ______ him by accusing him of dishonest use of city funds.
3. If I ask my sister to turn down the radio she makes it even louder; I can't understand why she is so ______.
4. He is in ______ in connection with the bribery affair.
5. ______ me up the trees and I'll get some apples for you.

解答 1. explicit 2. maligned 3. unruly 4. detention 5. Boost

第二部分

WORD	MEANING	TYPICAL USE
agile /ˈædʒaɪl/ *adj.* 活泼的；敏捷的 反 clumsy	active; able to move quickly and easily; lively; nimble	The boy had an ***agile*** mind, and could come up with excuses as quickly as his mother asked for them. 那男孩头脑机敏。当他母亲询问理由时，他马上就能想出来。
caprice /kəˈpriːs/ *n.* 反复无常；善变 反 steadfastness	a sudden change of mind without reason; whim	His lack of money was the result of ***caprice*** in spending on unnecessary things. 他缺钱是他乱花钱，买些不需要的东西导致的。

WORD	MEANING	TYPICAL USE
disconsolate /dɪsˈkɒnsəlɪt/ *adj*. 孤独的；绝望的 反 jubilant	hopelessly sad at the loss of something without comfort of hope	She is ***disconsolate*** about the death of her father. 父亲的死令她悲痛欲绝。
fallacy /ˈfæləsɪ/ *n*. 谬见；谬误 反 truth	a mistaken belief; a false idea; an error; delusion	It is a popular ***fallacy*** to suppose that riches always bring happiness. 认为财富永远会带来幸福是一种常见的谬见。
ingenuous /ɪnˈdʒenjʊəs/ *adj*. 坦白的；老实的 反 dissembling	frank and open; candid; straight forward; naive	She gave ***ingenuous*** answers to all of the strangers' questions. 她诚实地回答了所有陌生人提出的问题。
mirage /ˈmɪrɑːʒ, mɪˈ-/ *n*. 海市蜃楼；空想 反 reality	an optical illusion; illusion; delusion; fantasy	I saw a ***mirage*** that made the highway ahead seem to be flooded with water. 我看见一个幻影，前头的公路好似被水淹没一般。
preclude /prɪˈkluːd/ *v*. 妨碍；阻止；使不可能 反 permit	make impossible; prevent; exclude; hinder	The heavy thunderstorm ***precluded*** our going to the beach. 大的雷雨使我们不能去海滨。

WORD	MEANING	TYPICAL USE
sheer /ʃɪə/ *adj.* 1. 极薄的 反 opaque	1. very thin; almost transparent	***Sheer*** white curtains hung at the little window to let in as much light as possible. 小窗上挂着极薄的白窗帘,尽量让阳光照进来。
2. 垂直的	2. straight up and down; perpendicular	From the top of the wall there was a ***sheer*** drop of 100 feet to the water below. 水从墙的最上端垂直落下,落差达到100英尺。
succinct /səkˈsɪŋkt/ *adj.* 简明的;简洁的 反 verbose	expressed briefly and clearly; concise; precise	His letter was ***succinct***, with all the major points on one page. 他的信很简洁,所有的重点都写在一页上。

EXERCISE 6.2 从第二部分中选出最恰当的单词,填入空格内:

1. The ______ child had never thought of being suspicious of what others told her.
2. Walls and bars ______ the possibility of escape.
3. I could see the garden through the ______ curtains of the window.
4. The cat was ______ because her kitten died.
5. The travellers in the desert saw an oasis in the distance but it was only a ______.

答案 1. ingenuous　2. preclude　3. sheer　4. disconsolate　5. mirage

第三部分

WORD	MEANING	TYPICAL USE
arable /ˈærəbl/ *adj.* 适于耕种的 反 sterile	suitable for producing crops; fit for plowing	There is not much ***arable*** land on the side of a rocky mountain. 在覆满岩石的山坡上没有多少适于耕种的土地。
complacent /kəmˈpleɪsnt/ *adj.* 自满的 反 self-condemned	self-satisfied; pleased with oneself	The winner's ***complacent*** smile annoyed the loser in the football game. 胜利者洋洋自得的微笑让足球赛的失败者深感厌恶。
dismember /dɪsˈmembə(r)/ *v.* 1. 肢解	1. cut or tear the links from	The wolves ***dismembered*** the deer's dead body with their sharp teeth. 狼用锐利的牙齿撕碎了小鹿的死尸。
2. 分裂;分割 反 consolidate	2. cut to pieces; separate or divide into parts	After the war, the defeated country was ***dismembered*** and could no longer be called a nation. 战后,战败国被瓜分,不再称得上是个国家了。

WORD	MEANING	TYPICAL USE
glee /gliː/ *n.* 欢乐；高兴 反 agony	a feeling of joyful satisfaction at something which pleases one; mirth; gaiety	She danced with ***glee*** when she saw the new toys which her father bought for her birthday. 当她看到父亲为她的生日买的新玩具时，高兴得手舞足蹈。
implicit /ɪmˈplɪsɪt/ *adj.* 暗含的；含蓄的 反 explicit	meant, but not clearly expressed or distinctly stated; implied	He gave us ***implicit*** consent to take the apples, for he smiled when he saw us do it. 他暗示我们可以拿那些苹果，因为当他看见我们在拿时，他微微地笑了。
mischievous /ˈmɪstʃɪvəs/ *adj.* 恶作剧的；淘气的 反 beneficial	naughty; full of mischief; playful; teasing	Someone is spreading ***mischievous*** stories about the minister's private life. 有人在散布有关部长私生活的谣言。
redundant /rɪˈdʌndənt/ *adj.* 过多的 反 necessary	not needed; more than is necessary; superfluous	In the sentence "She lives alone by herself" the word "alone" is ***redundant***. 在句子"她自己独自生活中"，"独自"是多余的词。

WORD	MEANING	TYPICAL USE
solicitude /səˈlɪsɪtjuːd/ *n.* 焦虑;关怀 反 indifference	anxious care; anxiety	The ***solicitude*** shown to him by his neighbors after the robbery impressed him very deeply. 遭抢劫之后,邻居的关切之情给他留下了深刻的印象。
surplus /ˈsɜːpləs/ *n.* 过剩;剩余 反 deficit	an amount over and above what is needed; excess	The bank keeps a large ***surplus*** of money in reserve. 银行保存一笔巨额备用金。

EXERCISE 6.3 从第三部分中选出最适当的单词,填入空格内:

1. The children laughed with ______ at the circus man's humorous action.
2. She broke up her brother's marriage by spreading ______ rumors about his wife.
3. However many matches a team wins, it should never be allowed to get ______.
4. Her silence gave ______ consent when I asked her to go to the dance party tonight.
5. They were thankful for the ______ of the king over the well-being of their subjects.

答案 1. glee 2. mischievous 3. complacent 4. implicit 5. solicitude

第四部分

WORD	MEANING	TYPICAL USE
abate /əˈbeɪt/ *v.* 减少;减轻 反 enhance	become less strong; decrease; lessen	The doctor gave him some medicine to ***abate*** the pain. 那医生给他一些药以减轻痛苦。
consummate /ˈkɒnsəmeɪt/ *v.* 完成;实现 反 baffle	bring to completion; realize; fulfil	His ambition was ***consummated*** when he won the prize. 当他获奖时,他的抱负实现了。
dwindle /ˈdwɪndl/ *v.* 缩减;减少 反 increase	become gradually fewer or smaller; shrink; diminish	Our savings have ***dwindled*** since my wife was sent to hospital. 自从我太太住进医院以后,我们的存款减少了。
haphazard /ˌhæpˈhæzəd/ *adj.* 偶然的;随便的 反 deliberate	not to be planned; random; by chance	It is a ***haphazard*** timetable; sometimes lessons are held and sometimes they aren't. 这是个不确定的课程表;有时有课;有时没课。

WORD	MEANING	TYPICAL USE
obvious /ˈɒbvɪəs/ *adj.* 显然的;明白的 反 equivocal	easy to understand; clear; apparent; conspicuous	It is ***obvious*** that a blind man ought not to drive an automobile. 瞎子不应该开车是很明显的事。
overt /ˈəʊvɜːt/ *adj.* 公然的;明显的 反 stealthy	open or public; not hidden	I know only his ***overt*** reasons for refusing; he may have others. 我只知道他拒绝的表面理由;也许还有其他理由。
rebuff /rɪˈbʌf/ *n.* (对请求等)断然拒绝 反 admission	a rough or cruel answer when one is trying to be friendly or is asking for help	We tried to be friendly, but his ***rebuff*** made us think he wanted to be left alone. 我们试图表示友好,但他的拒绝让我们以为他不想被干扰。
somber /ˈsɒmbə(r)/ *adj.* 闷闷不乐的;阴沉的;幽暗的 反 cheerful	sad and gloomy; have deep shadows	He was sad and his thought about the future was very ***somber***. 他很不快乐,他对未来感到渺茫。

WORD	MEANING	TYPICAL USE
thwart /θwɔːt/ *v.* 反对；妨碍；挫折 反 encourage	oppose and defeat; keep from doing something; frustrate; baffle	The boy's lack of money ***thwarted*** his plans for college. 那男孩没钱，所以上大学的计划受阻。
vehement /ˈviːɪmənt/ *adj.* 强烈的；猛烈的 反 impassive	having or showing strong feeling; caused by strong feeling; eager; passionate	I have a ***vehement*** hatred of people who are cruel to animals. 我对残害动物的人很反感。

EXERCISE 6.4 从第四部分中选出最恰当的单词，填入空格内：

1. It was a(n) ______ room with dark furniture and heavy black hangings.
2. His happiness was ______ when she agreed to marry him.
3. When he did not drive the car home, it was ______ that he had an accident.
4. Although the rain has ______ somewhat, the wind is still blowing very hard.
5. I was ______ in my camping plans by the cold weather.

答案 1. somber 2. consummated 3. obvious 4. abated 5. thwarted

第五部分

WORD	MEANING	TYPICAL USE
benign /bɪˈnaɪn/ *adj*. 亲切的；和蔼的 反 malign	having a kind disposition; benevolent; generous	The ***benign*** old lady sent us a kind and warm smile. 那位和蔼的老婆婆冲我们露出亲切、温暖的微笑。
degrade /dɪˈgreɪd/ *v*. 降级；降格；免职 反 promote	reduce to a lower rank, often as a punishment; take away the position or an honor	The sergeant was ***degraded*** to private for the reason of disobeying orders. 那个中士因为不服从命令而被降为二等兵。
ephemeral /ɪˈfemərəl/ *adj*. 朝生暮死的；短命的 反 perpetual	lasting for only a very short time; transitory	My other writings are very ***ephemeral***, but this book will be remembered forever. 我其他的作品都很短命，但这本书将永远被人们记住。
illiterate /ɪˈlɪtərɪt/ *adj*. 文盲的 反 intelligent	uneducated; unable to read and write; ignorant	People who have never gone to school are usually ***illiterate***. 没上过学的人通常是目不识丁的。

WORD	MEANING	TYPICAL USE
lavish /ˈlævɪʃ/ 1. *adj.* 浪费的 反 stingy	1. very free or too free in giving or spending; prodigal	Not every rich man is ***lavish*** in spending money. 不是每一个富人都挥霍无度。
2. *v.* 滥用	2. give or spend very freely or too freely	It is a mistake to ***lavish*** kindness on ungrateful people. 对忘恩负义的人过于友好是错误的。
peddle /ˈpedl/ *v.* 沿街叫卖;兜售 反 wholesale	go from place to place trying to sell small goods	He is the one who is ***ped-dling*** the drugs unlawful-ly. 他非法兜售药品。
reprove /rɪˈpruːv/ *v.* 谴责;责骂 反 compliment	blame or find fault with in a gentle way; scold	She ***reproved*** the maid in an angry voice for breaking the dish. 她生气地责骂女用,因为她打碎了盘子。
synthetic /sɪnˈθetɪk/ *adj.* 人工制造的 反 natural	artificially made; man-made; artificial	Many kinds of fabrics, furs and drugs are ***synthet-ic*** products. 许多种布、毛皮和药物都是人造的。

WORD	MEANING	TYPICAL USE
unbounded /ʌnˈbaʊndɪd/ *adj.* 无限制的；无际的 反 limited	boundless; without limits; tremendous	His ***unbounded*** courage and compassion made him an excellent leader of the nation. 他那无穷的勇气和怜悯心，使他成为国家的优秀领导者。
wretched /ˈretʃɪd/ *adj.* 可怜的；不幸的 反 fortunate	very unfortunate or unhappy; miserable; pitiful	He was ***wretched*** when he failed the entrance examination again. 他很不走运，入学考试又没考好。

EXERCISE 6.5 从第五部分中选出最适当的单词，填入空格内：

1. Don't ______ yourself by answering such foolish charges against you.
2. He always ______ money and time on pets.
3. After the loss of their savings and their home they felt too ______ to see their old friends.
4. Giving money to help Red Cross is a(n) ______ act.
5. He writes in a very ______ way; there are many mistakes on every page.

答案 1. degrade 2. lavish 3. wretched
4. benign 5. illiterate

效果检测

EXERCISE 6.6 由第二栏中选出第一栏各词的反义词：

COLUMN Ⅰ	COLUMN Ⅱ
______ 1. disconsolate	(A) clumsy
______ 2. consummate	(B) release
______ 3. malign	(C) natural
______ 4. illiterate	(D) opaque
______ 5. agile	(E) jubilant
______ 6. synthetic	(F) reality
______ 7. detention	(G) intelligent
______ 8. succinct	(H) praise
______ 9. sheer	(I) dissatisfy
______ 10. mirage	(J) verbose

解答 1. E　2. I　3. H　4. G　5. A
6. C　7. B　8. J　9. D　10. F

EXERCISE 6.7 选出适当的词填入空格内：

1. They agreed to share in common any ______ of funds after all expenses were paid in full.
   (A) surplus　　(B) surpass
2. He is ______ over the death of his favorite wife and weary of his life.
   (A) disconsolate　　(B) invidious
3. The principal ______ the boy who had been smoking in the classroom.
   (A) satiated　　(B) reproved
4. The boy gave a(n) ______ account of his acts, concealing nothing.
   (A) complacent　　(B) ingenuous

5. My mother gave me ______ care and affection in my childhood.

(A) lavish (B) prudent

6. If your protest had been more ______, the dealer might have paid attention to it.

(A) vehement (B) agile

7. Her decision to wear only blue clothes was pure ______.

(A) misdemeanor (B) caprice

8. That politician didn't hesitate to eliminate his political enemies to fulfil his ______ ambition for power.

(A) unbounded (B) unruly

9. The cheer group clapped their hands in ______ at the defeat of their opponent.

(A) mirage (B) glee

10. Cotton is natural fiber, but rayon and nylon are ______.

(A) mandatory (B) synthetic

解答 1. A 2. A 3. B 4. B 5. A
6. A 7. B 8. A 9. B 10. B

EXERCISE 6.8 找出与斜体词意义相反的单词：

______ 1. *arable* (A) sterile (B) cruel (C) stingy (D) tedious

______ 2. *ephemeral* (A) consequent (B) hardy (C) mute (D) perpetual

______ 3. *fallacy* (A) success (B) truth (C) achievement (D) exploit

______ 4. *abhor* (A) agree (B) approve (C) adore (D) assess

______ 5. *preclude* (A) exclude (B) contend (C) permit (D) deplore

解答 1. A 2. D 3. B 4. C 5. C

EXERCISE 6.9 从下列单词中选出最适当的词，填入空格内：

VOCABULARY LIST

glee	ingenuous	abated	peddled
overt	redundant	maligned	wretched
implicit	dwindle	mischievous	lavish

1. The ______ boy went through the house hanging all the pictures upsidedown.
2. My mother didn't believe that Tom troubled me until she saw him in the ______ act of his pulling my hair.
3. The child shouted with ______ when the birthday cake was cut.
4. What a(n) ______ existence these poor people lead in the slums!
5. He ______ his innocent friend by calling him a robber.
6. The farmer ______ his fruit from house to house.
7. A teacher must give ______ praise to the pupils when they answer the questions correctly.
8. The ship waited till the storm ______ before sailing out to sea.
9. In "We two both ate an apple each" the word "two" is ______.
10. He agreed to give his ______ opinion if his name wasn't mentioned in the news story.

解答 1. mischievous 2. overt 3. glee 4. wretched 5. maligned 6. peddled 7. lavish 8. abated 9. redundant 10. ingenuous

LESSON 7

预备测验

选出最恰当的答案：

1. If there is anything *amiss* in the house, it must be ______ immediately.

   (A) bought (B) built (C) repaired

2. There are more feelings of ______ in the *haughty* person than in common men.

   (A) pride (B) angry (C) horror

3. His gym shoes were *immaculate* in spite of the ______.

   (A) pavement (B) rainy day (C) burden

4. He tries to *dissemble* his ______ by talking repeatedly about how brave he was in the army.

   (A) courage (B) cowardice (C) guilty

5. His death was *retarded* several days by the ______ of his doctor.

   (A) negligence (B) condition (C) skill

解答 1. C 2. A 3. B 4. B 5. C

第一部分

WORD	MEANING	TYPICAL USE
blithe /blaɪð/ *adj.* 快乐的 反 miserable	happy and cheerful; gay; joyful	She continued to work in a ***blithe*** spirit in spite of all difficulties. 虽然有许多困难,但她仍继续愉快地工作。
dejected /dɪˈdʒektɪd/ *adj.* 失望的;沮丧的 反 exuberant	in low spirits; sad; discouraged; depressed	She was feeling ***dejected*** and unhappy until the good news cheered her up. 她感到沮丧和不快,直到有了这好消息她才雀跃起来。
erratic /ɪˈrætɪk/ *adj.* 不稳定的;不规律的 反 regular	not steady; unconstant; irregular; uncertain	He is an ***erratic*** fellow whose actions are usually completely unpredictable. 他是一个难以捉摸的家伙,他的行为经常完全出乎预料。
immaculate /ɪˈmækjʊlɪt/ *adj.* 洁净的;无暇的 反 filthy	without a spot or stain; absolutely clean; pure	When he was a child, his life contained noble ambitions and ***immaculate*** thought. 小时候,他的生命中有高贵的理想和纯洁的思想。

WORD	MEANING	TYPICAL USE
loathe /ləʊð/ *v.* 厌恶;嫌恶 反 admire	hate very much; feel strong dislike and disgust for; abhor	The little girl ***loathed*** to leave her mother for studying abroad. 那小女孩不喜欢离开母亲到国外去读书。
pensive /ˈpensɪv/ *adj.* 忧愁的;哀思的 反 airy	thoughtful in a serious or sad way; meditative; reflective	The woman in this painting has a ***pensive*** smile. 画中的女人笑容很哀怨。
retard /rɪˈtɑːd/ *v.* 阻碍;妨碍 反 accelerate	make slow; cause to happen later; delay	I was ***retarded*** from keeping an appointment by a business conference that lasted most of the day. 开了几乎一整天的商业会议,所以我无法去赴约。
stalwart /ˈstɔːlwət/ *adj.* 强壮的;强健的 反 feeble	strongly and stoutly built; sturdy; courageous; valiant	She was proud of her ***stalwart***, good-looking grandson. 她以她那强壮、英俊的孙子为荣。

WORD	MEANING	TYPICAL USE
shun /ʃʌn/ *v.* 回避;避开 反 encounter	avoid with determination; keep away from; eschew	During his illness he ***shunned*** all society, and in particular those who had been his dearest friends. 在生病期间,他避开了所有交际活动,尤其是最亲爱的朋友。

EXERCISE 7.1 从第一部分中选出最恰当的单词,填入空格内:

1. Her husband simply ______ whatever food she cooked for him without any reason.
2. Cold weather and insufficient rain have ______ the growth of the crops.
3. The teacher was ______ because one of his students failed to greet him on the street.
4. The cowardly soldier ______ hazardous duty by pretending to be sick.
5. He made up his mind to separate from the ______ girl who proved to be inconstant in human relations.

解答 1. loathed 2. retarded 3. dejected 4. shuns 5. erratic

第二部分

WORD	MEANING	TYPICAL USE
audible /ˈɔːdəbl/ *adj*. 听得见的 反 inaudible	loud enough to be heard; hearable	They quarreled with such a loud noise that their voices were ***audible*** to the neighbors. 他们吵架的声音很大,邻居们都能听到。
auspicious /ɔːsˈpɪʃəs/ *adj*. 幸运的; 兴盛的 反 unfavorable	with signs of success; favorable; propitious	The new boy had an ***auspicious*** first day in the elementary school. 那刚上小学的男孩第一天很幸运。
elation /ɪˈleɪʃən/ *n*. 得意洋洋 反 depression	high spirits; joy or pride; exultancy; gladness	She was filled with ***elation*** at the news that she won the first prize in her class. 听说自己是班上的第一名时,她感到得意洋洋。
haughty /ˈhɔːtɪ/ *adj*. 傲慢的; 骄傲的 反 modest	having too much pride; arrogant; too proud of oneself and too scornful of others	The ***haughty*** man thinks highly of himself while holding others in contempt. 那傲慢的人自视甚高,轻视别人。

WORD	MEANING	TYPICAL USE
jeopardy /ˈdʒepədɪ/ *n.* 危险;危难 反 safety	danger; risk; peril	The officer's violation of a regulation is more of a ***jeopardy*** than the enlisted man's offense. 军官违反命令比士兵犯罪更危险。
mandatory /ˈmændətərɪ/ *adj.* 命令的;必须的 反 optional	required by a command or order; compulsory; obligatory	It is ***mandatory*** to pay a debt within a certain period of time. 必须在一定的期限内还债。
rebuke /rɪˈbjuːk/ *v.* 指责;非难 反 praise	reprove; reproach; express disapproval of	The teacher ***rebuked*** the student for throwing the examination paper on the floor. 老师指责学生把试卷丢在地上。
sparse/spɑːs/ *adj.* 稀少的;稀疏的 反 dense	scattered; with few members; scanty; occurring here and there	Not many people came to see the game; the ***sparse*** crowd was scattered thinly through the stadium. 去看那场比赛的人很少;稀疏的观众零星地散布在看台上。
undue/ˈʌnˈdjʊː/ *adj.* 过度的;过分的 反 reasonable	too much; excessive; not reasonable	A miser gives ***undue*** importance to making and saving money. 守财奴过度看重赚钱和存钱。

EXERCISE 7.2 从第二部分中选出最恰当的单词，填入空格内：

1. They threw the dice on the ground; the letter "7" was a(n) ______ sign that the victory would be theirs.
2. A(n) ______ girl is always unpopular among her friends at school.
3. She spoke in such a low voice that her quiet remarks were barely ______.
4. It is a(n) ______ regulation that we must keep silent in the school library.
5. The man's life was in ______ when the tree fell suddenly.

解答 1. auspicious 2. haughty 3. audible 4. mendatory 5. jeopardy

第三部分

WORD	MEANING	TYPICAL USE
allay /əˈleɪ/ *v.* 使(恐惧、愤怒、怀疑等)缓和 反 intensify	make (fear, anger, doubt) less; put at rest; quiet; pacify; alleviate	The doctor's friendly manner helped the patient ***allay*** his fear. 这位医生友善的态度帮助该病人消除了恐惧。
carnal /ˈkɑːnəl/ *adj.* 肉体的；性欲的 反 spiritual	of the flesh; bodily; sensual	Gluttony and drunkenness have been called ***carnal*** vices. 贪食和嗜酒被称为肉体上的罪恶。

WORD	MEANING	TYPICAL USE
defunct /dɪˈfʌŋkt/ *adj.* 死的 反 existent	no longer in existence; dead; extinct; deceased	A family name becomes ***defunct*** when the only heir dies without any son. 当唯一的继承人死去而他又没有儿子时，这个姓就不存在了。
feasible /ˈfiːzəbl/ *adj.* 可实行的 反 impractical	that can be done easily; practicable	Of the many plans submitted, the committee selected the plan that seemed most ***feasible***. 在提出的许多计划中，委员会选出了那项似乎最切实可行的计划。
ingenuity /ˌɪndʒɪˈnjʊ(uː)ɪtɪ/ *n.* 精巧；创造力 反 stupidity	skill in planning or inventing; cleverness	The boy showed ***ingenuity*** in making toys out of scraps of discarded wood. 那男孩在用废弃的小木片制作玩具上表现出了创造力。
mirth /mɜːθ/ *n.* 欢乐；欢笑 反 grief	merriness and gaiety expressed by laughter	My joke caused a great deal of ***mirth*** among the little children. 我的笑话引起了孩子们的欢笑。

WORD	MEANING	TYPICAL USE
precarious /prɪˈkɛərɪəs/ *adj.* 危险的；不稳固的 反 safe	unsafe; not firm or steady; full of danger; perilous; hazardous	Soldiers on the battlefield lead a ***precarious*** life. 战场上的士兵们过着危险的生活。
preordain /ˌpriːɔːˈdeɪn/ *v.* 预定；预先注定 反 improvise	predetermine; fix or decide before the beginning	Some people believe that fate has ***preordained*** whether they will be happy or unhappy. 有些人认为命运已注定他们将来是否会幸福。
taciturn /ˈtæsɪtɜːn/ *adj.* 沉默寡言的 反 loquacious	saying very little; not fond of talking; uncommunicative; silent	At the council broad he was ***taciturn*** and never opened his lips. 在会议桌上他沉默寡言，从没有开口。
venomous /ˈvenəməs/ *adj.* 有毒的；有害的 反 benevolent	poisonous; malicious; vindictive	His eldest brother died after the ***venomous*** bite from the rattlesnake. 他大哥被响尾蛇咬了一口，之后中毒而死。

EXERCISE 7.3 从第三部分中选出最恰当的单词,填入空格内:

1. The famous restaurant began to decline after the death of the host and is now ______.
2. Your explanation sounds ______, but I'm not sure I believe it.
3. His fears were ______ by the news that his family was safe in the storm.
4. His whole face was laughing; his face was full of ______.
5. You should be careful to drive on a(n) ______ path that winds its way along the mountainside.

解答 1. defunct 2. feasible 3. allayed 4. mirth 5. precarious

第四部分

WORD	MEANING	TYPICAL USE
amiss /əˈmɪs/ *adj.* 有差错;错误的 反 proper	improper; wrong; out of order	The doctor said there was nothing ***amiss*** with her. 医生说她没什么病。
comprise /kəmˈpraɪz/ *v.* 构成;包含 反 omit	be made up of; consist of; include	This anthology ***comprises*** samples from the work of ten authors. 这本文选包含了 10 位作家的作品范例。

WORD	MEANING	TYPICAL USE
dissemble /dɪˈsembl/ *v.* 隐藏;掩饰 反 disclose	conceal one's real feelings, or thought; disguise; dissimulate	Families that quarrel in the privacy of the home do well to ***dissemble*** when they go out to dinner. 在家中争吵的家庭出外用餐时都掩饰得很好。
glib /glɪb/ *adj.* 油腔滑调的 反 terse	speaking easily and smoothly; voluble; fluent; garrulous	A ***glib*** door-to-door salesman sold her a set of books that she did not want. 一位能说会道、挨家挨户兜售商品的销售员卖给她一套她本来不想要的书。
invincible /ɪnˈvɪnsəbl/ *adj.* 难以克服的 反 conquerable	too strong to be conquered; indomitable; insuperable	Before World War Ⅱ, the French thought their Maginot Line as an ***invincible*** bulwark against German invasion. 第二次世界大战前,法国人把马其诺防线视为对抗德国入侵的坚强堡垒。
perfunctory /pə(ɜː)ˈfʌŋktərɪ/ *adj.* 草率的 反 meticulous	done hastily and without thought, interest, or care; mechanical; indifferent	The lazy little boy gave his face a ***perfunctory*** washing. 那懒惰的小男孩草草地洗了一把脸。

WORD	MEANING	TYPICAL USE
replete /rɪˈpliːt/ *adj.* 充满的 反 vacuous	abundantly supplied; filled; full; abounding	The Disneyland tour was ***replete*** with unexpected thrills and suspense. 迪斯尼乐园充满了意想不到的刺激和悬念。
solicit /səˈlɪsɪt/ *v.* 恳求;请求 反 respond	ask earnestly; try to get; beg; request	We respectfully ***solicit*** your continuous friendship and patronage. 我们恭敬地请求您给予我们长久的友谊和鼓励。
thraldom /ˈθrɔːldəm/ *n.* 奴役 反 liberty	bondage; slavery	The nation will soon be liberated from the foulest ***thraldom***. 那个国家很快将从最邪恶、肮脏的奴役中被解放出来。
wilt /wɪlt/ *v.* 枯萎;凋谢 反 thrive	cause to become less fresh and start to die; wither	Give the flowers some water regularly, or they will ***wilt***. 按时给花浇水，否则它们会枯萎的。

EXERCISE 7.4 从第四部分中选出最恰当的单词,填入空格内:

1. Columbus had a(n) ______ belief that he would reach land by sailing west.

2. The United Kingdom ______ England, Wales, Scotland and Northern Ireland.
3. The hungry beggar felt ______ with food and drink, then slept.
4. The teacher ______ the earnest attention of his students to see the map on the blackboard.
5. From his angry looks, I knew something had gone ______ while I was away.

解答 1. invincible 2. comprises 3. replete 4. solicited 5. amiss

第五部分

WORD	MEANING	TYPICAL USE
abominable /əˈbɒmɪnəbl/ *adj.* 可憎的；可恶的 反 admirable	causing great dislike; hateful; detestable; disgusting; abhorrent	That ***abominable*** place was so dirty and evil smelling that he turned away in disgust. 这个鬼地方如此肮脏而且臭气薰天，他厌恶地走开了。
brainy /ˈbreɪnɪ/ *adj.* 聪明的；精明的 反 silly	intelligent; clever	***Brainy*** students could understand easily what the teacher explained to them. 聪明的学生很容易理解老师的讲解。

WORD	MEANING	TYPICAL USE
deteriorate /dɪˈtɪərɪəreɪt/ *v.* 使变坏 反 ameliorate	become worse; lessen in character	As the morning progressed, the weather ***deteriorated*** more and more. 早晨过去之后,天气变得愈来愈坏。
exquisite /ˈekskwɪzɪt/ *adj.* 精美的 反 common	very lovely; very finely made or done; delicate	In German he was an ***exquisite*** stylist, and he brought to that language a new sensitivity in the art of story-telling. 在德文方面,他是个才艺很高的文学批评家,他用讲故事的技巧带给德文一种新的感受。
incurable /ɪnˈkjʊərəbl/ *adj.* 无法治愈的 反 remediable	cannot be cured or remedied	Cancer is no longer an ***incurable*** disease nowadays; it can be remedied by using radioactivity. 如今,癌症不再是不治之症;它可以用放射线进行治疗。
manual /ˈmænjʊəl/ 1. *adj.* 手工的 反 spiritual	1. of or using the hands; done with hands	***Manual*** workers often earn more than office workers. 劳力工人通常比坐办公室的人赚得多。

WORD	MEANING	TYPICAL USE
2. *n.* 使用手册	2. a book that helps its readers to understand or use something; handbook	This workbook has a teacher's ***manual*** in which examination problems and their answers are included. 这本教学参考书附有教师手册，内容包括试题和答案。
potential /pəˈtenʃəl/ *adj.* 可能的；潜在的 反 exposed	existing in possibility; latent; covert	He is a ***potential*** leader to control this large state. 他是个有潜力的领导者，能管理这个国家。
ruthless /ˈruːθlɪs/ *adj.* 无情的；残忍的 反 lenient	having no pity; showing no mercy; cruel; merciless; relentless	They are such ***ruthless*** parents that they never give presents to the children on Christmas Day. 他们是非常无情的父母，从没给过孩子圣诞礼物。
voluble /ˈvɒljʊbl/ *adj.* 口若悬河的 反 taciturn	ready to talk much; having the habit of talking much; talkative	Her explanations for failure to do the work were ***voluble*** but not easily believed. 她对工作失败的解释口若悬河，但不易为人所相信。

WORD	MEANING	TYPICAL USE
vociferous /vəʊˈsɪfərəs/ *adj.* 嘈杂的；喧哗的 反 tranquil	shouting; loud and noisy; clamoring	Theater lobbies were filled with a ***vociferous*** crowd during the intermission. 中场休息时，电影院的走廊里挤满了喧闹的人群。

EXERCISE 7.5 从第五部分中选出最恰当的单词，填入空格内：

1. The ______ white fur coat that the lady has on is very expensive.
2. There is a(n) ______ danger of being bitten when one plays with a strange dog.
3. What a(n) ______ thing this is to treat the little boy so relentlessly!
4. Mother tried to control the unruly screaming and shouting of her ______ child.
5. A machine ______ rapidly in its function if it is not taken care of by its users.

解答 1. exquisite 2. potential 3. ruthless 4. vociferous 5. deteriorates

效果检测

EXERCISE 7.6 从第二栏中选出第一栏各词的反义词：

COLUMN Ⅰ	COLUMN Ⅱ
______ 1. modest	(A) taciturn
______ 2. elation	(B) filthy
______ 3. voluble	(C) jeopardy

______ 4. miserable (D) preordain

______ 5. ingenuity (E) depression

______ 6. stalwart (F) stupidity

______ 7. undue (G) blithe

______ 8. improvise (H) reasonable

______ 9. immaculate (I) haughty

______ 10. safety (J) feeble

解答 1. I 2. E 3. A 4. G 5. F

6. J 7. H 8. D 9. B 10. C

EXERCISE 7.7 选出恰当的词填入空格内：

1. The new nurse was ______; she did not really care about her work.

   (A) perfunctory (B) auspicious

2. The nobles used to treat the common people with ______ contempt.

   (A) undue (B) sparse

3. All the flowers are ______ for lack of sunshine and water.

   (A) wilting (B) wielding

4. In trying to solve the problem we seem to have exhausted all the ______ that the brain of man could suggest.

   (A) ingenuity (B) ingenuousness

5. The queen's table was set with ______ dishes and silvers.

   (A) exquisite (B) meticulous

6. He is a(n) ______ person who favored baseball one day and opposed it the next.

   (A) erratic (B) clumsy

7. Their cruel treatment of prisoners was so ______ that we couldn't see anymore.

(A) invincible (B) abominable

8. The manager ______ the clerk for the negligence of his duty.

(A) rebuked (B) rebuffed

9. Christmas is a time of ______, especially for children.

(A) misery (B) mirth

10. He ______ his hate by a false show of friendliness and a reluctant smile.

(A) disgusted (B) dissembled

解答 1. A 2. A 3. A 4. A 5. A
6. A 7. B 8. A 9. B 10. B

EXERCISE 7.8 找出与斜体词意义相反的单词：

______ 1. *retard* the progress

(A) detain (B) hinder

(C) abandon (D) accelerate

______ 2. *sparse* hair

(A) soft (B) straight

(C) dense (D) curved

______ 3. *invincible* courage

(A) visible (B) cowardly

(C) limited (D) conquerable

______ 4. *mandatory* order

(A) equivocal (B) optional

(C) compulsory (D) inconsistent

______ 5. *glib* answer

(A) uncertain (B) loquacious

(C) taciturn (D) sincere

解答 1. D 2. C 3. D 4. B 5. C

EXERCISE 7.9 从下列单词中选出最恰当的词，填入空格内：

VOCABULARY LIST

jeopardies	replete	invincible	pensive
comprises	potential	voluble	amiss
precarious	ruthless	retarded	shun

1. A virtuous man will ______ evil companions and practices.
2. His course of graduate study ______ English, mathematics, and management.
3. She was in a(n) ______ mood, and sat down alone staring out the window.
4. Your child is a ______ singer.
5. Something must be ______ with a boy if he doesn't eat anything for days.
6. Ted is a(n) ______ speaker at meetings; he doesn't give much chance to others to say anything.
7. The earliest pioneers in the West confronted a great many ______.
8. The climber had only a(n) ______ hold on the slipping rock.
9. The new apartment house is ______ with every modern furniture.
10. Economic progress in Latin America has been consistently ______ by a high birth rate.

解答 1. shun 2. comprises 3. pensive
4. potential 5. amiss 6. voluble
7. jeopardies 8. precarious 9. replete
10. retarded

LESSON 8

预备测验

选出最恰当的答案：

1. The stranger's *derogatory* remarks about the town and its people made him ______.

   (A) stupid　(B) unpopular　(C) honest

2. The motorist was *acquitted* of ______; he was therefore absolved from any claim for damages.

   (A) reckless driving　(B) witness

   (C) suffering from the wound

3. One's childhood life seems happier in *retrospect* than in ______.

   (A) fancy　(B) reality　(C) adulthood life

4. A man may utter an *insolent* remark; he may be ______ of his associates.

   (A) cautious　(B) considerate　(C) contemptuous

5. The *acme* of the development of space ships probably lies in the ______.

   (A) future　(B) fortitude　(C) sagacity

答案 1. B 2. A 3. B 4. C 5. A

第一部分

WORD	MEANING	TYPICAL USE
bleak /bliːk/ *adj.* 寒冷的;荒凉的 反 cheerful	cold and cheerless; without shelter from cold winds	The weather in early December was ***bleak*** and unpleasant. 12 月初的天气是寒冷且令人不快的。
castigate /ˈkæstɪgeɪt/ *v.* 惩罚;谴责;严厉批评 反 applaud	punish or scold severely in order to correct; rebuke; criticize	The electric inspector was ***castigated*** for having failed to check the wire as he was supposed to. 电工因没有把他分内的电线检查好而被谴责。
enmity /ˈenmɪtɪ/ *n.* 敌意;不和 反 sympathy	the state of feeling of being an enemy; hatred; hostility; animosity	We should overcome the worst that the tyrant's ***enmity*** can do. 我们应该克服那暴君的仇恨造成的最大程度的破坏。
impartial /ɪmˈpɑːʃəl/ *adj.* 公平的 反 prejudiced	giving equal attention to all concerned; fair; not partial	In any case, parents should be ***impartial*** toward each of their children. 无论如何,父母应该公平地对待他们的每一个孩子。

WORD	MEANING	TYPICAL USE
lucid /ˈljuːsɪd/ *adj*. 1. 明白的；清晰的 反 obscure	1. easy to follow or understand; plan	The teacher asked me to give a ***lucid*** explanation of my being late for class. 老师要求我解释清楚为什么上课迟到。
2. 神志清明的	2. clear in intellect; sane; rational	The old man is confused most of the time but he does have ***lucid*** moments. 那老人大部分时间头脑不清醒，但也有清醒的时候。
perpendicular /ˌpɜːpənˈdɪkjʊlə(r)/ *adj*. 垂直的 反 horizontal	exactly upright; vertical; erect	A square has four 90-degree angles made by its four ***perpendicular*** sides. 正方形的四个直角由它四条垂直的边所构成。
retrospect /ˈretrəʊˌspekt/ *n*. 反顾；回顾 反 prospect	the act of looking back towards the past; thinking about the past	In ***retrospect***, many good opportunities were neglected in my life. 回想起来，我一生中错失了很多良机。

WORD	MEANING	TYPICAL USE
sagacity /səˈgæsɪtɪ/ *n.* 睿智;聪敏 反 folly	good judgement and understanding; wisdom; mental acuteness; shrewdness	The politician showed a good ***sagacity*** in avoiding the mistakes he'd made in the previous campaign. 这回,那位政治家精明地避免了上一次选举中犯过的错误。
urbane /ɜːˈbeɪn/ *adj.* 温文的;文雅的 反 vulgar	having very good manners; refined; courteous	***Urbane*** speech is educated speech, as distinguished from the speech of the ignorant. 文雅的言语是受过教育的言辞,和无知者的言语大有区别。

EXERCISE 8.1 从第一部分中选出最恰当的单词,填入空格内:

1. The ______ between Arabs and Israelis threatened to break into open war at any time.
2. The tree was leaning against the house and no longer ______.
3. A neutral observer, not a participant, asked for a(n) ______ account of how the fight started.
4. Lonely and ill, the old woman having no children faced a(n) ______ future.
5. Impartiality as well as ______ is required to be a good judge.

解答 1. enmity 2. perpendicular 3. impartial 4. bleak 5. sagacity

第二部分

WORD	MEANING	TYPICAL USE
ardent /ˈɑːdənt/ *adj.* 极热心的；热情的 反 impassive	full of zeal; very enthusiastic; eager	After reading about the lives of several great Americans, John became an ***ardent*** student of American history. 读了几个美国伟人的生平事迹之后，约翰成为了一个热衷于美国历史的学生。
derogatory /dɪˈrɒgətərɪ/ *adj.* 损毁的；诽谤的 反 enhancive	showing or causing lack of respect; disparaging; belittling	I can't bear his ***derogatory*** remarks about my brother's character. 我无法忍受他对我弟弟的个性的诽谤。
discretion /dɪsˈkreʃən/ *n.* 1. 谨慎；明辨	1. the quality of being discreet; good judgment	I won't tell you what time to leave; you're old enough to use your own ***discretion***. 我不会告诉你什么时候离开；你已到了可以自己进行判断的年龄了。

WORD	MEANING	TYPICAL USE
2. 自由选择或决定 反 recklessness	2. freedom to judge or choose	The house of the meetings will be fixed at the chairman's ***discretion***. 会议厅将由主席决定。
hilarious /hɪˈlærɪəs/ *adj*. 高兴的；热闹的 反 depressed	full of laughter; very merry; noisily gay; mirthful	The party got quite ***hilarious*** after they brought more wine. 他们又拿来一些酒之后，晚会变得相当热闹。
paramount /ˈpærəmaʊnt/ *adj*. 最重要的；至上的 反 mediocre	supreme; predominant; chief in importance	It is a ***paramount*** responsibility of every officer to take care of his men before caring for himself. 每个军官的最高职责是在照顾自己之前先照料好他的弟兄。
recede /rɪ(iː)ˈsiːd/ *v*. 后退 反 approach	move back or away; retreat; retire	Houses and trees seem to ***recede*** as we ride past in a train. 当我们乘火车经过时，房屋和树木似乎在后退。
rife /raɪf/ *adj*. 充斥的 反 scanty	widespread; common; numerous; prevalent	The whole city was ***rife*** with rumors of political corruption and bribery. 全城都在传政治腐败和贿赂的谣言。

WORD	MEANING	TYPICAL USE
spontaneous /spɒnˈteɪnɪəs/ *adj.* 自然的;自发的 反 compulsive	caused by natural impulse or desire; of one's own choice; voluntary	Both sides burst into ***spontaneous*** cheers at the magician's skillful tricks. 双方对魔术师熟练的技艺都不由自主地发出赞叹声。
tenuous /ˈtenjʊəs/ *adj.* 细的;薄的 反 thick	very thin or slender; not dense; rare	The air ten miles above the earth is very ***tenuous***. 地面上 10 英里处的空气是非常稀薄的。

EXERCISE 8.2 从第二部分中选出最恰当的单词,填入空格内:

1. You must show more ______ in choosing your friends.
2. We consider lack of morale as the ______ cause for our defeat.
3. We thought his mistake was the most ______ joke we'd ever heard.
4. A pile of oily rags will sometimes break into a(n) ______ flame.
5. Superstition is still ______ in some countries.

答案 1. discretion 2. paramount 3. hilarious 4. spontaneous 5. rife

第三部分

WORD	MEANING	TYPICAL USE
acme /ˈækmɪ/ *n.* 顶点;极点 反 bottom	the highest point; culmination; climax	A baseball player usually reaches the ***acme*** of his skills before he is thirty. 一个棒球运动员通常在他 30 岁之前到达球技高峰。
candor /ˈkændə(r)/ *n.* 坦白;诚意 反 feint	fairness; impartiality; frankness and sincerity	He spared no one's feelings and expressed his views with great ***candor***. 他不顾他人的感受,坦白地表达了自己的意见。
dissuade /dɪˈsweɪd/ *v.* 劝阻 反 persuade	persuade not to do something	The father finally ***dissuaded*** his son from leaving school. 那父亲终于说服了他的儿子不要辍学。
gratuitous /grəˈtjʊ(uː)ɪtəs/ *adj.* 不需要的 反 warranted	not deserved or necessary; uncalled-for	Her advice was quite ***gratuitous***; I can think for myself. 她的忠告毫无用处;我会为自己着想。

WORD	MEANING	TYPICAL USE
impeach /ɪmˈpiːtʃ/ *v.* 检举；弹劾 反 exonerate	accuse of wrong conduct	The House of Representatives has the sole power to ***impeach*** an officer of the United States Government. 美国众议院有弹劾政府官员的特权。
ostensible /ɒsˈtensəbl/ *adj.* 表面的；假装的 反 substantial	according to appearance; apparent	Her ***ostensible*** purpose was to borrow some sugar, but she really wanted to see her neighbor's new furniture. 她表面上是来借糖，但她真正的目的是来看看她邻居的新家具。
paltry /ˈpɔːltrɪ/ *adj.* 无价值的；微不足道的 反 significant	worthless; unimportant; worthlessly small; trivial	The poor painter sold his paintings for a ***paltry*** sum of money. 那位穷画家贱卖了他的画。
sordid /ˈsɔːdɪd/ *adj.* 污秽的；不洁的 反 clean	dirty; filthy	The poor family lived in a ***sordid*** log cabin in the valley. 这个贫穷的家庭住在山谷中一座污秽的小木屋内。

WORD	MEANING	TYPICAL USE
tidy /ˈtaɪdɪ/ *adj.* 整洁的；整齐的 反 chaotic	neatly arranged; orderly	She makes it a rule to keep her room neat and ***tidy*** after coming back from school. 放学后，她习惯保持房间的整齐和清洁。

EXERCISE 8.3 从第三部分中选出最恰当的单词，填入空格内：

1. When he became prime minister, he reached the ______ of his hopes.
2. The father ______ the boy from being a doctor, but persuaded him to be a politician.
3. The team felt cheated and challenged the umpire to prove his ______.
4. Were it not for your ______ interference, the children would have quickly settled their dispute.
5. My daughter is very ______ and never goes out without combing her hair.

答案 1. acme 2. dissuaded 3. candor
4. gratuitous 5. tidy

第四部分

WORD	MEANING	TYPICAL USE
aloof /əˈluːf/ *adv.* 远离;躲开 反 nearly	at a distance but within view; apart	One tall boy stood ***aloof*** from all the small children. 一个高个子男孩远远地站着,离开所有矮个子的孩子。
cardinal /ˈkɑːdɪnəl/ *adj.* 首要的;主要的 反 insignificant	of highest importance; chief; principal	Regular meals and exercise are of ***cardinal*** importance to our health. 规律的饮食和运动对我们的健康是最重要的。
drab /dræb/ *adj.* 1. 暗黄灰色的;土褐色的 反 bright	1. lacking brightness or color	There are many ***drab*** houses in the smoky mining town. 冒烟的矿城内有许多土褐色的房子。
2. 单调的;枯涩的	2. not attractive; uninteresting; dull	The life of a person who never does anything is dull and ***drab***. 一个从未做过任何事的人的生活是索然无味的。
feud /fjuːd/ *n.* 世仇 反 intimacy	a long and deadly quarrel	The two families had been at ***feud*** with each other for three generations. 这两家已有三代的冤仇了。

WORD	MEANING	TYPICAL USE
insolent /ˈɪnsələnt/ *adj.* 粗野的；无礼的 反 humble	boldly rude; intentionally disregarding the feelings of others; insulting; impudent	His ***insolent*** speech and behavior upset everyone in the room. 他粗野的言论和行为让房间内的每个人都很不高兴。
mitigate /ˈmɪtɪgeɪt/ *v.* 使缓和；使减轻 反 aggravate	make less in force or degree; make less severe; temper	The judge said that nothing could ***mitigate*** the cruelty with which the man had treated the child. 法官说没有任何事能减轻那人对小孩的残暴行为。
pertinent /ˈpɜːtɪnənt/ *adj.* 中肯切题的 反 irrelevant	connected directly; to the point; relevant	A summary of the events leading up to this situation would be ***pertinent*** information. 把造成这种情况的事件作简略说明，才是适当的资料。
predecessor /ˌpredɪˈsesə, ˈpriːdɪsesə/ *n.* 某职位的前任 反 successor	a person holding a position or office before another	His ***predecessor*** quit because he was not in the least interested in this kind of job. 他的前任因为对这种工作毫无兴趣，所以离职了。

WORD	MEANING	TYPICAL USE
tardy /ˈtɑːdɪ/ *adj.* 延迟的 反 prompt	slow in acting or happening; delaying; dilatory	Let me apologize for my being ***tardy*** in answering your letter. 让我为我回信迟了而道歉。
whet /wet/ *v.* 刺激 反 quell	make someone wish for more; stimulate	You'd think she would never climb again, after falling down the mountain, but it just ***whetted*** her appetite. 你也许会认为她从山上摔下来后就不会再爬山了，然而正相反，那正好刺激了她的兴趣。

EXERCISE 8.4 从第四部分中选出最恰当的单词，填入空格内：

1. They did not speak when they met, for they were at deadly ______ with each other last week.
2. The teacher scolded the boy several times for being ______ for school.
3. Aspirin ______ the pain of his headache in about half an hour.
4. She held herself ______ from society, preferring to spend her days and nights dwelling on her memories.
5. Rumors of secret information on the actress' suicide ______ the curiosity of the public.

答案 1. feud 2. tardy 3. mitigated
4. aloof 5. whetted

第五部分

WORD	MEANING	TYPICAL USE
acquit /əˈkwɪt/ *v.* 宣告无罪 反 inculpate	say that a person is not guilty of wrongdoing	The man accused of stealing the money was ***acquitted*** for lack of witnesses. 那人被起诉偷钱，但因没有目击证人而被宣告无罪。
brittle /ˈbrɪtl/ *adj.* 脆的；易碎的 反 hard	easily broken; fragile; frail	Be careful not to break the box of glass; that thin glass is hard but ***brittle***. 小心不要打碎那个玻璃盒；那薄薄的玻璃虽然坚硬，但易碎。
detract /dɪˈtrækt/ *v.* 去掉；减损 反 exaggerate	remove some of the quality of worth; depreciate; derogate	The ugly frame ***detracts*** from the beauty of the famous picture. 难看的框子有损这幅名画的美。

WORD	MEANING	TYPICAL USE
extirpate /ˈekstɜːpeɪt/ *v.* 根除 反 establish	pull up by the roots; destroy completely; eradicate; annihilate	To ***extirpate*** weeds is not only to destroy their visible parts but to pull them out by the roots. 除草不只是破坏其可见部分，而是连根拔起。
indulgent /ɪnˈdʌldʒənt/ *adj.* 1. 放任的	1. too kind or agreeable; giving in to another's wishes or whims	The ***indulgent*** mother bought her children everything they wanted. 这个溺爱的母亲给孩子买他们想要的任何东西。
2. 宽容的 反 stern	2. not critical; lenient	The ***indulgent*** teacher praised every poem we wrote. 这位宽容的老师称赞我们写的每一首诗。
mendacious /menˈdeɪʃəs/ *adj.* 爱说谎的；不诚实的 反 candid	lying; untruthful; dishonest	The ***mendacious*** beggar told a different tale of woe at every house. 那个爱说谎的乞丐给每家讲不同的悲哀故事。

WORD	MEANING	TYPICAL USE
plausible /ˈplɔːzəbl/ *adj.* 似乎合理的；似乎公平的 反 incredible	appearing true; reasonable or fair	For my own sake, I've told a ***plausible*** lie at the club meeting, but the members did not believe me at all. 为了我自己，我在俱乐部的会议上说了一个似乎合情合理的谎言，但那些人根本不相信我。
sanction /ˈsæŋkʃən/ *n.* 批准；认可 反 rejection	permission with authority; support; approval	We have the ***sanction*** of the recreation department to play ball in this park. 康乐部门允许我们在这个公园里玩球。
shallow /ˈʃæləʊ/ *adj.* 浅的 反 profound	not deep; lacking deep or serious thinking; superficial	Youngsters usually rush into marriage with only the ***shallow*** notions of what love and responsibility mean. 年轻人通常对爱和责任只有一些肤浅的观念，就匆匆地结婚。
verge /vɜːdʒ/ *n.* 边；缘 反 interior	the edge or border; brim; the point at which something begins or happens	We parked the car on the grass ***verge*** at the side of the highway. 我们把车停在公路边的草坪上。

EXERCISE 8.5 从第五部分中选出最恰当的单词,填入空格内:

1. The scandal published in the newspaper, ______ much from the mayor's reputation.
2. A(n) ______ explanation is the one that appears to be believable on the surface.
3. It is illegal to translate a book without the ______ of the author and the publisher.
4. She tried to hide her grief, but she was on the ______ of tears.
5. We look forward to the day when disease and poverty will be ______.

答案 1. detracted 2. plausible 3. sanction 4. verge 5. extirpated

效果检测

EXERCISE 8.6 从第二栏中选出第一栏各词的反义词:

COLOUM I	COLOUM II
______ 1. gratuitous	(A) depressed
______ 2. ardent	(B) significant
______ 3. paramount	(C) inculpate
______ 4. mendacious	(D) obscure
______ 5. enmity	(E) warranted
______ 6. paltry	(F) impassive
______ 7. hilarious	(G) substantial
______ 8. acquit	(H) mediocre
______ 9. ostensible	(I) candid
______ 10. lucid	(J) sympathy

解答 1. E 2. F 3. H 4. I 5. J
6. B 7. A 8. C 9. G 10. D

EXERCISE 8.7 选出适当的词填入空格中：

1. The manager considered it ______ to his position to accept the demands of the trade union leaders.

   (A) derivative (B) derogatory

2. My mother tried to ______ me from going to see the movie, for I had not finished my homework.

   (A) dissuade (B) persuade

3. Discrimination and persecution have created an atmosphere of ______ between them.

   (A) amity (B) enmity

4. The appetizer was delicious and ______ the hungry and tired man's palate.

   (A) whetted (B) whipped

5. The spider hung from a ______ silky thread at the corner of the room.

   (A) tenuous (B) tentative

6. People who are ______ in paying their bills are poor customers.

   (A) tedious (B) tardy

7. After the severe storm the flag pole was no longer ______.

   (A) impartial (B) perpendicular

8. The rocky peaks of high mountains are always ______ and windy.

   (A) bleach (B) bleak

9. The judge decided to ______ the man's sentence in the light of his previous record.

   (A) malign (B) mitigate

10. The plan for the new building will be practised after all necessary ______ are obtained.

(A) sanctities　　(B) sanctions

解答 1. B　2. A　3. B　4. A　5. A
6. B　7. B　8. B　9. B　10. B

EXERCISE 8.8 找出与斜体词意义相反的单词：

______ 1. *urbane*

(A) rural　　(B) vulgar
(C) modern　　(D) neglect

______ 2. *castigate*

(A) agree　　(B) preserve
(C) obey　　(D) applaud

______ 3. *shallow*

(A) profound　　(B) relevant
(C) indifferent　　(D) humble

______ 4. *retrospect*

(A) antipathy　　(B) prospect
(C) reality　　(D) improvement

______ 5. *impeach*

(A) castigate　　(B) bestow
(C) exonerate　　(D) recede

解答 1. B　2. D　3. A　4. B　5. C

EXERCISE 8.9 从下列单词中选出最适当的词，填入空格内：

VOCABULARY LIST

whet	predecessors	indulgent	discretion
tardy	cardinal	castigate	impartial
recede	spontaneous	tidy	acme

1. A judge cannot remain ______ without being free of all political pressure.
2. They're very ______ parents; they give their children presents all the time.
3. He is always ______ in paying back the borrowed money.
4. The laughter at his joke is never forced but always ______.
5. The ______ idea of the Labor Party's political thought is that all people should be equal.
6. It requires ______ to criticize someone without hurting his feelings.
7. This is the 5th plan we have made but it's not better than its ______.
8. I watched the coast of Korea slowly ______ into the distance.
9. Schubert reached the ______ of his skill while he was quite young.
10. Their living room was so ______ that is seemed doubtful that anyone actually lived in it.

解答

1. impartial 2. indulgent 3. tardy
4. spontaneous 5. cardinal 6. discretion
7. predecessors 8. recede 9. acme
10. tidy

LESSON 9

预备测验

选出最恰当的答案：

1. Mr. Kim was a counsel for the *plaintiff* and Mr. Park for the ______.

   (A) lawyer　　(B) defendant　　(C) jury

2. The ______ entered the harbor and began to *plunder* the town.

   (A) policemen　　(B) pirates　　(C) sailors

3. He is very *scrupulous* about the ______.

   (A) choice of his words　　(B) manual labor

   (C) water pollution

4. Their ______ were drawn *aslant* over their brows, and they were chewing gum, leaning against the wall.

   (A) legs　　(B) gloves　　(C) caps

5. The crowd at the scene of the accident *impeded* the arrival of the ______.

   (A) jeopardy　　(B) ambulance　　(C) relish

解答 1. B 2. B 3. A 4. C 5. B

第一部分

WORD	MEANING	TYPICAL USE
adjacent /ə'dʒeɪsənt/ *adj.* 接近的；邻近的 反 distant	near or close; neighboring; next; bordering	No one in the ***adjacent*** apartments was awakened by their quarreling sounds. 他们的吵架声没有吵醒邻近公寓里的人。
calamity /kə'læmɪtɪ/ *n.* 不幸之事；灾难 反 bliss	a great misfortune; disaster; misfortune; misery	The spring floods were a great ***calamity*** to the farmers whose crops and houses were ruined. 春天的洪水对于农民来说是一大灾难，他们的农作物和房子都被毁坏了。
devastate /'devəsteɪt/ *v.* 毁灭；破坏 反 fertilize	make waste; make unfit to live in; desolate; destroy	The floods and storms which have no precedent in the recorded history ***devastated*** the country. 历史上前所未有的洪水和台风摧毁了这个国家。
exultant /ɪg'zʌltənt/ *adj.* 狂欢的；狂喜的 反 mournful	rejoicing greatly; triumphant	The ***exultant*** players were dancing on the ground over their team's victory. 欣喜若狂的球员为欢庆他们的胜利，在球场上跳起了舞。

WORD	MEANING	TYPICAL USE
inexhaustible /ˌɪnɪɡˈzɔːstəbl/ *adj*. 无穷无尽的 反 limited	cannot be exhausted; very abundant	The wealth of our country seems ***inexhaustible*** to many people abroad. 对许多海外人士而言,我们国家的财富似乎是无穷无尽的。
maudlin /ˈmɔːdlɪn/ *adj*. 易落泪的 反 unmoved	sentimental in a weak and silly way	We saw a ***maudlin*** movie about an orphan who lost his parents in the war. 我们看了部催人泪下的电影,内容是有关一个在战争中失去父母的孤儿。
plunder /ˈplʌndə(r)/ *v*. 抢夺 反 donate	rob; take by force; steal	The enemies ***plundered*** all the valuable things they could find in the village. 敌人把在村里能够发现的所有贵重物品都抢走了。
scrupulous /ˈskruːpjʊləs/ *adj*. 审慎的;诚实的 反 heedless	conscientious; exactly honest; very careful to do what is right	A ***scrupulous*** man never fails to give back the borrowed money to its owner. 诚实的人绝不会不把钱还给债主。

WORD	MEANING	TYPICAL USE
sundry /ˈsʌndrɪ/ *adj.* 种种的 反 unique	a number of; several; various	From ***sundry*** hints, I guessed I was to be given a bicycle for my birthday present. 通过种种暗示，我猜我生日时能得到一辆自行车作礼物。
zealous /ˈzeləs/ *adj.* 热心的 反 neglectful	eager; earnest; actively enthusiastic	The children made ***zealous*** efforts to clean up the house for the Christmas party. 孩子们为了圣诞宴会，热心努力地打扫屋子。

EXERCISE 9.1 从第一部分中选出最恰当的单词，填入空格内：

1. The troops in the besieged town gave a(n) ______ shout at the sight of new troops advancing to help them.
2. No one would think it ______ to weep at the death of a friend.
3. They were glad they had survived the ______ and met with no disaster.
4. We are told that the potentialities of the human brain are ______.
5. In olden times soldiers ______ a conquered city and often gained great wealth.

解答 1. exultant 2. maudlin 3. calamity 4. inexhaustible 5. plundered

第二部分

WORD	MEANING	TYPICAL USE
altruistic /ˌæltrʊˈɪstɪk/ *adj.* 利他的 反 selfish	thoughtful of the welfare of others; unselfish	We wonder if human beings are primarily ***altruistic*** or selfish. 不知道人类在根本上是利他还是利己。
clamor /ˈklæmə(r)/ *v.* 叫嚣 反 silence	a loud confused noise or shouting; uproar	The children were ***clamoring*** for candy. 孩子们吵着要糖果。
disintegrate /dɪsˈɪntɪɡreɪt/ *v.* 碎裂 反 assemble	break up into small pieces	The old manuscripts had ***disintegrated*** into a pile of fragments and dust. 陈旧的手稿已化成一堆碎片和纸屑。
forebear /ˈfɔːbɛə(r)/ *n.* 祖先 反 descendant	an ancestor; forefather	Although Napoleon was Corsican, he is considered by most modern Frenchmen to have been French as their own ***forebears***. 虽然拿破仑是科西嘉岛人，可是今天大多数的法国人仍然认为他是法国人，是他们的祖先。

WORD	MEANING	TYPICAL USE
intact /ɪnˈtækt/ *adj.* 原封不动的 反 damaged	as if untouched; uninjured; whole	The money was returned ***intact*** by the boy who found it on the street. 那男孩把在街上捡的钱原封不动地送了回去。
molest /məʊˈlest/ *v.* 骚扰 反 soothe	trouble or annoy intentionally; interfere with trouble	We did not ***molest*** the big dog, because we were afraid of him. 我们没有去惊扰那只大狗，因为我们怕它。
profuse /prəˈfjuːs/ *adj.* 很多的 反 sparing	very abundant; generous	The mourner's ***profuse*** tears at the burial were heartbreaking. 丧礼上，送葬人泪如雨下，让人哀伤。
slack /slæk/ *adj.* 懈怠的；疏忽的 反 agile	careless; not tight or firm; sluggish	He was ***slack*** in fulfilling his promises and responsibilities. 他对约定的事及其职责敷衍了事。
tart /tɑːt/ *adj.* 酸的 反 sweet	acid tasting; not sweet; sour; sarcastic	***Tart*** apples taste sharp and are pleasantly acid in their taste. 酸苹果的味道很酸，但酸得爽口。

WORD	MEANING	TYPICAL USE
viable /ˈvaɪəbl/ *adj.* 可成立的 反 impracticable	able to succeed in operation; able to keep alive; livable	This plan looks all right in principle, but in practice it wouldn't be ***viable***. 这个计划原则上没问题，可事实上却无法成立。

EXERCISE 9.2 从第二部分中选出最恰当的单词，填入空格内：

1. The speaker could hardly be heard above the ______ of the uproaring crowd.
2. Don't be ______ in your efforts till the work is completely finished.
3. The dog that ______ sheep has to be driven out immediately.
4. A(n) ______ person is thoughtful of welfare of the others.
5. Few buildings in the bombed city remained ______.

解答 1. clamor 2. slack 3. molests 4. altruistic 5. intact

第三部分

WORD	MEANING	TYPICAL USE
aslant /əˈslɑːnt/ *adj.* 斜的 反 straight	not straight or level; sloping	The carpenter made the roof ***aslant*** to allow water to run down. 木匠把屋顶造斜，使水能够流下。

WORD	MEANING	TYPICAL USE
concede /kən'siːd/ *v.* 承认 反 contradict	admit as true; acknowledge	They ***conceded*** that victory was no longer attainable and agreed to a negotiated surrender. 他们承认无法获胜，并同意谈判投降。
distrust /dɪs'trʌst/ *v.* 不信任 反 confide	have no confidence in; not trust; be suspicious of; doubt	She could not allow the stranger to enter her house, for she ***distrusted*** him. 她不允许那个陌生人进入房子，因为她不信任他。
groggy /'grɒgɪ/ *adj.*（生病之后）虚弱的；不稳的 反 steady	weak because of illness; unsteady	The table is very ***groggy***. I think the leg is going to fall off. 那桌子非常不稳。我想桌子腿快断了。
intrepid /ɪn'trepɪd/ *adj.* 勇敢的 反 timid	showing no fear; brave; fearless; courageous	The ***intrepid*** fireman saved people trapped in a burning building disregarding his own safety. 勇敢的消防队员不顾自己的安危，救出了困在失火的屋里的人。

WORD	MEANING	TYPICAL USE
overbearing /ˌəʊvəˈbɛərɪŋ/ *adj.* 傲慢的 反 humble	arrogant; forcing others to one's own will; haughty	We found it hard to like the boy because of his ***overbearing*** manners. 因为那男孩傲慢的态度，我们发现很难喜欢他。
rash /ræʃ/ *adj.* 鲁莽的；冒失的 反 deliberate	foolishly bold; not thinking enough of the results; reckless	Only a ***rash*** person would have rushed into the burning house to save some clothes. 只有鲁莽的人才会冲进失火的房子，去抢救一些衣服。
sporadic /spəˈrædɪk/ *adj.* 零星的；偶发的 反 regular	happening irregularly; scattered in time; occasional	Though polio has been practically wiped out, there have been ***sporadic*** cases of the disease. 虽然小儿麻痹症已差不多消灭了，但是仍有一些零星的病例。
toxic /ˈtɒksɪk/ *adj.* 有毒的 反 harmless	related to or caused by poisonous substance; poisonous	Fumes from automobiles and factory chimneys are ***toxic.*** 汽车和工厂烟囱排放出的烟是有毒的。

EXERCISE 9.3 从第三部分中选出最恰当的单词,填入空格内:

1. When I left my bed after my long illness, I felt too ______ to stand.
2. The government ______ defeat as soon as the election results were known.
3. He keeps his money at home because he ______ banks.
4. It is ______ to cross the street without looking at both ways.
5. The ______ persons travelled west in spite of hardships and constant danger of Indian attack.

解答 1. groggy 2. conceded 3. distrusts 4. rash 5. intrepid

第四部分

WORD	MEANING	TYPICAL USE
avert /əˈvɜːt/ *v.* 避免;防止 反 encounter	turn aside or away; prevent happening; avoid; prevent	The driver ***averted*** an accident by a quick turn of the steering wheel. 那司机急转方向盘,避免了一次意外事故的发生。
deduce /dɪˈdjuːs/ *v.* 推论 反 induce	reach a conclusion by reasoning; infer	Mother ***deduced*** from my loss of appetite what had happened to the cookies. 母亲从我没有食欲便可推知小甜饼的味道。

WORD	MEANING	TYPICAL USE
embark /ɪmˈbɑːk/ *v.* 1. 搭载 反 disembark	1. go on board a ship, aircraft, or other vehicle	Our ship ***embarked*** passengers and wool at an Australian port. 我们的船在澳大利亚的一个港口装载了乘客及羊毛。
2. 从事;着手	2. set out; start	After leaving college, the young man ***embarked*** on a new business career. 那年轻人大学毕业后,从事一项新的职业。
humiliate /hjʊ(uː)ˈmɪlɪeɪt/ *v.* 使丢脸 反 encourage	cause to feel humble; lower the pride or dignity; mortify	The boy ***humiliated*** his parents by behaving badly in front of the guests. 那男孩在客人面前表现不好,使父母很没面子。
jovial /ˈdʒəʊvɪəl/ *adj.* 快乐的 反 sorrowful	full of good humor; friendly; jolly; convivial	A gregarious man, he enjoyed the companionship of a large number of ***jovial*** friends. 他是个爱社交的人,喜欢和一大群快乐的朋友作伴。
pastime /ˈpɑːstaɪm;ˈpæs-/ *n.* 消遣;娱乐 反 labor	a pleasant way of passing time; amusement; recreation as a game or sport	Baseball has been called America's national ***pastime*** through four seasons. 棒球一直被称为美国全国性的四季皆宜的娱乐活动。

WORD	MEANING	TYPICAL USE
renounce /rɪˈnaʊns/ *v.* 放弃 反 claim	give up entirely; forego; relinquish	The prince ***renounced*** his right to the throne. 王子放弃了王位继承权。
snug /snʌg/ *adj.* 温暖的 反 uncomfortable	sheltered and warm; comfortable; cosy	My grandmother likes to read a newspaper in a ***snug*** corner near the fireplace. 我祖母喜欢在火炉旁的温暖角落里看报纸。
umpteen /ˈʌmptiːn/ *adj.* 很多的 反 few	of a very large number	She doesn't need to borrow a book because she's got ***umpteen*** books waiting to be read at home. 她不需要借书,因为家中已有大堆的书等着她去看。

EXERCISE 9.4 从第四部分中选出最恰当的单词,填入空格内:

1. Her instructions are so complicated that I cannot ______ from them what she wants.
2. The little cat has found a(n) ______ corner behind the stove.
3. Santa Claus is pictured as a(n) ______ old fellow with long beard on his face and a large bag on his back.
4. The shipwrecked sailors ______ all hope of rescue and were floating on the sea.
5. Hunting and fishing are ______ ardently followed by the devotees of those sports.

解答 1. deduce 2. snug 3. jovial 4. renounced 5. pastimes

第五部分

WORD	MEANING	TYPICAL USE
blur /blɜː/ *v.* 弄脏 反 purify	make less clear in form or outline	The boy ***blurred*** the picture by touching it before the paint was dry. 那男孩在颜料未干前用手去碰，把画弄脏了。
demolish /dɪˈmɒlɪʃ/ *v.* 破坏 反 construct	destroy; pull or tear down	The slums were ***demolished*** before the town was extended. 该镇在扩展前，先拆除了贫民窟。
enslave /ɪnˈsleɪv/ *v.* 奴役 反 liberate	make into a slave; take away freedom from	Education makes people easy to govern but impossible to ***enslave***. 教育使人易于被管理，但不可能被奴役。
impede /ɪmˈpiːd/ *v.* 阻碍 反 spur	get in the way of; make something difficult to do; hinder; obstruct	Many a man is ***impeded*** in his career by a lack of belief in himself. 许多人因缺乏自信而阻碍了自己的成功。

WORD	MEANING	TYPICAL USE
lull /lʌl/ *v.* 使入睡;使安静 反 excite	soothe with sounds or caresses; make calm; quiet	The mother ***lulled*** the baby to sleep by singing a song. 母亲唱歌哄婴儿入睡。
plaintiff /ˈpleɪntɪf/ *n.* 原告 反 defendant	a person who begins a lawsuit	In the court the ***plaintiff*** asserted that the thief had stolen two hundred dollars from his store. 法庭上,原告声称小偷从他店里偷走了200美元。
robust /rəˈbʌst,rəʊ-/ *adj.* 强壮的 反 weak	having or showing very good health; strong and healthy	He was strong and healthy, but he's never been ***robust*** since his illness. 他原本健康有力,可是自从生病后,就不再强壮了。
strenuous /ˈstrenjʊəs/ *adj.* 辛苦的 反 idle	very active; full of energy; requiring much effort	We had a ***strenuous*** day moving into our new house. 我们辛苦了一天,搬进了新居。
vitiate /ˈvɪʃɪeɪt/ *v.* 1. 使污浊 反 purge 2. 使无效	1. weaken or spoil; harm the quality of 2. destroy the legal force or authority of; invalidate	Pollution from smoke and dust ***vitiates*** the air. 烟尘的污染使空气变得污浊。 All his attempts to improve were ***vitiated*** by his lack of will-power. 由于缺乏意志力,他想改良的尝试全都没有效果。

EXERCISE 9.5 从第五部分中选出最恰当的单词，填入空格内：

1. The child's hysterical crying ______ the doctor from completing his examination.
2. They are going to ______ that old building to clear the road for a new highway.
3. Water spilled on the letter and ______ the writing.
4. He has a(n) ______ appearance though he is not actually well.
5. The contract was ______ because one person signed it under compulsion.

解答 1. impeded 2. demolish 3. blurred
4. robust 5. vitiated

效果检测

EXERCISE 9.6 从第二栏中选出第一栏各词的反义词：

	COLUMN Ⅰ	COLUMN Ⅱ
______	1. tart	(A) steady
______	2. intrepid	(B) purge
______	3. sporadic	(C) unmoved
______	4. devastate	(D) build
______	5. vitiate	(E) heedless
______	6. groggy	(F) plaintiff
______	7. demolish	(G) fertilize
______	8. maudlin	(H) sweet
______	9. defendant	(I) cowardly
______	10. scrupulous	(J) regular

解答 1. H 2. I 3. J 4. G 5. B
6. A 7. D 8. C 9. F 10. E

EXERCISE 9.7 选出最符合句意的单词：

1. The decay of moral principles rapidly ______ Roman society.

   (A) thwarted (B) disintegrated

2. She has ______ all hope of going to Europe this year for lack of money.

   (A) embarked (B) renounced

3. The whole town was ______ by the war flames.

   (A) devastated (B) extorted

4. The ______ soldier carries out a dangerous mission, without letting fear prevent him from doing.

   (A) intrepid (B) viable

5. We had a(n) ______ day moving into our new house.

   (A) overbearing (B) strenuous

6. The nurse treated the wounded soldier with the most ______ care.

   (A) scrupulous (B) venomous

7. We've ______ all her arguments and she has nothing more to say.

   (A) plundered (B) demolished

8. It is ______ to cross the street without looking both ways.

   (A) indulgent (B) rash

9. The fumes from furnaces and motor vehicles have ______ the air we breathe and shortened our life expectancy.

   (A) vitiated (B) averted

10. He had no choice but to ______ that he had been guilty of bad judgment.

    (A) concede (B) conceit

解答 1. B 2. B 3. A 4. A 5. B
6. A 7. B 8. B 9. A 10. A

EXERCISE 9.8 找出与斜体词意义相反的单词:

______ 1. *altruistic* social animal

(A) critical (B) gregarious

(C) temporary (D) selfish

______ 2. *adjacent* farmhouse

(A) wealthy (B) noisy

(C) distant (D) splendid

______ 3. *sundry* articles

(A) fine (B) opposed

(C) gloomy (D) unique

______ 4. a *rash* promise

(A) deliberate (B) sluggish

(C) rare (D) reckless

______ 5. *exultant* over success

(A) mournful (B) lack

(C) zealous (D) indifferent

解答 1. D 2. C 3. D 4. A 5. A

EXERCISE 9.9 从下列单词中选出最适当的词,填入空格内:

VOCABULARY LIST

scrupulous	rash	intrepid	calamity
zealous	deduced	inexhaustible	intact
impeded	viable	distrusted	concede

1. The salesman seems very ______ to persuade the housewife to buy the book.

2. When the fire broke out the party turned to be a complete ______.

3. The deep snow and the extreme cold ______ our travel to Canada.
4. I'm willing to ______ that a large car would have cost more, but I still think we should have bought one.
5. A(n) ______ judge is careful to weigh all the evidence and excludes all personal feelings.
6. From the fact that Socrates was a man and the principle all men die, I ______ that Socrates would die.
7. The new president is a man of a(n) ______ energy.
8. They didn't believe him. In fact, they ______ him in all matters.
9. Only controlled disarmament can make a(n) ______ world in this nuclear age.
10. The heiress kept her father's art collection completely ______.

解答 1. zealous 2. calamity 3. impeded
4. concede 5. scrupulous 6. deduced
7. inexhaustible 8. distrusted 9. viable
10. intact

LESSON 10

预备测验

选出最恰当的答案：

1. He was *suspended* from school for a week ______.

   (A) to help his father (B) for bad conduct

   (C) to study more

2. Though they *disapproved* of the details, they were in ______ agreement over the plan.

   (A) eccentric (B) substantial (C) nebulous

3. A cowardly soldier *eludes* hazardous duty by ______.

   (A) aggrieving (B) wrangling (C) malingering

4. The *offence* was such a minor ______ of manners that everyone overlooked it.

   (A) breach (B) obstruction (C) overdue

5. The Romen Empire rapidly *waned* in ______ in the 5th century.

   (A) victory (B) power (C) success

解答 1. B 2. B 3. C 4. A 5. B

第一部分

WORD	MEANING	TYPICAL USE
aggrieve /ə'griːv/ *v.* 迫害 反 console	cause grief or trouble to; injure unjustly	The entire population was ***aggrieved*** by the tyranny of the king. 全国人民受到那国王暴政的迫害。
callous /'kæləs/ *adj.* 1. 心肠硬的 反 sensitive	1. unfeeling; not sensitive; insensible	Only a ***callous*** person can see suffering without trying to relieve it. 只有铁石心肠的人才能看到苦难而不设法拯救。
2. 变硬的(如脚底起硬茧)	2. hard and thick; hardened	Walking barefoot on the asphalt pavement makes the bottom of your feet ***callous***. 赤脚走在柏油路上会使你的脚底生硬茧。
disapprove /ˌdɪsə'pruːv/ *v.* 不赞成 反 consent	have an unfavorable or bad opinion of; express an opinion against	She wants to continue her study in the United States, but her parents ***disapprove*** of her plan. 她想在美国继续求学，可是父母不同意她的计划。

WORD	MEANING	TYPICAL USE
fabulous /ˈfæbjʊləs/ *adj.* 惊人的 反 true	nearly unbelievable; hard or impossible to believe	Ten dollars is a ***fabulous*** price for an ordinary pencil. 一支普通的铅笔要10美元，价格真让人难以相信。
infuriate /ɪnˈfjʊərɪeɪt/ *v.* 激怒 反 placate	make very angry; make furious	He was ***infuriated*** by the policeman's rough treatment of his wife. 他因警察粗鲁地对待他的妻子而大怒。
mordant /ˈmɔːdənt/ *adj.* 尖酸的；讽刺的 反 mild	biting and cutting; severe; sarcastic	His political opponents feared his ***mordant*** tongue, and even more his ***mordant*** pen. 他的政治对手害怕他尖酸刻薄的口才，更怕他讽刺的文章。
prowess /ˈpraʊɪs/ *n.* 勇敢 反 cowardice	great personal bravery; daring; courage; valor	The Indians sang a song of victory, describing their ***prowess*** in battle. 印第安人唱起一首胜利之歌，描述他们在战斗中的勇敢。

WORD	MEANING	TYPICAL USE
subversive /sʌbˈvɜːsɪv/ *adj.* 颠覆的 反 constructive	tending to overthrow; causing ruin; destructive	He was arrested as a member of a ***subversive*** organization. 他以一名颠覆组织分子的身份被捕。
temporary /ˈtempərərɪ/ *adj.* 暂时的 反 permanent	lasting only a limited time; not permanent; transient	Many students find ***temporary*** jobs during their summer holidays. 许多学生在暑假找到临时工作。

EXERCISE 10.1 从第一部分中选出最恰当的单词，填入空格内：

1. Do you think it is right for women to paint their lips or do you ______?
2. Two firemen showed great ______ by repeatedly rushing into the burning building to save many lives.
3. The parent was deeply ______ by his children's disobedience.
4. The teacher's ______ comment about the girl's essay made her cry.
5. The hunter made a(n) ______ shelter out of branches to avoid the heavy rain.

解答 1. disapprove 2. prowess 3. aggrieved 4. mordant 5. temporary

第二部分

WORD	MEANING	TYPICAL USE
amass /əˈmæs/ *v.* 积蓄 反 dissipate	heap together; gather; accumulate	Through the years he ***amassed*** a large fortune to buy a farm after he retired. 退休以后，他用多年积蓄的大笔财富买了一座农场。
colossal /kəˈlɒsəl/ *adj.* 巨大的 反 trivial	of huge size; gigantic; vast; tremendous	The Empire State Building is a ***colossal*** structure. 帝国大厦是一座巨大的建筑物。
dismal /ˈdɪzməl/ *adj.* 沮丧的 反 joyous	dark and gloomy; dreary; somber	Sickness or bad luck often makes a person feel ***dismal.*** 生病或噩运经常让人沮丧。
genial /ˈdʒiːnjəl/ *adj.* 亲切的；友好的 反 sullen	cheerful and friendly; smiling and pleasant; kindly; jovial	She was glad to see us again and gave me a ***genial*** welcome. 她很高兴再见到我们，并亲切地对我表示欢迎。
inveterate /ɪnˈvetərɪt/ *adj.* 习惯性的 反 occasional	confirmed in habit, practice, or feeling; habitual	It is hard for an ***inveterate*** smoker to give up tobacco. 烟瘾很大的人很难戒烟。

WORD	MEANING	TYPICAL USE
offence /əˈfens/ *n.* 犯罪;触犯 反 defence	the act of breaking the law; sin; wrong; crime	The punishment for that ***offence*** is two years in prison. 对那项罪行的刑罚是监禁两年。
sojourn /ˈsɒdʒɜːn, -ən/ *v.* /*n.* 寄居 反 departure	stay for a time; a brief stay	During his ***sojourn*** in Africa he learned much about native customs. 在寄居非洲期间,他了解了许多当地的风俗。
turmoil /ˈtɜːmɔɪl/ *n.* 混乱 反 tranquility	a state of confusion, excitement, and trouble, disturbance; tumult	Six robberies in one night put our village in a ***tur-moil.*** 一夜发生六起抢劫案使得我们全村陷入一场混乱之中。
suspend /səsˈpend/ *v.* 暂停 反 schedule	put off or stop for a period of time; postpone	A scientist ***suspends*** judgment and refrains from drawing conclusions until all the facts are in. 科学家在未掌握全部事实前,暂时不作判断或下结论。

EXERCISE 10.2 从第二部分中选出最恰当的单词,填入空格内:

1. It is sometimes difficult to acknowledge that another person's lot may be more ______ than one's own.

2. Disturbing the place and breaking most traffic laws are ______ in this country.
3. My acquaintance made a(n) ______ fortune in the last ten years.
4. Train service will be ______ from midnight to 4 a. m. to permit repair.
5. The noise of cars passing along the road is a continual ______ to our quiet at home.

答案 1. dismal 2. offences 3. colossal 4. suspended 5. turmoil

第三部分

WORD	MEANING	TYPICAL USE
assent /əˈsent/ *v.* 同意 反 disagree	agree to a suggestion; express agreement; agree	She ***assented*** to the doctor's assertion that her son was ill, but could not consent to having him hospitalized. 她同意医生的诊断，即她儿子生病了，但不同意让他住院。
cosy /ˈkəʊzɪ/ *adj.* 温暖而舒适的 反 uncomfortable	warm and comfortable; snug	The couple wish to live in a ***cosy*** little home rather than in a big mansion. 那对夫妇宁愿住在温暖舒适的小屋中，而不愿住在大厦里。

WORD	MEANING	TYPICAL USE
diversify /daɪˈvɜːsɪfaɪ, dɪ-/ *v.* 使多样化 反 simplify	make different or various in form or quality; vary	That factory is trying to ***diversify*** its products to sell in different markets. 那家工厂试着使产品多样化,以卖给不同的市场。
haggard /ˈhægəd/ *adj.* 憔悴的 反 fat	looking worn from pain, fatigue, or hunger; gaunt	The ***haggard*** faces of the rescued miners showed that they had a great deal of suffering. 获救矿工们憔悴的脸色表明他们遭受了极大的痛苦。
irreparable /ɪˈrepərəbl/ *adj.* 无法挽救的 反 reparable	cannot be repaired or made good	Careless drivers cause many ***irreparable*** accidents. 大意的司机造成许多无法挽救的意外事故。
paternal /pəˈtɜːnəl/ *adj.* 父系的 反 maternal	of or like a father; fatherly	Everyone has two ***paternal*** grandparents and two maternal grandparents. 每个人都有两个属于父系的祖父母和属于母系的外祖父母。
replica /ˈreplɪkə/ *n.* 复制品 反 original	a copy of a work of art, especially one made by the original artist	The young artist made a ***replica*** of the famous painting. 那位年轻的画家照着名画摹仿了一幅。

WORD	MEANING	TYPICAL USE
seclusion /sɪˈkluːʒən/ *n.* 隔离;隐居 反 publicity	the act of keeping away from others	His ***seclusion*** of the rabbit in the barn was kept secret from everyone else. 他把兔子藏在谷仓里,不为人知。
wrangle /ˈræŋgl/ *v.* 争吵 反 coincide	argue or dispute in a noisy or angry way; quarrel	The two friends ***wrangled*** and now they don't speak to each other. 那两个朋友争吵后,现在不再和对方说话。

EXERCISE 10.3 从第三部分中选出最恰当的一个单词,填入空格内:

1. The little boy was a(n) ______ of his father in looks and voice.
2. To ______ one's reading is to read about a number of different subjects.
3. The house is not ______ tonight because our air conditioner is not working.
4. Hunger and suffering made the lost hikers ______.
5. She lives in ______ apart even from her closest friends.

答案 1. replica 2. diversify 3. cosy 4. haggard 5. seclusion

第四部分

WORD	MEANING	TYPICAL USE
bigoted /ˈbɪgətɪd/ *adj.* 固执己见的 反 tolerant	holding fast to an opinion, belief, party, or other position; intolerant; prejudiced	Most ***bigoted*** people are intolerant of opposition. 多数固执己见的人受不了反对意见。
deficient /dɪˈfɪʃənt/ *adj.* 不足的 反 sufficient	not complete; defective; imperfect	Most of the food they eat is ***deficient*** in iron and protein. 他们吃的大部分食物缺乏铁和蛋白质。
elude /ɪˈljuːd/ *v.* 躲避 反 encounter	escape from by means of a trick	The sly fox ***eluded*** the hunters by running back in the opposite direction. 狡猾的狐狸向相反的方向跑,躲过了猎人。
ignoble /ɪgˈnəʊbl/ *adj.* 卑微的 反 noble	without honor; disgraceful; mean	Some very great men have come from ***ignoble*** families. 有些非常伟大的人物来自卑微的家庭。

WORD	MEANING	TYPICAL USE
kindred /ˈkɪndrɪd/ *adj.* 同类的 反 foreign	related; belonging to the same group	We are studying about dew, frost, mist, and other ***kindred*** facts of nature. 我们正在研究有关露、霜、雾以及其他同类的自然现象。
melancholy /ˈmelənkəlɪ/ *adj.* 忧郁的 反 exhilerated	sad; gloomy; depressed in spirits; lamentable; deplorable	During the Romantic period it was fashionable in literature to have a ***melancholy*** outlook on the world. 浪漫主义时期,文学界流行悲观的世界观。
poltroon /pɒlˈtruːn/ *n.* 懦夫 反 valor	a wretched coward	No one likes to be regarded as a ***poltroon.*** 没有人喜欢被认为是懦夫。
rout /raʊt/ *v.* 溃败 反 surrender	defeat completely and drive away	The enemy was ***routed.*** 敌军被击溃了。
vulnerable /ˈvʌlnərəbl/ *adj.* 难防守的 反 protected	open to attack; can be easily wounded or injured	The most massive defence system would still leave the nation ***vulnerable*** to nuclear attack. 最强大的防卫系统仍然难以防止国家遭受核武器的攻击。

EXERCISE 10.4 从第四部分中选出最恰当的单词,填入空格内:

1. Weak teeth are usually caused by your diet in which calcium is ______.
2. Pollution of its drinking water left the city ______ to many diseases.
3. In the slums of some cities even small children learn ______ language.
4. The ______ news that the king is seriously ill made all of us pray God for his quick recovery.
5. The baseball team ______ its opponents by a score of ten to one.

解答 1. deficient 2. vulnerable 3. ignoble 4. melancholy 5. routed

第五部分

WORD	MEANING	TYPICAL USE
abide /əˈbaɪd/ *v.* 居住 反 depart	remain; stay; wait	The child ***abided*** with his grandparents for three years before being returned to his parents. 那孩子被送回父母身边之前,跟祖父祖母住了三年。
boisterous /ˈbɔɪstərəs/ *adj.* 喧闹的 反 silent	noisily cheerful and rough; exuberant	The audience in the theater was irritated by the unruly and ***boisterous*** children. 戏院的观众被孩子们的不守秩序和喧闹所激怒。

WORD	MEANING	TYPICAL USE
despicable /dɪˈspɪkəbl/ *adj.* 卑鄙的 反 admirable	deserving to be despised; contemptible	To spit in the classroom is ***despicable***. 在教室里吐痰是卑劣的行为。
exotic /ɪgˈzɒtɪk/ *adj.* 外来的 反 domestic	from a foreign country; not native; strange and unusual	We saw many ***exotic*** plants at the flower exhibition, which we had never seen before. 花展上，我们看到许多以前从未见过的外来植物。
imperative /ɪmˈperətɪv/ *adj.* 1. 必需的 反 unnecessary	1. urgent; essential; must be done	For the mountain climber, it is ***imperative*** to get food and water before sunset. 那个登山者必须在日落前得到食物和水。
2. 命令的	2. expressing a command, request, or warning	My wife has such an ***imperative*** voice that everyone obeys her. 我妻子有一种命令式的声音，每个人都服从她。
nonplus /ˈnɒnpləs/ *v.* 使困惑 反 hearten	puzzle completely; make unable to say or do something; confuse	He was ***nonplused*** by the strange customs he saw everywhere in the country. 他在这个国家各地看到的奇怪习俗令他感到困惑。

WORD	MEANING	TYPICAL USE
pompous /ˈpɒmpəs/ *adj.* 夸大的 反 informal	foolishly solemn and self-important; pretentious	The leader of the band bowed in a ***pompous*** manner. 乐队队长用夸张的姿势鞠了个躬。
sever /ˈsevə(r)/ *v.* 分开;断绝 反 connect	break or cut apart; cut off; separate	He ***severed*** connection with Tom. 他和汤姆断绝了关系。
sultry /ˈsʌltrɪ/ *adj.* 闷热的 反 cold	hot and moist; oppressively hot	The day was so ***sultry*** that they had little energy left. 天气如此闷热,他们都筋疲力尽了。
wane /weɪn/ *v.* (月)亏;减弱 反 wax	grow gradually smaller or less after being full or complete; diminish	The moon was ***waning***, and in such a ***waning*** light, it is very difficult to see the enemy. 月亮渐亏,而在如此微弱的月光下,很难看见敌人。

EXERCISE 10.5 从第五部分中选出最恰当的单词,填入空格内:

1. We were ______ to see two roads where we had expected only one.
2. The railway guard was a(n) ______ little official, who thought he controlled the whole railway system himself.
3. It is ______ that this very sick child should stay in bed at least for two

weeks.

4. According to Greek mythology, my wife had been ______ from my own body.
5. It is ______ of you to leave your wife and children without food and money.

解答 1. nonplused 2. pompous 3. imperative 4. severed 5. despicable

效果检测

EXERCISE 10.6 从第二栏中选出第一栏各词的反义词：

COLUMN Ⅰ	COLUMN Ⅱ
______ 1. schedule	(A) constructive
______ 2. melancholy	(B) occasional
______ 3. callous	(C) publicity
______ 4. exotic	(D) suspend
______ 5. assent	(E) nonplus
______ 6. seclusion	(F) exhilerated
______ 7. subversive	(G) sensitive
______ 8. hearten	(H) domestic
______ 9. inveterate	(I) surrender
______ 10. rout	(J) disagree

解答 1. D 2. F 3. G 4. H 5. J
6. C 7. A 8. E 9. B 10. I

EXERCISE 10.7 选出最符合句意的单词：

1. He had a(n) ______ habit of winking one eye.

   (A) mordant (B) inveterate

2. Bus service will be ______ until the highway is repaired.

   (A) suspended (B) mendacious

3. The constant noise from the machine ______ all the secretaries in the office.

   (A) infuriated (B) placated

4. If a bill to be paid is ten dollars and you have only six dollars, four dollars is ______.

   (A) irreparable (B) deficient

5. There are several ______ buildings in the business district of Seoul.

   (A) colossal (B) pompous

6. Everyone ______ to the dance party on Christmas Eve.

   (A) assented (B) abided

7. Where to go, and what to do when we get there, are two ______ questions.

   (A) diversified (B) kindred

8. The government dislikes this magazine because it prints ______ ideas.

   (A) subversive (B) substantial

9. I remember his name very well, but his name ______ me for the moment.

   (A) wrangles (B) eludes

10. She ______ with some relatives in London for three months.

    (A) sojourned (B) rambled

解答 1. B 2. A 3. A 4. B 5. A
6. A 7. B 8. A 9. B 10. A

EXERCISE 10.8 找出与斜体词意义相反的单词：

______ 1. *elude* (A) enlarge (B) enclose (C) extend (D) encounter

______ 2. *dismal* (A) joyous (B) certain (C) easy (D) stern

______ 3. *wane* (A) sane (B) real (C) control (D) wax

______ 4. *seclusion* (A) protection (B) combination (C) publicity (D) salvage

______ 5. *ignoble* (A) graceful (B) calm (C) mordant (D) genial

解答 1. D 2. A 3. D 4. C 5. A

EXERCISE 10.9 从下列单词中选出最适当的词，填入空格内：

VOCABULARY LIST

elude	seclusion	boisterous	offence
infuriated	prowess	turmoil	suspended
diversify	wrangled	despicable	ignoble

1. The sailor's voices could not be heard above the ______ of the storm.
2. The man was highly praised for having the ______ to go into the burning house to save the little girl.
3. To steal from the collection plate in church or from a blind beggar is ______.
4. The hurricane ______ all ferry service for three days.
5. She was simply ______ by her husband's cold indifference about her new dress.

6. The children ______ about who should sit in the front seat of the car.
7. To ______ one's routine work is to break up one's day into segments devoted to various aspects of one's job.
8. That dirty old house is a(n) ______ to everyone who lives in the street.
9. He was amazed that no one else seemed to notice the ______ cruelty with which she treated her stepsons.
10. He rented a cottage in the woods for the summer, in which he could be in ______ while he was writing.

解答

1. turmoil	2. prowess	3. ignoble
4. suspended	5. infuriated	6. wrangled
7. diversify	8. offence	9. despicable
10. seclusion		

LESSON 11

预备测验

选出最恰当的答案:

1. Department stores are often *congested* ______.

   (A) after 9 o'clock in evening (B) before Christmas

   (C) on cold, windy days

2. A *judicious* parent ______ his children to decide many things for themselves.

   (A) forbids (B) encourages (C) dissuades

3. A(n) ______ person treats his work with *apathy*.

   (A) lazy (B) wise (C) old

4. ______ *simulate* flowers or leaves of a tree.

   (A) Most gardeners (B) Some people

   (C) Certain insects

5. Constant *vigilance* is necessary in order to ______ in driving.

   (A) avoid accidents (B) save gasoline

   (C) prevent engine trouble

解答 1.B 2.B 3.A 4.C 5.A

第一部分

WORD	MEANING	TYPICAL USE
acclimate /ˈæklɪmeɪt/ *v.* 习惯于 *n.* acclimation	get used to a new climate	We are becoming ***acclimated*** to New York weather. 我们渐渐习惯了纽约的天气。
assail /əˈseɪl/ *v.* 攻击；质问 *n./adj.* assailant	attack with violence or continuous criticism; assault	The senators ***assailed*** the President on the subject of the treaty between the two countries. 议员们质问总统有关两国间的条约的问题。
congest /kənˈdʒest/ *v.* 充满 *n.* congestion	fill too full; overcrowd	His face was ***congested*** with anger as the argument grew more heated. 争辩变得愈发激烈时，他的脸上满是愤怒之情。
effusive /ɪˈfjuːsɪv/ *adj.* 热情的 *n.* effusion	showing too much feeling; too demonstrative and emotional	Her ***effusive*** welcome made us feel most uncomfortable. 她热情的迎接使我们非常不自在。

WORD	MEANING	TYPICAL USE
frugal /ˈfruːgəl/ *adj.* 节约的 *n.* frugality	without waste; not wasteful; saving; thrifty	A good manager is ***frugal*** in the use of his funds. 一个好的经营者节约资金的使用。
insolvent /ɪnˈsɒlvənt/ *adj.* 无力偿还的；破产的 *n.* insolvency	unable to pay one's debt; bankrupt	The newspapers accused the government of being ***insolvent*** in its debts. 报纸指责政府无力偿还债务。
nausea /ˈnɔːsɪə/ *n.* 恶心；晕船 *v.* nauseate	the feeling that one is about to vomit; seasick	Most passengers of the ship were seized with ***nausea*** during the storm at sea. 船上大多数乘客在风暴中晕船。
redeem /rɪˈdiːm/ *v.* 赎回 *n.* redemption	get back by payment; set free by payment; regain	She had no way to ***redeem*** her furniture out of pawn. 她无法赎回当掉的家具。
seep /siːp/ *v.* 渗入 *n.* seepage	leak slowly; ooze; trickle	They used waterproof cement to prevent water from ***seeping*** through the roof of the tunnel. 他们用防水的水泥防止水从隧道顶部渗入。

WORD	MEANING	TYPICAL USE
symmetry /ˈsɪmɪtrɪ/ *n.* 对称 *adj.* symmetrical	exact likeness in shape between the opposite sides of something	A swollen cheek spoiled the ***symmetry*** of his handsome face. 一边肿的面颊让他英俊的脸庞不再对称。

EXERCISE 11.1 从第一部分中选出最恰当的单词，填入空格内：

1. John is not ______; he does not pour out his emotions.
2. After paying the money, he ______ his watch from the pawnshop.
3. My aunt is a(n) ______ housekeeper who buys and uses food carefully.
4. Main Street is ______ with the traffic of people driving to work each morning.
5. Country girls cannot easily ______ themselves to working in an office.

答案 1. effusive 2. redeemed 3. frugal 4. congested 5. acclimate

第二部分

WORD	MEANING	TYPICAL USE
aggravate /ˈægrəveɪt/ *v.* 使更坏 *n.* aggravation	make worse or more severe	New York's hot weather is often ***aggravated*** by its humidity. 潮湿使纽约炎热的天气更加恶劣。

WORD	MEANING	TYPICAL USE
balmy /ˈbɑːmɪ/ *adj.* 温和的	soft and gentle; mild	A ***balmy*** breeze was blowing across the beautiful lake. 一阵温和的微风吹过美丽的湖面。
culmination /ˌkʌlmɪˈneɪʃən/ *n.* 极点,顶点 *v.* culminate	the highest point; climax	The ***culmination*** of the doctor's life's work was his discovery of a cure for cancer. 那位医生一生工作的最高成就便是在癌症治疗上的发现。
endorse /ɪnˈdɔːs/ *v.* 签名于(票据等的)背面 *n.* endorsement	write one's name on the back of (a check, note, or other document)	The storekeeper ***endorsed*** my bill when I paid the full amount. 当我把钱付清时,店主在账单背面签了名。
hygiene /ˈhaɪdʒiːn/ *n.* 卫生学 *adj.* hygienic	the science of keeping good health; rules of health	The main field of ***hygiene*** is concerned with healthy living and cleanliness. 卫生学包含的主要范围和健康的生活及清洁有关。
intangible /ɪnˈtændʒəbl/ *adj.* 不能触摸的 *n.* intangibility	not capable of being touched or felt; impalpable	Sound is ***intangible*** and the same is true of light. 声和光都是无法触摸的。

WORD	MEANING	TYPICAL USE
oblivious /əˈblɪvɪəs/ *adj.* 忘记的 *n.* oblivion	not mindful; forgetful	Grandfather sat by the fireplace, ***oblivious*** of everything around him. 祖父坐在火炉旁，忘却了周遭的一切。
rite /raɪt/ *n.* 仪式 *adj.* ritual	a solemn ceremony; formal procedure in a religious or other observance	The funeral will be performed according to church ***rites.*** 葬礼将依据教会的仪式举行。
simulate /ˈsɪmjʊleɪt/ *v.* 假装 *adj.* simulative	put on a false appearance of; pretend; feign	Her story was boring, but he ***simulated*** interest to please her. 虽然她的故事令人厌倦，但为了让她高兴他假装有兴趣听。
transcribe /trænsˈkraɪb/ *v.* 用另一种文字或符号写出 *n.* transcript	copy in writing or in typewriting	The account of the trial was ***transcribed*** from the stenographer's shorthand notes. 庭审记录是由速记员的速记符号翻译过来的。

EXERCISE 11.2 从第二部分中选出最恰当的单词，填入空格内：

1. The book was so interesting that I was completely ______ of my

surroundings.

2. Sharon was the heroine of the play. She ______ the bewildered mother successfully.
3. His bad temper was ______ by a headache.
4. A priest administered the last ______ to the dying man.
5. The next day his speech was ______ in the newspapers, word for word.

解答 1. oblivious 2. simulated 3. aggravated 4. rite 5. transcribed

第三部分

WORD	MEANING	TYPICAL USE
annex /ə'neks/ *v.* 合并 *n.* annexation	join or add to something larger or more important	Outlying districts were ***annexed*** by the city. 边远郊区被并入该市。
brew /bruː/ *v.* 1. 酿造 *n.* brewage	1. make (beer, ale, or mash) by soaking, boiling, and fermenting grain	Some people ***brew*** beer at home for home use. 有些人在家中酿啤酒以供自用。
2. 图谋	2. bring about; plan; plot; contrive	The boys whispering in the corner are ***brewing*** some mischief. 那些在角落里说悄悄话的男孩们正企图捣乱。

WORD	MEANING	TYPICAL USE
deride /dɪˈraɪd/ *v.* 嘲笑 *adj.* derisive	make fun of; laugh at in scorn	The boys ***derided*** him for his fear of the darkness. 男孩们嘲笑他怕黑。
evaluate /ɪˈvæljʊeɪt/ *v.* 评估 *n.* evaluation	find out the value or the amount of; appraise	She always ***evaluates*** people by their clothes. 她总是根据衣着来评价人。
imminent /ˈɪmɪnənt/ *adj.* 即将来临的 *n.* imminence	likely to happen soon; about to occur; impending; urgent	Swept along by the swift current, he was in ***imminent*** danger of going over the waterfall. 被一阵急流卷走之后,他正面临着被冲下瀑布的危险。
judicious /dʒʊ(uː)ˈdɪʃəs/ *adj.* 明智的 *n.* judiciousness	having, using, or showing good judgment; wise; sensible; prudent; discreet	A ***judicious*** historian selects and weighs facts carefully and critically. 明智的历史学家用小心翼翼、批判性的态度来权衡事实。
preponderance /prɪˈpɒndərəns/ *n.* (数目、重量、力量之)优势 *adj.* preponderant	greater number; greater power or influence	There is a ***preponderance*** of hot days in July and August. 七八月间炎热的日子最多。

WORD	MEANING	TYPICAL USE
sage /seɪdʒ/ *adj.* 明智的 *n.* sageness	showing wisdom or good judgment; wise	Many ***sage*** staffs around the commander helped him win the battle. 司令官身旁许多明智的参谋帮助他打赢了那场战役。
specter /ˈspektə(r)/ *n.* 幽灵 *adj.* spectral	a phantom or ghost, especially one of a terrifying nature or appearance; ghost; phantom	Some superstitious people said that the ***specter*** of the murdered man haunted the house. 一些迷信的人说，那个被谋杀者的鬼魂常在这间屋子里出没。
tumult /ˈtjuːmʌlt/ *n.* 骚动 *adj.* tumultuous	the confused noise and excitement of a big crowd; uproar	The shout of "Fire" caused a great ***tumult*** in the theater. "失火"的喊叫声使剧院大乱。

EXERCISE 11.3 从第三部分中选出最恰当的单词，填入空格内：

1. The defeated team was greeted by a(n) ______ of angry voices in the crowd.
2. There is a(n) ______ of tigers in the forest, and only a small number of monkeys and elephants.
3. The expedition has now returned, and its members are beginning to ______ and integrate the facts gathered in the field and at the base.
4. The old professor gave us ______ advice, which we have never forgotten.

5. Her little daughter cried in her bed, saying she had seen a dreadful ______ in her dream.

答案 1. tumult 2. preponderance 3. evaluate 4. sage 5. specter

第四部分

WORD	MEANING	TYPICAL USE
apathy /ˈæpəθɪ/ *n.* 漠不关心；冷漠 *adj.* apathetic	lack of interest or desire for activity; indifference; unconcern	Her ***apathy*** since her husband's death worries her children. 自从她丈夫死后，她的冷漠让孩子们感到忧虑。
collide /kəˈlaɪd/ *v.* 冲突 *n.* collision	rush against each other; crush	If the aims of two countries ***collide***, there may be a war. 两国的目标如果发生冲突，就可能引起战争。
drape /dreɪp/ *v.* 悬挂 *n.* drapery	cover or hang with cloth falling loosely in folds as a decoration	The buildings were ***draped*** with red, white, and blue bunting. 屋子上悬挂着红白蓝三色的旗帜。

WORD	MEANING	TYPICAL USE
fatuous /ˈfætjʊəs/ *adj.* 愚昧的 *n.* fatuity	stupid; foolish; ridiculous; silly	After his boring speech for over an hour, the ***fatuous*** speaker waited for applause from the audience. 进行了一个多小时令人厌倦的演讲后,那无知的演说者期待着听众的掌声。
impudent /ˈɪmpjʊdənt/ *adj.* 厚颜的 *n.* impudence	without shame or modesty; rudely bold; insolent; impertinent	The ***impudent*** boy made faces at the teacher. 那厚颜的男孩对老师扮鬼脸。
meditate /ˈmedɪteɪt/ *v.* 考虑 *adj.* meditative	think quietly; consider carefully for a long time; reflect	I could have given a much better answer if I had had enough time to ***meditate***. 如果我有足够的时间来考虑,便能回答得好些。
purify /ˈpjʊərɪfaɪ/ *v.* 洗除罪恶;使纯净 *n.* purification	make pure; cleanse	This music seems to ***purify*** one's spirit of evil thoughts. 这音乐似乎能消除人罪恶的念头。

WORD	MEANING	TYPICAL USE
sagacious /səˈɡeɪʃəs/ *adj.* 精明的 *n.* sagacity	having a sharp or keen mind and good judgment; shrewd	A ***sagacious*** businessman seldom fails in his business. 精明的商人在生意上很少失败。
suave /swɑːv, sweɪv/ *adj.* 文雅的 *n.* suavity	smoothly agreeable or polite; showing good manners	The secretary's beautiful figure and ***suave*** manners made the office bright. 秘书窈窕的身材及文雅的举止使得办公室为之一亮。
vigilance /ˈvɪdʒɪləns/ *n.* 警醒 *adj.* vigilant	watchful care; watchfulness; alertness	The watchman who caught the thief was praised for his ***vigilance***. 那抓到小偷的巡夜者因其警觉而受到赞赏。

EXERCISE 11.4 从第四部分中选出最恰当的单词,填入空格内:

1. After we had waited for about twenty minutes, a(n) ______ man came along and tried to get in at the head of our line.
2. The citizen's ______ to local affairs resulted in poor government.
3. This salt has been specially ______ for use in medicine.
4. The cat watched the mousehole with ______.
5. He ______ for two days before giving his final answer.

解答 1. impudent 2. apathy 3. purified
4. vigilance 5. meditated

效果检测

EXERCISE 11.5 将各词不同词性的适当形式填入空格内：

	ADJECTIVE	NOUN	VERB	ADVERB
1.	______	preponderance	______	______
2.	______	______	deride	______
3.	______	______	redeem	××××
4.	______	nausea	______	______
5.	sagacious	______	××××	______
6.	______	balm	××××	______
7.	______	______	simulate	______
8.	effusive	______	______	______
9.	××××	______	seep	××××
10.	______	______	meditate	______

解答

	ADJECTIVE	NOUN	VERB	ADVERB
1.	preponderant	(preponderance)	preponderate	preponderantly
2.	derisive	derision	(deride)	deridingly
3.	redemptive	redemption	(redeem)	××××
4.	nauseous	(nausea)	nauseate	nauseously
5.	(sagacious)	sagacity	××××	sagaciously
6.	balmy	(balm)	××××	balmily
7.	simulative	simulation	(simulate)	simulatively
8.	(effusive)	effusion	effuse	effusively
9.	××××	seepage	(seep)	××××
10.	meditative	meditation	(meditate)	meditatively

EXERCISE 11.6 将题前的斜体词转换为恰当的形式，填入空格内：

1. *endorse* You have to sign your ______ on the back of a check, in evidence of its transfer of assuring its payment.
2. *oblivious* Drug addicts like to use narcotic because it causes complete ______ of all sorrows.
3. *suave* Before I asked her name, she introduced herself with perfect ______.
4. *symmetry* Notice the ______ looks of the human body; the right side is the counterpart of the left.
5. *drape* The gay colors of the ______ made the living room bright and cheery.
6. *vigilance* While she was out, the faithful dog kept ______ guard over the baby.
7. *frugal* Riches are achieved with industry and kept by ______.
8. *apathy* The lazy boy's ______ attitude toward schoolwork annoyed both his teacher and his parents.
9. *tumult* I couldn't hear what she said because of the sailor's ______ voice.
10. *transcribe* The college wanted a ______ of the student's high-school record.

解答

1. endorsement 2. oblivion 3. suavity
4. symmetrical 5. drapery 6. vigilant
7. frugality 8. apathetic 9. tumultuous
10. transcript

EXERCISE 11.7 找出与其他三个不相关的词：

______ 1. (A) fatuous (B) grateful
(C) ridiculous (D) stupid

______ 2. (A) ghost (B) phantom
(C) specter (D) perfume

______ 3. (A) cynical (B) impending
(C) imminent (D) urgent

______ 4. (A) impalpable (B) insubstantial
(C) intangible (D) indulgent

______ 5. (A) elastic (B) judicious
(C) prudent (D) discreet

______ 6. (A) annex (B) subjoin
(C) split (D) affix

______ 7. (A) uproar (B) savor
(C) riot (D) tumult

______ 8. (A) insolent (B) impudent
(C) impertinent (D) insane

______ 9. (A) indifference (B) contour
(C) apathy (D) unconcern

______ 10. (A) ooze (B) seep
(C) peep (D) trickle

解答 1. B 2. D 3. A 4. D 5. A
6. C 7. B 8. D 9. B 10. C

EXERCISE 11.8 从下列单词中选出最恰当的词，填入空格内：

VOCABULARY LIST

collided	aggravate	insolvent	meditate
symmetry	imminent	culmination	hygiene
endorse	seeped	annexed	redeemed

1. He had to ______ the check before the bank would cash it.
2. Water had ______ into the house through the walls and roof.
3. The property on which the money was lent was ______ when the loan was paid back.
4. The black clouds, thunder, and lightning show that a storm is ______.
5. Telling a lie in the court will only ______ your guilt.
6. The Hawaiian Islands were ______ to the United States by act of Congress, July 7, 1898.
7. The ______ of the Christmas Party was the appearance of Santa Claus.
8. The terrible earthquake killed thousands of people in the city, and it led me to ______ on the weakness of human beings.
9. The bump on the left side of her forehead spoiled the ______ of her face.
10. Two large ships ______ in the harbor and both sank.

解答
1. endorse 2. seeped 3. redeemed
4. imminent 5. aggravate 6. annexed
7. culmination 8. meditate 9. symmetry
10. collided

LESSON 12

预备测验

选出最恰当的答案：

1. A(n)______ surgeon works with *dexterity*.

   (A) good (B) unskilled

2. In ______ weather the air is very *humid*.

   (A) windy (B) rainy

3. The little girl was in *ecstasy* over ______.

   (A) the pitiful beggar (B) her new puppy

4. Work is *repugnant* to ______ people.

   (A) lazy (B) diligent

5. The doctor said that ______ would *suffice* the patient.

   (A) smoking or drinking (B) two meals a day

解答 1. A 2. B 3. B 4. A 5. B

第一部分

WORD	MEANING	TYPICAL USE
accelerate /æk'seləreɪt/ *v.* 加速进行 *n.* acceleration	cause to move faster; speed up	The engineer *accelerates* a train by turning on more power. 火车司机启动更多的动力，使火车加速前进。

WORD	MEANING	TYPICAL USE
averse /əˈvɜːs/ *adj.* 反对的；不愿的 *n.* aversion	turned away in mind or feeling; having a strong dislike; opposed	I will keep it secret; I feel ***averse*** to telling it to someone. 我会保密的，我不愿告诉任何人。
corroborate /kəˈrɒbərɪt/ *v.* 证实 *adj.* corroborative	make more certain; give support or certainty to; confirm	Two persons who saw the road accident ***corroborated*** the driver's statement. 两个目睹了车祸的人证实了驾驶员的陈述。
encamp /ɪnˈkæmp/ *v.* 扎营 *n.* encampment	make camp; settle in tents	It took the soldiers only half an hour to ***encamp*** in the heavy rain. 士兵们在大雨中扎营只花了半小时。
humid /ˈhjuːmɪd/ *adj.* 潮湿的 *n.* humidity	slightly wet; moist; damp	The air is very ***humid*** near the sea or large lake. 靠近海或大湖的地方，空气非常潮湿。
irrigation /ˌɪrɪˈgeɪʃən/ *n.* 灌溉 *adj.* irrigational	the act of supplying water	It is impossible to make plants grow in a desert without ***irrigation***. 没有灌溉，植物在沙漠中不可能生长。

WORD	MEANING	TYPICAL USE
preeminent /prɪ(iː)ˈemɪnənt/ *adj.* 卓越的 *n.* preeminence	standing out above all others; superior to others, outstanding	Every baseball player envies him, for he is ***pre-eminent*** above all his rivals for pitching. 每个棒球球员都羡慕他，因为在投球方面，他胜过任何竞争者。
rudiment /ˈruːdɪmənt/ *n.* 初步 *adj.* rudimentary	the first steps or stages; a part to be learned first; beginning	Everyone learns the ***rudiments*** of arithmetic in elementary school. 每个人在上小学的时候都学初级算术。
stifle /ˈstaɪfl/ *v.* 使窒息 *adj.* stifling	stop the breath of; cause difficulty in breathing; smother	When they got in the boiler room they were almost ***stifled*** by the heat. 进入锅炉房时，他们热得几乎透不过气来。
versatile /ˈvɜːsətaɪl/ *adj.* 多才多艺的 *n.* versatility	able to do many things well; having many kinds of skills	He is a very ***versatile*** performer; he can act, sing, dance and play the piano. 他是个多才多艺的表演者：他会演戏、唱歌、跳舞，还会弹钢琴。

EXERCISE 12.1 从第一部分中选出最恰当的单词,填入空格内:

1. ______ is needed to make crops grow in dry regions.
2. It is almost impossible to learn multiplication without knowing the ______ of addition.
3. Witnesses ______ her statement that there were two men in the room around that time.
4. Theodore Roosevelt was a(n) ______ man; he was successful as a statesman, soldier, sportsman, explorer and author.
5. The black smoke filled the building and almost ______ the firemen in it.

解答 1. irrigation 2. rudiments 3. corroborated 4. versatile 5. stifled

第二部分

WORD	MEANING	TYPICAL USE
anatomy /əˈnætəmɪ/ *n.* 身体结构 *adj.* anatomical	the structure of animals and plants; structure	The *anatomy* of an earthworm is much simpler than that of a man. 和人相比,蚯蚓的身体结构要简单得多。
brawn /brɔːn/ *n.* 肌肉(尤指强壮的肌肉) *adj.* brawny	muscular strength; muscle	Football requires brain as well as *brawn*. 踢足球需要智力和体力。

WORD	MEANING	TYPICAL USE
dexterity /deks'terɪtɪ/ *n.* 灵巧;机敏 *adj.* dexterous	skill in using the hands and brain	***Dexterity*** in questioning the witnesses helped the lawyer win many cases. 这位律师擅长询问目击者,这帮助他打赢了许多官司。
erupt /ɪ'rʌpt/ *v.* 爆发 *n.* eruption	explode and pour out of fire; burst forth	Mount Vesuvius hasn't ***erupted*** for a good many years. 维苏威火山已经有许多年没有爆发了。
hypothesis /haɪ'pɒθɪsɪs/ *n.* 假说 *adj.* hypothetical	an idea of suggestion put forward as a starting point for reasoning	Let's discuss this topic on the ***hypothesis*** that it is true. 我们假定它是真的,来讨论这主题。
manipulate /mə'nɪpjʊleɪt/ *v.* 操纵 *n.* manipulation	handle or control with skill	To drive an automobile, you must learn how to ***manipulate*** the steering wheel and pedals. 要想驾驶汽车,你必须学习如何操纵方向盘和踏板。
prowess /'praʊɪs/ *n.* 英勇 *adj.* prowessful	great personal bravery; daring	The tribesmen sang a song of victory, describing their ***prowess*** in battle. 族人唱着胜利之歌,歌颂他们在战场上的英勇。

WORD	MEANING	TYPICAL USE
scrupulous /ˈskruːpjʊləs/ *adj.* 1. 正直的；诚实的 *n.* scrupulosity	1. very careful to do what is right; conscientious	A less ***scrupulous*** man wouldn't give the money back to its owner. 稍不诚实的人就不会将钱送还给失主。
2. 谨慎小心的	2. attending thoroughly to details; very cautious	The nurse treated the wounded soldiers with the most ***scrupulous*** care. 护士无微不至地照顾受伤的士兵。
suffice /səˈfaɪs/ *v.* 足够 *n.* sufficiency	meet the desires, need or requirement; satisfy	One hundred dollars a month will ***suffice*** for the old lady's need. 一个月100美元足够那老妇人花销。

EXERCISE 12.2 从第二部分中选出最恰当的单词,填入空格内:

1. His new ______ gives a possible reason for the existence of life on the moon.
2. Mother told me that fifty dollars would ______ for my summer travel, but as it truned out, it was not enough.
3. His ______ and skill as a footballer makes it certain that he'll be chosen for the team.
4. A clever politician knows how to ______ his supporters.
5. Steve is ______ about returning books to the library on time; he has never paid a late fine.

解答 1. hypothesis 2. suffice 3. prowess 4. manipulate 5. scrupulous

第三部分

WORD	MEANING	TYPICAL USE
antique /æn'tiːk/ *adj.* 古代的 *n.* antiquity	of a time long past; out of date; old-fashioned	He really likes ***antique*** art much more than modern art. 他的确喜爱古典艺术远胜于现代艺术。
coherent /kəʊ'hɪərənt/ *adj.* 连贯的 *n.* coherence	being naturally or reasonably connected; consistent; sticking together	In ***coherent*** writing, every sentence is connected in thought to the previous sentence. 在连贯的写作中,每一个句子在思想上都要和前面的句子相连。
doze /dəʊz/ *v.* 小睡 *adj.* dozy	sleep lightly; be half asleep	After dinner my father often ***dozes*** in his chair for a while. 晚饭后,我父亲常在他的椅子上打个盹。
fascinate /'fæsɪneɪt/ *v.* 使迷惑,着迷 *n.* fascination	attract very strongly; enchant by charming qualities	The actress's beauty and cleverness ***fascinated*** everyone in the room. 那女演员的美貌与聪明迷住了屋里的每一个人。

WORD	MEANING	TYPICAL USE
innovate /ˈɪnəʊveɪt/ *v.* 革新 *n.* innovation	make change; bring in something new	Some people like to ***innovate*** the old systems and traditions; others like to preserve them. 有些人喜欢改革旧有的制度及传统,而有些人却喜欢保留它们。
mystify /ˈmɪstɪfaɪ/ *v.* 使困惑 *n.* mystification	bewilder purposely; perplex; puzzle to make mysterious	The magician's tricks ***mystified*** the audience in the theater. 那位魔术师的把戏让剧院里的观众感到困惑。
recur /rɪˈkɜː/ *v.* 再发生 *n.* recurrence	come up again; occur again; be repeated	Leap year ***recurs*** every four years, and in that year February has 29 days. 每四年有一个闰年,而在那一年中,二月份是29天。
shimmer /ˈʃɪmə(r)/ *v.* 闪烁发光 *n.* shimmery	shine with a soft trembling light; gleam faintly	The sky was clear, and moonlight was ***shimmering*** on the lake. 天空中没有一片云,月光照在湖面上,闪闪发光。

WORD	MEANING	TYPICAL USE
technicality /ˌteknɪˈkælɪtɪ/ *n.* 专门的事项 *v.* technicalize	a technical matter, term or expression	The general explained the military ***technicalities*** of the matter to the newspaper reporters. 那将军向报社记者解释该事件在军事上专门的事项。

EXERCISE 12.3 从第三部分中选出最恰当的单词,填入空格内:

1. The children were ______ by all the marvellous toys in the shop window of the store.
2. He bought a(n) ______ chair at a high price, which had been made in 1860.
3. A(n) ______ sentence is easy to read and clear to understand.
4. The magician put an egg in an empty box, and in a few seconds a hen came out of it. I was completely ______ about what happened.
5. It is difficult to ______ when people prefer the old, familiar way of doing things.

答案 1. fascinated 2. antique 3. coherent 4. mystified 5. innovate

第四部分

WORD	MEANING	TYPICAL USE
articulate 1. /ɑːˈtɪkjʊlɪt/ *adj.* 发音清晰的 *n.* articulation	1. spoken in distinct syllables or words; clear	A baby cries and gurgles but does not use ***articulate*** speech. 婴儿仅仅是啼哭和咯咯作声，却无法清晰地发音。
2. /ɑːˈtɪkjʊleɪt/ *v.* 发音清晰	2. speak distinctly; express in clear sounds or words.	The speaker was careful to ***articulate*** his words so that everyone in the hall could understand him. 那说话者小心地清晰吐字，以便使大厅中的每个人都能听懂。
confront /kənˈfrʌnt/ *v.* 面对 *n.* confrontation	meet face to face; face boldly; stand facing	The soldiers were ***confronted*** by two terrorists as they left their camp. 士兵们离开营帐时，迎面来了两个恐怖分子。
ecstasy /ˈekstəsɪ/ *n.* 出神 *v.* ecstasize	a condition of very great joy; rapture	While she was waiting for her boyfriend in the tea room, a sweet melody filled her with ***ecstasy***. 她在茶室里等男朋友时，一阵美妙的旋律使她出神。

WORD	MEANING	TYPICAL USE
foster /ˈfɒstə(r)/ *v.* 助长 *n.* fosterage	help the growth or development of; promote; help to grow	The mother tried to ***foster*** her son's interest in music by taking him to concerts frequently. 那母亲常带儿子去听音乐会，尝试着借此培养他对音乐的兴趣。
irradiate /ɪˈreɪdɪeɪt/ *v.* 照耀 *n.* irradiation	shine upon; light up; make bright; illuminate	The hall is not dim; the four large lamps ***irradiate*** it. 厅内并不暗；有四盏灯照明。
obstinate /ˈɒbstɪnɪt/ *adj.* 固执的 *n.* obstinacy	firmly holding to one's opinion or purpose; stubborn	The ***obstinate*** man would go his own way, in spite of all warning. 那固执的人不顾所有的警告，依然我行我素。
repugnant /rɪˈpʌgnənt/ *adj.* 使人讨厌的 *n.* repugnance	disagreeable or offensive; distasteful	Some people eat foods that are ***repugnant*** to others. 某些人讨厌的食物，有些人却爱吃。

WORD	MEANING	TYPICAL USE
soporific /ˌsɒpəˈrɪfɪk, ˌsəʊ-/ *adj.* 催眠的 *adv.* soporiferously	causing or tending to cause sleep; drowsy	After his ***soporific*** speech for an hour, the speaker received no applause from the audience. 在那催眠般的一小时演讲后，演说者没有得到任何来自听众的掌声。
triumph /ˈtraɪəmf/ *n.* 巨大的成功 *adj.* triumphant	a notable success or achievement; great victory	The conquest of outer space is one of the greatest ***triumphs*** of modern science. 征服外层空间是现代科学最伟大的成就之一。

EXERCISE 12.4 从第四部分中选出最恰当的单词，填入空格内：

1. We ______ the little girl while her mother was in hospital.
2. John was a really ______ man; we tried to get him to change his mind, but in vain.
3. The little band of settlers, with rifles in their hands, ______ the bandits.
4. The general achieved a glorious ______ over the enemy in the battle.
5. A(n) ______ sermon cannot get the audience to pay attention to the speaker; it merely makes the listeners fall asleep.

答案 1. fostered 2. obstinate 3. confronted 4. triumph 5. soporific

效果检测

EXERCISE 12.5 将题前的斜体词转换为恰当的形式，填入空格内：

1. *doze* Most people feel unwilling to work in a ______ summer afternoon.
2. *dexterity* A successful manager should be ______ in handling people as well as managing money.
3. *antique* That vase is of such great ______ that nobody knows how old it is.
4. *brawn* The muscles of his ______ arms are as strong as iron bands.
5. *foster* The chairman stood at the head of ______ of community development.
6. *recur* More care in the future will prevent ______ of the same mistake.
7. *suffice* The ship had a ______ of provisions for a voyage of two months.
8. *articulate* If you read slowly, your ______ will be much better.
9. *humid* On a hot, sultry day it is very difficult to work because of the ______.
10. *averse* She always put three spoons of sugar in her coffee; she has an ______ to the bitter taste of it.

解答 1. dozy 2. dexterous 3. antiquity 4. brawny 5. fosterage 6. recurrence 7. sufficiency 8. articulation 9. humidity 10. aversion

EXERCISE 12.6 找出与斜体词意义最接近的单词：

______ 1. the final *triumph* over the enemy

(A) warning (B) victory

(C) attack (D) fire

______ 2. the *articulate* speech

(A) boring (B) amusing

(C) solemn (D) clear

______ 3. an *obstinate* man

(A) stubborn (B) soporific

(C) repugnant (D) coherent

______ 4. to *corroborate* his testimony

(A) confirm (B) confess

(C) conceal (D) conclude

______ 5. an *antique* gown

(A) beautiful (B) precious

(C) old-fashioned (D) dirty

解答 1. B 2. D 3. A 4. A 5. C

EXERCISE 12.7 将各词不同词性的适当形式填入空格内：

	ADJECTIVE	NOUN	VERB	ADVERB
1.	______	ecstasy	______	______
2.	××××	______	encamp	××××
3.	______	______	cohere	______
4.	______	hypothesis	______	______
5.	______	shimmer	shimmer	××××
6.	______	______	recur	______

7. antique	______	______	××××
8. ______	______	fascinate	______
9. ______	______	______	sufficiently
10. ______	______	erupt	______

解答

ADJECTIVE	NOUN	VERB	ADVERB
1. ecstatic	(ecstasy)	ecstasize	ecstatically
2. ××××	encampment	(encamp)	××××
3. coherent	coherence	(cohere)	coherently
4. hypothetical	(hypothesis)	hypothesize	hypothetically
5. shimmery	(shimmer)	(shimmer)	××××
6. recurrent	recurrence	(recur)	recurrently
7. (antique)	antiquity	antiquate	××××
8. fascinating	fascination	(fascinate)	fascinatingly
9. sufficient	sufficiency	suffice	(sufficiently)
10. eruptive	eruption	(erupt)	eruptively

EXERCISE 12.8 从下列单词中选出最恰当的词，填入空格内：

VOCABULARY LIST

coherent	irradiated	recur	prowess
accelerate	erupt	averse	manipulated
confronted	hypothesis	foster	ecstasy

1. He likes to talk about political problems among his friends, but was ______ to discussing politics in public.
2. The clerk stole money from the firm and ______ the accounts to conceal his theft.
3. Sunshine, fresh air and rest often ______ a person's recovery from

sickness.

4. The driver was so upset that he could not give a(n) ______ account of the accident.
5. We hope his illness will not ______; no longer can he afford to pay his medical expenses.
6. Films and pictures about recent wars sometimes ______ angry memories and feelings of hatred between nations.
7. Mystics, religious prophets and poets have been known to go into ______ when meditating or seeking inspiration.
8. The volcano suddenly began to ______ lava and ashes, and the inhabitants took refuge to a safe place.
9. When Columbus first presented his ______ that the earth is round, very few believed it.
10. Two firemen showed great ______ by repeatedly rushing into the burning to save many lives.

解答

1. averse	2. manipulated	3. accelerate
4. coherent	5. recur	6. foster
7. ecstasy	8. erupt	9. hypothesis
10. prowess		

LESSON 13

预备测验

选出最恰当的答案：

1. It takes years of hard work to *compile* ______.

   (A) a good dictionary　　(B) a foreign language

2. The early ______ lives were full of *tribulations.*

   (A) Christians'　　(B) emperors'

3. The soldier was ______ for *valor* in battle.

   (A) heavily punished　　(B) given a medal

4. The coach's *autocratic* manner made him ______ among the players of the team.

   (A) popular　　(B) unpopular

5. She was greatly *encumbered* on the trip by ______.

   (A) the big radio　　(B) a good companion

答案 1. A 2. A 3. B 4. B 5. A

第一部分

WORD	MEANING	TYPICAL USE
abound /əˈbaʊnd/ *v*. 富于 *adj*. abundant	be plentiful or numerous; exist in large numbers	Our nation ***abounds*** in opportunities for well-educated young men and women. 国内受过良好教育的青年拥有许多机会。
arrogant /ˈærəgənt/ *adj*. 傲慢的 *n*. arrogance	in a proud, superior manner; showing too much pride	He behaved in such ***arrogant*** manners in his firm that he was at last fired. 他在公司里的行为如此傲慢，以致终于被解雇了。
compile /kəmˈpaɪl/ *v*. 编纂 *n*. compilation	make or form a book or a list out of various materials	It takes a long time as well as many experts working together to ***compile*** an encyclopedia. 编一本百科全书，不仅要花很长的时间，还要有许多专家一起工作才行。
entreat /ɪnˈtriːt/ *v*. 恳求 *n*. entreaty	keep asking earnestly; beg and pray; implore	The murderer ***entreated*** the judge to show mercy, but was sentenced to death. 那杀人犯恳求法官怜悯，但还是被判了死刑。

WORD	MEANING	TYPICAL USE
filth /fɪlθ/ *n.* 污物 *adj.* filthy	foul, disgusting dirt; obscenity	The alley was filled with lots of garbage and other ***filth***. 这条巷子遍地是大堆的垃圾及其他污物。
incumbent /ɪnˈkʌmbənt/ *adj.* 负有义务的 *n.* incumbency	resting as a duty; being the moral duty of (someone)	It is ***incumbent*** on you to give a father's advice before your son leaves home. 在儿子离家前给他一点忠告,是你做父亲应尽的义务。
monotony /məˈnɒtənɪ/ *n.* 单调 *adj.* monotonous	sameness of tone or pitch; lack of variety	At sea, everything that breaks the ***monotony*** of the surrounding expanse attracts attention. 在茫茫的大海上,每件能打破单调的事物都能引起注意。
reciprocate /rɪˈsɪprəkeɪt/ *v.* 回报 *n.* reciprocation	give in return; give and receive	I hope I can ***reciprocate*** your hospitality some time. 我希望下次能回报你的殷勤招待。
shaggy /ˈʃægɪ/ *adj.* 多粗毛的 *n.* shagginess	covered with a mass of hair or wool	The ***shaggy*** dog always sleeps in the bed with her. 那条长毛狗总是和她一起睡在床上。

WORD	MEANING	TYPICAL USE
tribulation /ˌtrɪbjʊˈleɪʃən/ *n.* 苦难 *v.* tribulate	great trouble or misery; hardship; affliction	Hunger, cold and sickness were among the ***tribulations*** of pioneer life. 饥饿、寒冷和病痛是开拓者生活中苦难的一部分。

EXERCISE 13.1 从第一部分中选出最恰当的单词,填入空格内:

1. She invited me to her birthday party, and I ______ by wishing her a happy Christmas.
2. The blue whale once ______ in the Antarctic, but is becoming more and more scarce.
3. She ______ her father to send her to the United States for further study.
4. He ______ enough information on his tour of South Africa to write a book.
5. It is ______ upon you to warn the boy of the harm of smoking.

答案 1. reciprocated 2. abounded 3. entreated 4. compiled 5. incumbent

第二部分

WORD	MEANING	TYPICAL USE
adolescent /ˌædəʊˈlesənt/ 1. *adj.* 青少年的 *n.* adolescence	1. growing up from childhood to adulthood	He read many books in the ***adolescent*** stage of his life. 他在青年时代读了不少书。
2. *n.* 青少年	2. a person growing up from childhood to manhood or womanhood	One who is 15 years old is not an adult, but an ***ado-lescent***. 15 岁的人不能算是成人,不过是个青少年。
autocratic /ˌɔːtəˈkrætɪk/ *adj.* 独裁的 *n.* autocracy	of or like an autocrat; having absolute power or authority; dictatorial	Adolf Hitler commanded ***autocratic*** power; no one could rigorously oppose his plans or decisions. 希特勒独裁,没有人能够强硬地反对他的计划或决定。
congenial /kənˈdʒiːnjəl/ *adj.* 意气相投的;适合的 *n.* congeniality	having similar tastes and interests; agreeable	All the furniture of the room was very ***congenial*** to my taste. 屋里所有的家具都非常符合我的品味。

WORD	MEANING	TYPICAL USE
encumber /ɪnˈkʌmbə(r)/ *v.* 堆满 *n.* encumbrance	make free action or movement difficult; hinder; obstruct; hamper	The room was ***encumbered*** with heavy furniture. 屋里堆满了笨重的家具。
horrify /ˈhɒrɪfaɪ/ *v.* 使恐惧 *n.* horror	cause to feel horror; shock very much	The little girl was ***horrified*** by the scaring story. 小女孩被这个恐怖的故事吓坏了。
manifest /ˈmænɪfest/ *adj.* 明白的 *n.* manifestation	apparent to the eye or to the mind; obvious; evident	It is now ***manifest*** that if you don't return the book to the library right now, you will have to pay a late fine. 现在情况很明白了，如果你不立刻把书送回图书馆，你就得付逾时罚金。
nutrition /njʊ(uː)ˈtrɪʃən/ *n.* 营养 *adj.* nutritious	the action of providing or state of being provided with food	Good health is not always obtained by good ***nutrition***. 健康未必靠好的营养就能得到。
repress /rɪˈpres/ *v.* 镇压 *n.* repression	keep down; hold back; prevent from acting; suppress	They could ***repress*** the uprising with the help of the army. 依靠军队的帮助，他们能够镇压暴动。

WORD	MEANING	TYPICAL USE
smuggle /ˈsmʌgl/ *v.* 走私 *n.* smuggler	bring into or take out of a country secretly and against the law	They were accused of ***smuggling*** diamonds from foreign countries. 他们被起诉从国外走私钻石。
tangible /ˈtændʒəbl/ *adj.* 确实的 *n.* tangibility	can be touched or felt by touch; physical; material	There has been a ***tangible*** improvement in his school work. 他的功课确实有进步。

EXERCISE 13.2 从第二部分中选出最恰当的单词,填入空格内:

1. I enjoyed the party last night; the ______ atmosphere of the party pleased me.
2. Milk, meat, fruits and vegetables provide good ______.
3. It is a crime to ______ jewelry.
4. They are ______ by their parents, who prevent them from playing or shouting.
5. Rubbish and old boxes on the passage ______ the fire escape.

解答 1. congenial 2. nutrition 3. smuggle 4. repressed 5. encumbered

第三部分

WORD	MEANING	TYPICAL USE
analogy /əˈnælədʒɪ/ *n.* 相似之处 *adj.* analogous	a degree of likeness or sameness; likeness in some ways between things	The teacher drew an ***analogy*** between the human heart and a pump. 老师把人的心脏和水泵作类比。
billow /ˈbɪləʊ/ *n.* 巨浪 *adj.* billowy	a very large wave of water	The ship was tossed by the ocean ***billows*** in the storm. 暴风雨中，这艘船被海上的巨浪击得颠簸不平。
detonate /ˈdetəneɪt/ *v.* 使爆裂 *n.* detonation	(cause to) explode suddenly with a loud noise	The bomb was ***detonated*** from several miles away; it caused no damage to our town. 那炸弹在几英里以外爆炸了，对我们的城镇并未构成损害。
entangle /ɪnˈtæŋgl/ *v.* 与……纠缠 *n.* entanglement	get twisted up and caught; tangle	The fly became ***entangled*** in the spider's web. 这只苍蝇与蜘蛛网纠缠在一起。

WORD	MEANING	TYPICAL USE
hibernate /ˈhaɪbɜːneɪt/ *v.* 冬眠；过冬 *n.* hibernation	pass the winter in a state like sleep; spend the winter	During long severe winters, some animals, such as badgers, ground squirrels and some insects, ***hibernate***. 在漫漫寒冬里，有些动物，例如獾、地鼠和一些昆虫会冬眠。
intuition /ˌɪntjʊ(uː)ˈɪʃən/ *n.* 直觉 *adj.* intuitive	the immediate perception or understanding of truths or facts without reasoning	By experience with all kinds of people the doctor has developed great powers of ***intuition***. 有了治疗各种人的疾病的经验，这位医生具备了很强的直觉。
pollute /pəˈljuːt/ *v.* 污染 *n.* pollution	make impure, foul or dirty; destroy the purity of; contaminate	Many rivers in that city are ***polluted*** with filthy waste from factories. 那座城市里的许多河流被工厂排放的污物所污染。
revere /rɪˈvɪə/ *v.* 尊敬 *n.* reverence	give great respect and admiration to; respect deeply	She ***reveres*** her grandfather; he is strict in decision, but shows great affection to her. 她尊敬她的祖父。他在作决定时虽然严厉，却深爱着她。

WORD	MEANING	TYPICAL USE
solitary /ˈsɒlɪtərɪ/ *adj.* 单一的 *n.* solitudc	alone or single; without companions; lonely	The hermit led a ***solitary*** life in the deep mountains far away from the town. 那位隐士在远离市镇的深山中独自生活。
valor /ˈvælə(r)/ *n.* 勇气 *adj.* valiant	courage; bravery	They owed their lives to the ***valor*** of the firemen. 由于消防队员们的勇敢，他们才得以保住生命。

EXERCISE 13.3 从第三部分中选出最恰当的单词,填入空格内:

1. The bird flew into the net, and the more it struggled, the more it ______ itself.
2. The company commander showed great ______ in leading his men despite a painful wound in his leg.
3. The water along the beach was ______ by refuse from those factories.
4. In February, my parents returned from Florida where they had ______ since Christmas.
5. The students ______ the old professor; he has wisdom as well as profound knowledge in his field.

解答 1. entangled 2. valor 3. polluted 4. hibernated 5. revere

第四部分

WORD	MEANING	TYPICAL USE
antagonist /æn'tægənɪst/ *n.* 对手 *adj.* antagonistic	one who is opposed to another; opponent; adversary	The brave knight defeated each ***antagonist*** who came against him. 这个勇敢的武士把向他挑战的对手一一击败。
cognizant /'kɒgnɪzənt/ *adj.* 认知的 *n.* cognizance	having knowledge; being fully aware of; conscious	As the doctor was fully ***cognizant*** of the patient's serious condition, he acted swiftly to relieve it. 由于医师完全了解病人病情的严重,所以他快速地采取措施以消除其病痛。
doleful /'dəʊlfʊl/ *adj.* 悲哀的 *n.* dolefulness	very sad or dreary; mournful; dismal	His ***doleful*** expression showed that he had failed in the examination. 从他悲哀的表情就可以看出他考试没通过。
facility /fə'sɪlɪtɪ/ *n.* 1. 方便 *v.* facilitate	1. the quality of being able to be done easily	The ***facility*** of communication is far greater now than it was a hundred years ago. 现在的交通比100年前方便多了。

WORD	MEANING	TYPICAL USE
2. 便利	2. an advantage; convenience	A free bus to the airport is a ***facility*** offered only by this hotel. 到机场的免费公共汽车是这家旅馆独家提供的便利条件。
improvise /ˈɪmprəvaɪz/ *v.* 即席而作 *n.* improvisation	make up on the spur of the moment; sing or speak without preparation	He ***improvised*** a new stanza for the school song at the football game. 他在足球赛中临时为校歌作了新词。
inquisitive /ɪnˈkwɪzɪtɪv/ *adj.* 好奇的 *n.* inquiry	asking many questions; prying into other people's affairs	The old lady was very ***inquisitive*** about what her neighbors were doing. 这位老妇人对邻居的所作所为非常好奇。
protrude /prəˈtruːd/ *v.* 突出 *n.* protrusion	(cause to) stick out or stretch outwards from a place; thrust forth	The policeman stopped the man when he saw a gun ***protruding*** from his pocket. 警察看见那人口袋中露出一截枪，立即挡住了他的去路。
savor /ˈseɪvə(r)/ *n.* 滋味 *adj.* savory	a taste or smell; flavor; relish	He used to say that argument adds a ***savor*** to conversation. 他以前一向认为争论为谈话增添情趣。

WORD	MEANING	TYPICAL USE
subvert /sʌbˈvɜːt/ *v.* 败坏 *n.* subversion	overthrow; cause the downfall of; ruin; destroy	Much of the city was ***subverted*** by the earthquake and a great fire. 这座城市的大部分都被地震和大火毁坏了。

EXERCISE 13.4 从第四部分中选出最恰当的单词,填入空格内:

1. A normal child is very ______ about what animals live on the moon or stars.
2. The soup had been boiled too long and lost its peculiar ______.
3. Keep your feet under your desk; do not let them ______ into the aisle.
4. The boys ______ a tent out of two blankets and a long pole.

解答 1. inquisitive 2. savor 3. protrude
4. improvised

效果检测

EXERCISE 13.5 将各词不同词性的适当形式填入空格内:

	ADJECTIVE	NOUN	VERB	ADVERB
1.	______	valor	××××	______
2.	______	facility	______	______
3.	inquisitive	______	______	______
4.	______	______	reciprocate	______
5.	______	______	abound	______
6.	______	______	revere	______

7. ______	horror	______	______
8. ______	______	compile	××××
9. ______	______	subvert	______
10. ______	______	protrude	______

解答

ADJECTIVE	NOUN	VERB	ADVERB
1. valiant	(valor)	××××	valiantly
2. facile	(facility)	facilitate	facilely
3. (inquisitive)	inquisition inquiry	inquire	inquisitively
4. reciprocal	reciprocation	(reciprocate)	reciprocally
5. abundant	abundance	(abound)	abundantly
6. reverent	reverence	(revere)	reverently
7. horrible	(horror)	horrify	horribly
8. compilatory	compilation	(compile)	××××
9. subversive	subversion	(subvert)	subversively
10. protrusive	protrusion	(protrude)	protrusively

EXERCISE 13.6 将题前的斜体词转换为恰当的形式,填入空格内:

1. *nutrition* Apples and oranges are very ______ food.
2. *savor* The ______ smell of roasting turkey greeted us as we entered the house.
3. *solitary* Both the prospector in the desert and the shy person in the city live in ______.
4. *analogy* The wing of an airplane is ______ to the wing of a bird.

5. *cognizant* The judge took ______ of the accused man's ill health in handing down the sentence.

6. *facility* The broken lock ______ my entrance into the empty house.

7. *encumber* Shoes or long hair must be an ______ to a swimmer.

8. *manifest* Entering the burning building was a ______ of his courage.

9. *reciprocate* Although I gave him many presents, I had no ______ gifts from him.

10. *entreat* The savages paid no attention to their captive's ______ for mercy.

解答 1. nutritious 2. savory 3. solitude
4. analogous 5. cognizance 6. facilitated
7. encumbrance 8. manifestation
9. reciprocal 10. entreaty

EXERCISE 13.7 找出与其他三个不相关的词:

______ 1. (A) encumber (B) obstruct
(C) irradiate (D) hamper

______ 2. (A) cognizant (B) averse
(C) aware (D) conscious

______ 3. (A) pollute (B) restrain
(C) suppress (D) repress

______ 4. (A) savor (B) relish
(C) flavor (D) billow

______ 5. (A) kindred (B) congenial
(C) shaggy (D) sympathetic

______ 6. (A) affliction (B) hardship
(C) tribulation (D) nutrition

______ 7. (A) ecstasy (B) antagonist
(C) opponent (D) adversary

______ 8. (A) obvious (B) manifest
(C) obstinate (D) evident

______ 9. (A) doleful (B) dismal
(C) mournful (D) autocratic

______ 10. (A) upset (B) smuggle
(C) overthrow (D) subvert

解答 1. C 2. B 3. A 4. D 5. C
6. D 7. A 8. C 9. D 10. B

EXERCISE 13.8 从下列单词中选出最恰当的词，填入空格内：

VOCABULARY LIST

filth	detonated	incumbent	protruded
congenial	analogy	repress	improvise
tangible	adolescent	monotony	entangled

1. He ______ his feet in the coil of rope and fell down.
2. No one lives in the old house; it is full of ______.
3. The police need ______ proof of his guilt before they can act against him.
4. If an actor forgets his words on the stage, he has to ______ the scene.
5. He is not an adult; he is still in the ______ stage of growth.
6. He enjoyed his trip to Europe very much; some ______ companions made

the trip successful.

7. It is a(n) ______ responsibility of all military officers to maintain the dignity of the uniform.

8. The saucy child ______ her tongue when her mother blamed her for her laziness.

9. When she was given a Christmas gift from her boyfriend, she could not ______ her desire to open it immediately.

10. There is a(n) ______ between the way water moves in waves and the way light travels.

解答

1. entangled	2. filth	3. tangible
4. improvise	5. adolescent	6. congenial
7. incumbent	8. protruded	9. repress
10. analogy		

LESSON 14

预备测验

选出最恰当的答案：

1. The young man took the vows of *chivalry* to become a ______.

   (A) scholar　(B) knight　(C) judge

2. *Diagnosis* is one of the most important parts of the ______.

   (A) doctor's work　(B) nuclear warfare

   (C) mechanical engineering

3. It is difficult to ______ someone who is *elusive*.

   (A) marry　(B) teach　(C) find

4. The woman was often *persecuted* by the man, and she ______ him.

   (A) likes　(B) knows　(C) hates

5. He is so *vindictive* that he never ______ anybody.

   (A) dislikes　(B) forgives　(C) despises

答案 1. B 2. A 3. C 4. C 5. B

第一部分

WORD	MEANING	TYPICAL USE
addict 1. /əˈdɪkt/ *v.* 对……有瘾 *n.* addiction	1. give oneself up to a habit	He is ***addicted*** to alcohol and drugs. 他对酒和毒品成瘾。

WORD	MEANING	TYPICAL USE
2. /ˈædɪkt/ *n.* 沉溺于不良嗜好者	2. a person who is a slave to a habit	Doctors and policemen disagree on how to control drug distribution and handle ***addicts***. 医生和警察对于如何管制药量的分配及管理有药瘾者的意见并不一致。
assiduous /əˈsɪdjʊəs/ *adj.* 刻苦的 *n.* assiduity	having or showing careful and continual attention	He is ***assiduous*** at his studies; he works hard and steadily and pays continual attention to his teacher. 他刻苦学习，努力工作，并时时注意老师所说的话。
conspire /kənˈspaɪə(r)/ *v.* 图谋 *n.* conspiracy	plan secretly with others to do something unlawful or wrong; plot	The two men ***conspired*** to steal the jewels and then sell them to a jeweler in another country. 那两个人企图盗取珠宝，然后卖给另一个国家的珠宝商。

WORD	MEANING	TYPICAL USE
elusive /ɪˈljuːsɪv/ *adj.* 令人困惑的 *n.* elusion	hard to catch or find; evasive; hard to understand	He is such an ***elusive*** person; you never know where he is when you want him. 他就是这样一个谜一般的人物，当你需要他时，你永远不知道他在何处。
gaudy /ˈɡɒdɪ/ *adj.* 华而不实的 *n.* gaudiness	too bright and gay to be in good taste; cheap and showy	A cheap, ***gaudy*** steamboat arrive at the wharf from St. Louis. 一艘来自圣路易、低廉且华而不实的汽船到达了码头。
ignite /ɪɡˈnaɪt/ *v.* 使燃烧 *n.* ignition	set on fire; cause to start to burn; kindle	He ***ignited*** the match by scratching it on the desk. 他将火柴在桌上一划，便点着了。
negotiate /nɪˈɡəʊʃɪeɪt/ *v.* 商定 *n.* negotiation	talk with another person to settle disagreement; arrange by discussion	The trade union is ***negotiating*** with the employers to get a better contract. 工会正与雇主商议确定一个较好的合约。

WORD	MEANING	TYPICAL USE
respiration /ˌrespəˈreɪʃən/ *n.* 呼吸 *adj.* respiratory	the act of inhaling and exhaling; breathing	***Respiration*** is difficult at great heights and some mountaineers wear oxygen masks to overcome such difficulty. 在很高的地方呼吸是困难的，有些登山者戴上氧气面罩来克服这个困难。
spice /spaɪs/ *n.* 调味；调料 *n.* spicery	a vegetable substance used to flavor foods	The speaker made a few funny jokes to add ***spice*** to his speech. 这位演说者开了一些有趣的玩笑，来为演说添加趣味。
unanimous /jʊ(uː)ˈnænɪməs/ *adj.* 全体一致的 *n.* unanimity	in complete accord or agreement; mutually agreed; with no opposition	The proposal was accepted with ***unanimous*** approval by the committee. 这个建议是经委员会全体一致同意后采用的。

EXERCISE 14.1 从第一部分中选出最恰当的单词，填入空格内：

1. She would be attractive if she did not wear such ______ jewelry.
2. The children were ______ in their wish to go to the beach in summer.
3. The government has to ______ with the opposition party on the new law.
4. The criminals had ______ to rob the First National Bank, but their plot was detected in advance of their action.
5. A drug ______ finds it almost impossible to stop using drugs.

答案 1. gaudy 2. unanimous 3. negotiate 4. conspired 5. addict

第二部分

WORD	MEANING	TYPICAL USE
aggregate /ˈæɡrɪɡɪt/ *v.* 1. 集合 *n.* aggregation	1. cause to come together into a group or mass	The power of the allies ***aggregated*** together was great, though individually some were quite weak. 尽管个体的力量相当微弱，但只要团结起来，便可汇成一股强大的力量。
2. 合计	2. amount as a whole to; add up to	His various wages for the year ***aggregated*** $22,000. 一年内，他的各种工资总计22,000美元。
banal /ˈbeɪnəl/ *adj.* 平庸的 *n.* banality	not new or interesting; very common; trite	Their conversation was ***banal***, full of uninteresting remarks, such as "nice weather" and "slow traffic today". 他们谈话的内容琐碎，都是些乏味之词，例如"天气不错"和"今天交通不畅"。

WORD	MEANING	TYPICAL USE
curative /ˈkjʊərətɪv/ *adj.* 有疗效的 *n.* curativeness	having the power to cure; tending to cure; remedial	Taking a rest in the mountains is very ***curative*** for breathing difficulties. 在山上休息对治疗呼吸困难非常有效。
enforce /ɪnˈfɔːs/ *v.* 迫使 *n.* enforcement	urge with force; cause to be carried out; compel	The robbers ***enforced*** obedience to their demand by threat of violence. 匪徒用暴力威胁使受害者服从他们的要求。
hypocrite /ˈhɪpəkrɪt/ *n.* 伪君子 *adj.* hypocritical	a person who pretended to be very good or religious	No one in the village likes the man because he is a shameless ***hypocrite***. 村子里没有一个人喜欢那人，因为他是一个无耻的伪君子。
intercept /ˌɪntə(ɜː)ˈsept/ *v.* 中途拦截 *n.* interception	stop or seize on the way from one place to another	It is illegal to ***intercept*** a letter or parcel before it is delivered. 在信件或包裹尚未送达收件人的时候中途将其拦截是违法的。

WORD	MEANING	TYPICAL USE
persecute /ˈpɜːsɪkjuːt/ *v.* 迫害 *n.* persecution	treat badly; cause to suffer constantly; do harm to; oppress; harass	Some early religious leaders were ***persecuted*** by their enemies. 一些早期的宗教领袖遭到他们敌人的迫害。
sarcasm /ˈsɑːkæzəm/ *n.* 讥讽 *adj.* sarcastic	the act of making fun of a person to hurt his feelings; harsh or bitter irony	"Don't hurry!" said her father in ***sarcasm*** as she slowly dressed. 当她慢吞吞地穿衣服时,她父亲讽刺地说:"别着急!"
superfluous /sjʊ(uː)ˈpɜːflʊəs/ *adj.* 多余的 *n.* superfluity	more than is needed or desired; excessive; surplus	We have enough food for the picnic; any more would be ***superfluous***. 我们有足够的野餐食物,再多的食物就会多余。
vindicate /ˈvɪndɪkeɪt/ *v.* 辩解 *n.* vindication	show or prove the truth and justice; exculpate	The report of the committee of inquiry completely ***vindicates*** him and declares his action to have been right and proper. 调查委员会的报告完全是在替他辩护,而且声称他的行为是正确而且恰当的。

EXERCISE 14.2 从第二部分中选出最恰当的单词,填入空格内:

1. A person who says one thing and does another is called a(n) ______.
2. "How unselfish you are!" said the girl in ______ as her brother took the biggest piece of the cake.
3. The cruel boy ______ the kitten by throwing stones at it whenever it came near to him.
4. I have already stated quite clear what I think about your idea; any further comment on the subject would be ______.
5. Do not drink so much; you might take away 50 percent from the ______ power of the medicine.

答案 1. hypocrite 2. sarcasm 3. persecuted 4. superfluous 5. curative

第三部分

WORD	MEANING	TYPICAL USE
animate /ˈænɪmeɪt/ 1. *v.* 使有生气	1. make lively; arouse to action; inspire	A smile ***animated*** her face as she went to the gate to meet her husband. 当她到门口迎接丈夫时,脸上的微笑使她显得朝气蓬勃。

WORD	MEANING	TYPICAL USE
/ˈænɪmɪt/ 2. *adj.* 有生命的	2. having life; alive	Many scientists now believe that there are some worlds in outer space having ***animate*** beings. 现在许多科学家相信在外层空间的某些星球上有生物存在。
chivalry /ˈʃɪvəlrɪ/ *n.* 骑士精神 *adj.* chivalrous	the qualities of an ideal knight; the rules or beliefs of a knight	***Chivalry*** includes bravery, loyalty, honor, courtesy, respect for woman, protection of the weak and generosity. 骑士精神包含勇敢、忠诚、荣誉感、礼貌、尊敬妇女、保护弱者和慷慨。
diagnosis /ˌdaɪəgˈnəʊsɪs/ *n.* 诊断;调查 *adj.* diagnostic	the act or process of finding out diseases; a careful study of the facts	A doctor cannot treat an illness until he has made a ***diagnosis***. 医生未作诊断前不能治病。
exemplify /ɪgˈzemplɪfaɪ/ *v.* 例证 *n.* exemplification	show or illustrate by example	The teacher ***exemplified*** the use of the word for the students. 这位老师为学生们举例说明这个词的用法。

WORD	MEANING	TYPICAL USE
impend /ɪmˈpend/ *v.* 逼近 *adj.* impending	be likely to happen soon; be about to happen	When a war ***impends***, wise men try to prevent it in advance. 战争逼近时，智者设法预先阻止它。
modulate /ˈmɒdjʊleɪt/ *v.* 调整；改变(嗓音的)音量 *n.* modulation	regulate or adjust; alter the voice in pitch, tone, or volumn	The speaker had a really noble voice which he could ***modulate*** with great skill. 这位演说者有副相当好的嗓子；他能很有技巧地调整它。
prophecy /ˈprɒfɪsɪ/ *n.* 预言 *v.* prophesy	the act of telling what will happen in the future; foretelling future events	The teacher's ***prophecy*** that the boy would become a great national leader was later fulfilled. 老师曾预言这个男孩将会成为一位伟大的国家领袖，这个预言后来实现了。
sensuous /ˈsensjʊəs/ *adj.* 感官的 *n.* sensuousness	of the senses; derived from the senses; perceived by the senses	After hard work we could feel the ***sensuous*** delight of a hot bath. 辛苦工作后，我们能够感到洗热水澡让全身舒畅的快感。

WORD	MEANING	TYPICAL USE
tact /tækt/ *n.* 机智 *adj.* tactful	the ability to say or do the right things; skill in handling difficult situations	A minister of foreign affairs who lacks ***tact*** is a dangerous man. 缺乏机智的外交部长是个危险的人物。
vindictive /vɪnˈdɪktɪv/ *adj.* 欲报复的 *adv.* vindictively	having or showing a desire for revenge; revengeful; unforgiving; spiteful	The ***vindictive*** little girl tore up her sister's papers. 那个充满报复心的小女孩把她姐姐的作业撕了。

EXERCISE 14.3 从第三部分中选出最恰当的单词,填入空格内:

1. The two doctors made different ______ of my disease.
2. Our teacher is able to ______ a lecture on a dull subject with witty remarks.
3. Black clouds and the flashes of lightning are signs that a storm ______.
4. The cat stretched itself with ______ pleasure in the warm sun.
5. Some people are able to ______ their voices according to the size of the room in which they speak.

解答 1. diagnoses 2. animate 3. impends 4. sensuous 5. modulate

第四部分

WORD	MEANING	TYPICAL USE
append /ə'pend/ *v.* 附加 *n.* appendix	add to a large thing; attach as a supplement	If you hand in your report late, ***append*** a note explaining the reason for the delay. 如果你迟交报告，就附上一张纸条说明理由。
communal /'kɒmjʊnəl/ *adj.* 公有的 *v.* communalize	of or for a community; owned jointly by all; public	The Plains Indian has a plentiful and regular supply of meat and skins by the ***communal*** buffalo hunting. 大草原上的印第安人猎取公有的水牛，获得很多肉和皮。
ecology /ɪ(iː)'kɒlədʒɪ/ *n.* 生态学 *adj.* ecological	a branch of biology that deals with the habits of living things	After learning ***ecology*** I could see the relation of living things to their environment and to each other. 读过生态学之后，我能了解生物和环境以及生物彼此间的关系。

WORD	MEANING	TYPICAL USE
forbear /fɔːˈbɛə(r)/ *v.* 忍住 *n.* forbearance	hold back; keep from doing; refrain	He's deserved to be punished several times, but I've ***forborne*** from doing so. 他应受几倍于此的处罚，但我忍住了，没有那么做。
indifference /ɪnˈdɪfrəns/ *n.* 漠不关心；冷淡 *adj.* indifferent	lack of interest or attention; unconcern	It was a matter of ***indifference*** to him whether his hands were clean or dirty. 他的手是干净还是脏，对于他来说是无所谓的。
mediocre /ˌmiːdɪˈəʊkə(r)/ *adj.* 普通的；平凡的 *n.* mediocrity	of average quality; neither bad nor good; ordinary	He was a ***mediocre*** student; his academic records were not excellent, but not bad, either. 他是中等水平的学生，成绩不优秀也不差。
rehearse /rɪˈhɜːs/ *v.* 1. 详述 *n.* rehearsal	1. tell in detail; say over again	He ***rehearsed*** the story of all his sufferings in prison. 他详细叙述了自己在监狱中遭遇的一切。
2. 预演	2. learn and practice for later performance	We ***rehearsed*** our parts for the school play. 我们排演学校话剧中的角色。

WORD	MEANING	TYPICAL USE
singular /ˈsɪŋgjʊlə(r)/ *adj.* 奇异的 *n.* singularity	extraordinary; unusual; queer; odd	It is unwise to make yourself so ***singular*** in your clothes. 通过服饰来标新立异是不明智的。
transient /ˈtrænzɪənt/ *adj.* 短暂的 *n.* transiency	passing quickly or soon; not lasting; transitory; momentary	My mood is only ***transient***; it will go away pretty soon. 我的情绪只是一时的，很快就会过去。

EXERCISE 14.4 从第四部分中选出最恰当的单词，填入空格内：

1. I decided to ______ telling her the truth because I knew it would upset her.
2. The children ______ all the happenings of the day to their parents in the evening.
3. The detectives and the policemen were greatly puzzled by the ______ nature of the crime.
4. The boy's ______ to his school work worried both his teacher and his parents.
5. The author ______ a list of troublesome words at the end of the book.

解答 1. forbear 2. rehearsed 3. singular 4. indifference 5. appended

效果检测

EXERCISE 14.5 将各词不同词性的适当形式填入空格内：

	ADJECTIVE	NOUN	VERB	ADVERB
1.	______	chivalry	××××	××××
2.	banal	______	______	______
3.	______	______	respire	××××
4.	××××	______	rehearse	××××
5.	unanimous	______	××××	______
6.	______	______	intercept	××××
7.	______	______	elude	______
8.	××××	______	forbear	××××
9.	______	diagnosis	______	______
10.	mediocre	______	××××	××××

解答

	ADJECTIVE	NOUN	VERB	ADVERB
1.	chivalrous	(chivalry)	××××	××××
2.	(banal)	banality	banalize	banally
3.	respiratory	respiration	(respire)	××××
4.	××××	rehearsal	(rehearse)	××××
5.	(unanimous)	unanimity	××××	unanimously
6.	interceptive	interception	(intercept)	××××
7.	elusive	elusion	(elude)	elusively
8.	××××	forbearance	(forbear)	××××
9.	diagnostic	(diagnosis)	diagnose	diagnostically
10.	(mediocre)	mediocrity	××××	××××

EXERCISE 14.6 将题前的斜体词转换为恰当的形式，填入空格内：

1. *conspire* The leaders of the ______ against the government were caught and punished.
2. *singular* The ______ of the woman's appearance attracted much attention in the party.
3. *persecute* Religious and political ______ drove many people to the United States.
4. *enforce* Strict ______ of the laws against speeding will reduce automobile accidents.
5. *assiduous* He plans everything with unfailing ______.
6. *indifference* The boy was so excited to see snow that he was ______ to the cold.
7. *prophecy* I wouldn't dare to try to ______ who will win the election.
8. *superfluous* I have a ______ of pencils for the exam; you may borrow one if you want.
9. *append* The history book has an ______ containing an account of what has happened since 1950.
10. *sarcasm* The teacher's ______ comment about the girl's essay made her cry.

解答 1. conspiracy 2. singularity 3. persecution 4. enforcement 5. assiduity 6. indifferent 7. prophesy 8. superfluity 9. appendix 10. sarcastic

EXERCISE 14.7 找出与斜体词意义最接近的单词：

1. artificial *respiration*
   (A) fiber (B) flower
   (C) light (D) breathing
2. *append* a word list
   (A) make (B) copy
   (C) submit (D) attach
3. a *gaudy* dress
   (A) old-fashioned (B) bright and showy
   (C) very precious (D) too long
4. a man of *singular* ability
   (A) common (B) imaginative
   (C) exceptional (D) creative
5. the *mediocre* student
   (A) ordinary (B) excellent
   (C) arrognant (D) diligent

解答 1. D 2. D 3. B 4. C 5. A

EXERCISE 14.8 从下列单词中选出最恰当的词，填入空格内：

VOCABULARY LIST

ignites	negotiate	communal	tact
indifference	transient	addicted	unanimous
spices	prophecy	intercepted	exemplify

1. His ______ that a war between the two countries would soon break out turned out real.
2. It rained all day in Guangzhou, but here we had only a(n) ______

shower for minutes.

3. You will not become ______ to smoking if you refuse cigarettes when they are offered.
4. The town swimming pool is a(n) ______ property; every member of the community can swim in the pool freely.
5. A diligent person works very hard, but a lazy person usually treats his work with ______.
6. She used several kinds of ______ in cooking the meat.
7. A wise politician should have a great ______ in dealing with his supporters.
8. We gained possession of the ball when John ______ a forward pass.
9. He was elected president of the committee by a(n) ______ vote.

解答 1. prophecy 2. transient 3. addicted
4. communal 5. indifference 6. spices
7. tact 8. intercepted 9. unanimous

LESSON 15

预备测验

选出最恰当的答案：

1. The ______ was *apprehended* as he tried to cross the river.

   (A) conscientious policeman　　(B) little girl

   (C) escaped prisoner

2. ______ *diverted* the audience's attention from the play.

   (A) The luxurious furniture on the stage

   (B) The actor's mature performance

   (C) The siren of the fire engine

3. The ______ was made by *excavating* the side of a mountain.

   (A) road　　(B) dam　　(C) tunnel

4. If a man ______, he becomes *intoxicated*.

   (A) drinks too much whisky

   (B) makes a large fortune

   (C) fails in an important examination

5. Most people who live ______ are *urban* dwellers.

   (A) near the coast　　(B) in apartments

   (C) in jungles

解答 1. C 2. C 3. C 4. A 5. B

第一部分

WORD	MEANING	TYPICAL USE
adhere /əd'hɪə(r)/ *v.* 黏附 *n.* adherence	stick firmly to another or each other; cling; hold closely	The two surfaces ***adhered*** to each other, and we couldn't get them apart. 这两个表面彼此黏在一起了,我们无法把它们分开。
audacity /ɔː'dæsɪtɪ/ *n.* 大胆无耻 *adj.* audacious	too much boldness; impudence; reckless daring; boldness	He had the ***audacity*** to go to the party without being invited. 尽管未被邀请,他也敢厚着脸皮去参加宴会。
contiguity /ˌkɒntɪ'gjuːətɪ/ *n.* 接近 *adj.* contiguous	the state of being very close together; nearness; proximity; adjacency	The ***contiguity*** of the house and the garage was a convenience in bad weather. 房屋与车库离得近,在天气不好时是一大便利条件。
enchant /ɪn'tʃɑːnt/ *v.* 施魔法于 *n.* enchantment	use magic on; bewitch; delight greatly; charm	The witch had ***enchanted*** the princess so that she would sleep for a month. 这个女巫对公主施了魔法,所以公主将会沉睡一个月。

WORD	MEANING	TYPICAL USE
grandeur /ˈgrændʒə(r)/ *n.* 伟大 *adj.* grand	great beauty, power or size; greatness; majesty	As he watched the Niagara Falls, he thought of the ***grandeur*** of nature. 当他注视着尼亚加拉瀑布时，他想到了大自然的伟大。
infer /ɪnˈfɜː/ *v.* 推论出 *n.* inference	find out by reasoning; come to believe after thinking	From her story we ***in-ferred*** that they went to the United States unwill-ingly. 从她的故事里，我们推测他们去美国不是自愿的。
numb /nʌm/ *adj.* 失去知觉的 *n.* numbness	without ability to feel or move; unable to feel anything	I cannot write a letter; my fingers are ***numb*** with cold. 我无法写信。我的手指冻僵了。
remit /rɪˈmɪt/ *v.* 1. 汇寄 *n.* remittance	1. send money in payment to a person or place	Please ***remit*** the amount of your bill by check. 请将你账单的总钱数用支票汇寄过来。
2. 赦免 *n.* remission	2. forgive all or a portion of a debt or punishment	The girl was accused of stealing a pair of shoes, but because of her young age the judge ***remitted*** the prison sentence. 那女孩被指控偷了一双鞋子，但由于她年幼，法官赦免了对她的监禁。

WORD	MEANING	TYPICAL USE
skeptical /ˈskeptɪkəl/ *adj.* 怀疑的 *n.* skepticism	unwilling to believe a claim or promise; distrustful; incredulous	His ***skeptical*** remark about the team's chances of winning made us gloomy. 他怀疑这支队伍胜算的言论，使我们沮丧。
urban /ˈɜːbən/ *adj.* 都市的 *v.* urbanize	of or having to do with cities or towns	The ***urban*** population of China has greatly increased during the last several years. 近几年来，中国的城市人口大幅度地增加了。

EXERCISE 15.1 从第一部分中选出最恰当的单词，填入空格内：

1. The ______ of the little girl and the policeman prevented her from being kidnapped.
2. The audience was ______ by the grace of the young dancer.
3. In the United States today, the ______ population far outnumbers the farm population.
4. Apply the sticker on the dry surface, or it will not ______ properly.
5. I ______ from your letter that you did not wish to see us.

解答 1. contiguity 2. enchanted 3. urban 4. adhere 5. inferred

第二部分

WORD	MEANING	TYPICAL USE
amputate /ˈæmpjʊteɪt/ *v.* 锯掉 *n.* amputation	remove a part of the body by cutting it off for medical reasons	This is serious; I am afraid we'll have to ***amputate*** his leg. 情况很严重，恐怕我们必须锯掉他的腿。
bawdy /ˈbɔːdɪ/ *adj.* 淫秽的 *n.* bawdry	not decent; indecent; unchaste; lewd; obscene	All the people in the party were disgusted with his ***bawdy*** jokes. 所有参加宴会的人都厌恶他那淫秽的笑话。
deformity /dɪˈfɔːmɪtɪ/ *n.* 畸形 *adj.* deformed	an abnormal shape of a body; malformation; disfigurement	She is very attractive in spite of her slight ***deformity***. 虽然有轻微的畸形，她仍然非常迷人。
excavate /ˈekskəveɪt/ *v.* 挖掘 *n.* excavation	make a hole by digging; hollow out	It took a long time to ***excavate*** the ancient city of Troy. 人们花了很长时间挖掘古老的特洛伊城。
harass /ˈhærəs, həˈræs/ *v.* 侵袭 *n.* harassment	make worried by causing trouble; bother; vex	In olden times the coasts of England were frequently ***harassed*** by the Vikings. 古时候，英国海岸常受北欧海盗的侵袭。

WORD	MEANING	TYPICAL USE
intoxicate /ɪnˈtɒksɪkeɪt/ *v.* 使喝醉 *n.* intoxication	make drunk; excite beyond self-control	He does not drink at all; a little wine may ***intoxicate*** him. 他根本不喝酒，因为一点酒就能让他醉倒。
placid /ˈplæsɪd/ *adj.* 平静的 *n.* placidity	pleasantly calm or peaceful; quiet; tranquil; serene	The ***placid*** lake reflected the image of the old castle. 平静的湖面上映着古堡的倒影。
retaliate /rɪˈtælɪeɪt/ *v.* 报复 *adj.* retaliatory	pay back a wrong or injury; return evil for evil	Mary kicked Susan, and Susan ***retaliated*** against her by biting. 玛丽踢了苏珊一脚，而苏珊咬了玛丽一口作为报复。
stealthy /ˈstelθɪ/ *adj.* 秘密的 *adv.* stealthily	done in a secret manner; sly; secret; furtive	The cat found a bird sitting on the branch and crept with ***stealthy*** movements toward it. 猫发现枝头上有只鸟，便偷偷地向它爬过去。
wary /ˈwɛərɪ/ *adj.* 机警的，小心的 *n.* wariness	on one's guard against danger, deception, etc.; cautious; vigilant	He lied to me about my friend, and I have been very ***wary*** of him ever since. 他对我撒了个关于我朋友的谎，从那时起，我便非常提防他。

EXERCISE 15.2 从第二部分中选出最恰当的单词，填入空格内：

1. Better food has reduced the number of children born with ______.
2. He has been ______ by business troubles and his nagging wife.
3. I like the small restaurant at the foot of the mountain; it has an intimate and ______ atmosphere.
4. If we insult them, they will probably ______ against us sometime.
5. The joy of victory so ______ the members of the team that they jumped and sang and behaved like crazy men.

解答 1. deformity 2. harassed 3. placid 4. retaliate 5. intoxicated

第三部分

WORD	MEANING	TYPICAL USE
annihilate /əˈnaɪəleɪt/ *v.* 消灭 *n.* annihilation	destroy completely; wipe out of existance; obliterate; exterminate; abolish	Three survivors told us in detail how the regiment was ***annihilated*** by the enemy. 三个生还者详细地告诉了我们该军团是如何被敌人消灭的。
chronological /ˌkrɒnəˈlɒdʒɪkəl/ *adj.* 按年代次序的 *n.* chronicle	arranged according to the order of time	In telling a story, we usually follow ***chronological*** order. 我们通常依照年代次序来叙述故事。

WORD	MEANING	TYPICAL USE
divert /daɪˈvɜːt/ *v.* 使转向 *n.* diversion	turn aside or in a different direction; turn the attention away	They are planning to ***divert*** the river to supply water somewhere else. 他们正计划着使这河流转向,以便让别处也能得到供水。
enhance /ɪnˈhɑːns/ *v.* 增加 *n.* enhancement	add up; make greater; heighten	The moonlight on the lake ***enhanced*** the beauty of the scene. 湖上的月光使得风景更美了。
imprison /ɪmˈprɪzən/ *v.* 禁锢 *n.* imprisonment	put in prison; keep in prison	The criminal has been ***imprisoned*** in a dark cell for almost 10 years. 这个罪犯被关在暗室里,差不多有10年了。
malice /ˈmælɪs/ *n.* 恶意 *adj.* malicious	a wish to hurt or make one suffer; active ill will; enmity; spitefulness	Do not bear ***malice*** toward him; he is a good man by nature. 不要对他怀有恶意,他是个性情善良的人。
prosecute /ˈprɒsɪkjuːt/ *v.* 1. 检举 *n.* prosecution	1. bring before a court of law	The driver was ***prosecuted*** for exceeding the speed limit on the express way. 那司机因在高速公路上超速行驶而被检举。

WORD	MEANING	TYPICAL USE
2. 进行	2. carry out; carry on	He started an inquiry into the cause of the fire, and ***prosecuted*** it for several weeks. 他着手调查失火的原因,已经进行好几个星期了。
satirical /səˈtɪrɪkəl/ *adj*. 讽刺的 *v*. satirize	exhibiting something in a scornful light; sarcastic; sardonic	We were all amused by the ***satirical*** comparison of life at college and in the army. 大学和军中生活的讽刺性对比,让我们都感到好笑。
subscribe /səbˈskraɪb/ *v*. 1. 订购 *n*. subscription	1. pay money for the regular delivery of a newspaper, magazine, etc.	They ***subscribe*** to a monthly magazine in addition to several daily newspapers. 除了几份日报之外,他们还订了一份月刊。
2. 捐助	2. give or pay a sum of money	He ***subscribed*** a large amount of money for the hospital. 他为医院捐助了一大笔钱。
weird /wɪəd/ *adj*. 奇异的 *n*. weirdness	unnatural; mysterious; queer; unearthly	We heard a ***weird*** shriek from the darkness of the ruined castle. 我们听到一声来自黑暗的废弃城堡的奇怪的尖叫。

EXERCISE 15.3 从第三部分中选出最恰当的单词，填入空格内：

1. The growth of a city often ______ the value of land close to it.
2. Bryan tripped me so that I couldn't be able to play tomorrow. He did it not as a joke but out of ______.
3. No one survived the great avalanche; it ______ the whole village.
4. The teacher gave the pupils a(n) ______ list of events which had caused the First World War.
5. A juggler or magician ______ audience's attention from one hand by making feints with the other.

答案 1. enhances 2. malice 3. annihilated 4. chronological 5. diverts

第四部分

WORD	MEANING	TYPICAL USE
apprehend /ˌæprɪˈhend/ *v.* 1. 忧惧 *n.* apprehension	1. look forward to with fear; expect anxiously; dread	A guilty man ***apprehends*** danger in every sound. 犯了罪的人一听到响动就感到害怕。
2. 逮捕	2. seize a person who breaks the law; arrest	The thief who had stolen the jewels was ***apprehended*** by the police and was put in jail. 那偷珠宝的小偷被警方逮捕了，而且进了监狱。

WORD	MEANING	TYPICAL USE
commute /kəˈmjuːt/ *v.* 每天往返上下班 *n.* commutation	travel regularly to and from work	She ***commutes*** from Cambridge to London every day. 她每天往返于剑桥和伦敦之间。
emit /ɪˈmɪt/ *v.* 放射 *n.* emission	send out heat, light or sound; discharge; exude; eject	Heat and smoke ***emitted*** by the fire made it difficult for the firemen to put it out. 大火发出的热和烟,使得消防队员很难将火熄灭。
fortify /ˈfɔːtɪfaɪ/ *v.* 设立防御工事 *n.* fortification	build forts on; strengthen	The soldiers ***fortified*** the position on the hill by building earthworks and erecting log walls. 士兵们在山上的这个地方大兴土木工程并设立木墙,以建立防御工事。
inflict /ɪnˈflɪkt/ *v.* 使负担 *n.* infliction	give a blow; cause to suffer; impose	The government ***inflicted*** excessively heavy income taxes on the people. 那个政府从人民身上征收了过重的所得税。

WORD	MEANING	TYPICAL USE
mimic /ˈmɪmɪk/ *v.* (为了逗乐而)模仿 *n.* mimicry	make fun of by imitating; copy closely; imitate	She cut and painted pieces of paper that ***mimicked*** flowers so well that some people thought they were real. 她剪绘了些纸花，做得惟妙惟肖，以至于有人以为那是真的。
reassure /ˌriːəˈʃʊə/ *v.* 使安心 *n.* reassurance	comfort and make free from fear	Her calm voice ***reassured*** the frightened child, and he felt much better. 她平静的声音使那吓坏了的孩子安下心来，而且他感到好多了。
serial /ˈsɪərɪəl/ *adj.* 连载的 *v.* serialize	of a series; arranged in a series; making a series	An exciting new ***serial*** story will begin in our next week's issue. 下周出版的期刊上，我们将开始连载一部动人的新小说。
tactics /ˈtæktɪks/ *n.* 战略 *adj.* tactical	the art of organizing and using military forces in war; method to gain advantages or success	The ***tactics*** of pretending to cross the river and of making a retreat fooled the enemy. 假装渡河和撤退的战略愚弄了敌人。

EXERCISE 15.4 从第四部分中选出最恰当的单词,填入空格内:

1. Hundreds of thousands of suburban residents regularly ______ to the city.
2. He ______ his uncle's voice and gestures very cleverly.
3. The captain's confidence during the storm ______ all the passengers of the ship.
4. Place volumes one to five on the shelf in a(n) ______ order.
5. If you want to be a successful politician you must make yourself able in ______.

答案 1. commute 2. mimicked 3. reassured 4. serial 5. tactics

效果检测

EXERCISE 15.5 将各词不同词性的适当形式填入空格内:

ADJECTIVE	NOUN	VERB	ADVERB
1. ××××	______	mimic	××××
2. ______	______	retaliate	______
3. grand	______	××××	××××
4. ______	______	adhere	______
5. ______	satire	______	______
6. ______	______	emit	××××
7. bawdy	______	××××	××××
8. ××××	______	enhance	××××
9. ______	chronicle	______	______
10. numb	______	××××	××××

解答

	ADJECTIVE	NOUN	VERB	ADVERB
1.	××××	mimicry	(mimic)	××××
2.	retaliatory	retaliation	(retaliate)	retaliatorily
3.	(grand)	grandeur	××××	××××
4.	adherent	adherence	(adhere)	adherently
5.	satirical	(satire)	satirize	satirically
6.	emissive	emission	(emit)	××××
7.	(bawdy)	bawdry	××××	××××
8.	××××	enhancement	(enhance)	××××
9.	chronological	(chronicle)	chronologize	chronolo-gically
10.	(numb)	numbness	××××	××××

EXERCISE 15.6 将题前的斜体词转换为恰当的形式,填入空格中:

1. *malice* I think that story is nothing more than ______ gossip.
2. *infer* He never arrives on time, and my ______ is that he feels the meetings are useless.
3. *apprehend* Her ______ about the dangers of travelling were increased by the recent accident.
4. *chronological* Columbus kept a careful and detailed ______ of his voyage.
5. *enchant* In the Greek story, Circe turned men into pigs by her ______.

6. *audacity*	The ______ boy went to the party without being invited.
7. *prosecute*	The ______ will be stopped if the stolen money is returned.
8. *contiguity*	No one wants to buy the house even at a considerably lower price, because it is ______ to a cemetery.
9. *subscribe*	Your ______ to the newspaper expires next week.
10. *reassure*	The doctor told her that she would soon recover her health, but she didn't believe it in spite of all his ______.

解答

1. malicious
2. inference
3. apprehensions
4. chronicle
5. enchantment
6. audacious
7. prosecution
8. contiguous
9. subscription
10. reassurance

EXERCISE 15.7 找出与其他三个不相关的词：

______ 1. (A) abolish (B) exterminate
(C) annihilate (D) deride

______ 2. (A) symmetry (B) contiguity
(C) adjacency (D) proximity

______ 3. (A) harass (B) bother
(C) meditate (D) vex

______ 4. (A) enmity (B) anatomy
(C) malice (D) spitefulness

______ 5. (A) vigilant (B) wary
(C) cautious (D) coherent

_____ 6. (A) cling (B) stifle
(C) stick (D) adhere

_____ 7. (A) satirical (B) sarcastic
(C) sardonic (D) sagacious

_____ 8. (A) sly (B) furtive
(C) arrogant (D) stealthy

_____ 9. (A) congenial (B) serene
(C) tranquil (D) placid

_____ 10. (A) elusive (B) skeptical
(C) incredulous (D) distrustful

解答 1. D 2. A 3. C 4. B 5. D
6. B 7. D 8. C 9. A 10. A

EXERCISE 15.8 从下列单词中选出最恰当的词，填入空格内：

VOCABULARY LIST

inflict	prosecuting	chronological	diverted
inferred	adhere	amputated	audacity
intoxicated	tactics	apprehend	mimicking

1. The newspapers in this file are arranged in _____ order so that everyone can easily find the issue he wants.
2. The boy made all his friends laugh by _____ the teacher's slow and solemn way of talking.
3. When coaxing failed, she changed her _____ and began to cry.
4. Be careful when you use the keen ax; it can _____ a bad wound on your leg.
5. The doctor _____ the wounded soldier's leg in order to save his life.
6. Now I see how foolish I was to _____ the outcome of the test. I passed

it easily.

7. A loud noise ______ my attention from cooking and everything was burnt.
8. A glass of whisky ______ him, and he could not drive his car.
9. Glue and paste are used to make one surface ______ to another.
10. I looked at his boots and ______ that he was a policeman.

解答

1. chronological
2. mimicking
3. tactics
4. inflict
5. amputated
6. apprehend
7. diverted
8. intoxicated
9. adhere
10. inferred

LESSON 16

预备测验

选出最恰当的答案：

1. *Barometers* are used for measuring the ______ of the atmosphere.

   (A) pressure　　(B) humidity　　(C) temperature

2. She found ______ quite a *chore*.

   (A) smoking　　(B) fishing　　(C) housekeeping

3. *Coral* is often used for making ______.

   (A) powerful weapon

   (B) precious jewellery

   (C) winter coat

4. We can ______ by *twining* strings.

   (A) make a rope　　(B) pull a car　　(C) climb the cliff

5. Most of ______ comes from this *reservoir.*

   (A) the passengers of this bus

   (B) the city's drinking water

   (C) leather for making shoes

解答 1. A　2. C　3. B　4. A　5. B

第一部分

WORD	MEANING	TYPICAL USE
adversity /ədˈvɜːsətɪ/ *n.* 不幸	a condition of unhappiness, misfortune or distress	He who never was acquainted with ***adversity*** has seen the world but on one side. 从未遭遇逆境的他只了解世界的一面。
blister /ˈblɪstə(r)/ *n.* 水泡	a little bag-like place in the skin filled with water	My new shoes have made ***blisters*** on my heels. 我的新鞋使我的脚后跟长了水泡。
clatter /ˈklætə(r)/ *n.* 哗啦声	a number of rapid short knocking sounds	The ***clatter*** of metal plates was heard from the kitchen. 金属盘子的哗啦声从厨房传出。
digital /ˈdɪdʒɪtl/ *adj.* (阿拉伯)数字的	having to do with or using digits	Most of telephone dials use ***digital*** numbers. 大部分电话盘都使用阿拉伯数字。
gash /gæʃ/ *n.* 创伤;切伤	a long deep cut or wound; incision	He cannot work today; he got a ***gash*** in his hand while axing. 他今天无法工作,因为他用斧头时把手砍伤了。

WORD	MEANING	TYPICAL USE
impunity /ɪmˈpjuːnɪtɪ/ *n.* 免罚	freedom from punishment, injury or other bad consequences	For 20 years the same political party has run that country with absolute ***impunity***. 20 年来,就是这个政党安然无恙地统治着那个国家。
manure /məˈnjʊə(r)/ *n.* 肥料	a substance put on the soil as fertilizer	Plants grow much faster and stronger when they are given ***manure***. 施过肥的植物长得快多了,也强壮多了。
porous /ˈpɔːrəs/ *adj.* 多孔的	full of pores or tiny holes	Glass is not ***porous***, and it doesn't allow liquid to pass through. 玻璃是毫无空隙的,液体无法穿透它。
shack /ʃæk/ *n.* 破烂小木屋	a roughly-built hut or cabin	There are a lot of ***shacks*** in the run-down part of the town near the railroad. 在这座城市的落后地区,铁路附近有许多破烂的小木屋。

WORD	MEANING	TYPICAL USE
span /spæn/ *n.* 全长	a stretch between two limits; the distance between two supports	The average life ***span*** of people has increased considerably since the 19th century. 19 世纪以来,人类的平均寿命已经大幅度地延长了。
twitch /twɪtʃ/ *v.* 急拉;猛夺	pull with a sudden jerk; give a sudden quick pull	The strong winds ***twitched*** the paper out of her hand. 强风吹走了她手上的纸。

EXERCISE 16.1 从第一部分中选出最恰当的一个单词,填入空格内:

1. Sunburn has made a lot of ______ on my back.
2. The farmers spread ______ on the field to make it produce better crops.
3. The ______ in the cafeteria made it hard to hear one another talk.
4. A good friend will not desert you in time of ______.
5. A(n) ______ clock shows the time by displaying it in numbers, such as 2:30, instead of by hands moving around the dial.

解答 1. blisters 2. manure 3. clatter 4. adversity 5. digital

第二部分

WORD	MEANING	TYPICAL USE
armistice /ˈɑːmɪstɪs/ *n.* 休战	a stop in fighting; temporary peace; truce	November 11 is the ***Armistice*** Day of World War I. 11 月 11 日是第一次世界大战结束的纪念日。
breach /briːtʃ/ *n.* 违反(法纪)	an opening made by breaking something solid; act of breaking	It would be a ***breach*** of duty for the guard to leave before his replacement comes. 警卫在替补者尚未到来之前便离开岗位是不忠于职守的行为。
comity /ˈkɒmɪtɪ/ *n.* 团结	friendly, polite and respectful behavior and manners; courtesy; civility	To help a new student get oriented furthers the ***comity*** of the school. 帮助新生适应环境能促进学校的团结。
dungeon /ˈdʌndʒən/ *n.* 地牢	a dark underground room or cell to keep prisoners in	Some prisoners in the ***dungeon*** will be released tomorrow. 明天，地牢里的一些犯人将被释放。

WORD	MEANING	TYPICAL USE
gregarious /grəˈgɛərɪəs/ *adj.* 合群的	living in groups; fond of living with others	He is a ***gregarious*** man; he enjoys the companionship of a large number of friends. 他是个合群的人，喜欢和一大堆朋友在一起。
incur /ɪnˈkɜː/ *v.* 遭遇	run into something unpleasant	The explorers ***incurred*** great dangers when they tried to cross the rapids. 当那些探险者越过急流时，他们遇到了很大的危险。
mole /məʊl/ *n.* 1. 痣	1. a spot on the skin, usually brown	She has a small ***mole*** on the left side of her nose. 她鼻子左侧有一颗小痣。
2. 鼹鼠	2. a small animal that lives underground most of time	The ***mole*** digs holes and passages underground and makes its home in them. 那只鼹鼠在地下挖掘洞穴和通道，并且把家造于其间。
patent /ˈpeɪtənt, ˈpætənt/ *n.* 专利	a government grant giving a person the sole right to make and use his/her invention	He has applied for a ***patent*** on his latest invention. 他已经替他最新的发明申请了专利。

WORD	MEANING	TYPICAL USE
sip /sɪp/ *v.* 啜饮	drink little by little; drink only a little at a time	This coffee is very hot. Do not drink it quickly, but ***sip*** it. 这咖啡非常烫，不要喝得太快，只能小口啜饮。
sulfur /ˈsʌlfə(r)/ *n.* 硫磺	a light-yellow nonmetallic chemical element	***Sulfur*** is found abundantly in volcanic regions. 在火山地区发现了丰富的硫磺。
upsurge /ˈʌpsɜːdʒ/ *n.* 上升	an upward turn or trend; rise; upturn	This year's ***upsurge*** in rice production is due to the new method of cultivation. 今年稻米产量的提高是由于使用了新的栽培方法。

EXERCISE 16.2 从第二部分中选出最恰当的单词，填入空格内：

1. Strong disagreement produced a(n) ______ between the business partners.
2. During the ______, they deveolped a plan for ending the war.
3. ______ is used in making gunpowder, matches or various kinds of medicine.
4. He ______ a great many debts during his illness.
5. Hundreds of prisoners are still confined in the ______.

答案 1. breach 2. armistice 3. Sulfur 4. incurred 5. dungeon

第三部分

WORD	MEANING	TYPICAL USE
austere /ɒsˈtɪə(r)/ *adj.* 严厉的	severe or stern in manner or appearance	Grandfather was an ***austere*** man; he used to be silent and very strict to us. 祖父是个严厉的人。他一向沉默，而且对我们非常严格。
bouquet /ˈbʊ(uː)keɪ, bʊˈkeɪ/ *n.* 花束	a bunch of flowers	When I was in hospital, she called on me with a ***bouquet*** of roses in her hand. 我住院的时候，她捧着一束玫瑰花来探望我。
coral /ˈkɒrəl/ *n.* 珊瑚	a stone-like substance formed from the bones of a kind of small sea animals	In the Pacific Ocean there are many ***coral*** atolls that are ringlike islands. 太平洋中有许多环状珊瑚岛。

WORD	MEANING	TYPICAL USE
forum /ˈfɔːrəm/ *n.* 讨论会	the place for public discussion; public discussion	A group of schoolmasters are holding a ***forum*** on new ways of teaching history. 一些老师正在召开一个新的历史教学方法的讨论会。
gym /dʒɪm/ *n.* 体育馆	a building for physical training or indoor sports	On rainy days the students play games in the ***gym***. 下雨天，学生们在体育馆里做游戏。
interject /ˌɪntə(ɜː)ˈdʒekt/ *v.* 突然插入	throw in between other things; insert; interpose	"Not like that!" he ***interjected*** while explaining how to take the machine into pieces. 当讲解如何拆卸机器时，他突然插了一句"不是那样！"。
mushroom /ˈmʌʃrʊm/ *n.* 菌类植物；蘑菇	a small fungus shaped like an umbrella; toadstool	Some ***mushrooms*** are good to eat; some, such as toadstools, are poisonous. 有些蘑菇很好吃，然而有些却是有毒的，例如伞菌。

WORD	MEANING	TYPICAL USE
raft /rɑːft/ *n.* 救生艇	logs fastened together to make a floating platform	They escaped from the wrecked ship on a ***raft.*** 他们驾着救生艇逃离遇难的船。
smear /smɪə(r)/ *v.* 涂抹,弄脏	cover or stain with anything sticky, greasy or dirty	The children looked like black people; their faces were ***smeared*** with soot. 这些孩子看起来像黑人似的;他们的脸被煤烟给弄脏了。
taper /ˈteɪpə(r)/ *v.* 逐渐变细	make gradually smaller toward one end	One end of a pencil is ***tapered*** off to a point. 铅笔的一端逐渐变细,最后成了一个尖头。
via /ˈvaɪə,ˈviːə/ *prep.* 经由	by way of; by means of	I have read this French play ***via*** an English translation. 我已读过了这部法国戏剧的英译本。

EXERCISE 16.3 从第三部分中选出最恰当的单词,填入空格内:

1. Every now and then the speaker ______ a joke or story to keep us interested.
2. In tropical areas ______ grows in shallow water.
3. We could find no boats around the ferry, and we had to cross the river on

a(n) ______.

4. The judge had a(n) ______ look on his face as he spoke to the criminal.

5. The carpenter ______ the end of the fence post with an ax.

解答 1. interjected 2. coral 3. raft 4. austere 5. tapered

第四部分

WORD	MEANING	TYPICAL USE
barometer /bəˈrɒmɪtə(r)/ *n.* 气压计；反应指标	an instrument for measuring the atmospheric pressure	Newspapers are often called ***barometers*** of public opinion. 报纸常被称为反应舆论的晴雨表。
comply /kəmˈplaɪ/ *v.* 顺从	act in agreement with a request or a command	He ***complied*** with the doctor's order that he should take a rest at home. 他遵从医生的规定，在家中休息。
coxcomb /ˈkɒkskəʊm/ *n.* 花花公子	a vain, emptyheaded man; conceited dandy; fop	A ***coxcomb*** spends too much money and time on his clothes and appearance. 花花公子在自己的服饰及外表上花费了太多的金钱和时间。

WORD	MEANING	TYPICAL USE
foliage /ˈfəʊlɪɪdʒ/ *n.* 叶子的总称	the leaves of a plant, especially growing leaves	In summer the house next door is hidden in luxuriant ***foliage***. 夏天,隔壁的房子被繁茂的叶子掩盖。
hegira /ˈhedʒɪrə/ *n.* 穆罕默德从麦加到麦地那的逃亡;离开	the flight of Muhammed from Mecca to Medina; flight	She made her plan for her annual summer ***hegira*** to the Miami beach. 她计划到迈阿密海滩去度一年一次的暑假。
lair /lɛə(r)/ *n.* 野兽的巢穴	the den or resting place of a wild animal	The hunters traced the footmarks of a tiger and at last they found him in his ***lair***. 猎人们循着老虎的足迹前进,最后他们在它的巢穴中找到了它。
nightmare /ˈnaɪtmɛə(r)/ *n.* 恶梦	an unpleasant and terrible dream; dream causing fear	The child had a terrible ***nightmare*** and awoke crying. 那孩子做了个恶梦,哭醒了。
reservoir /ˈrezəvwɑː(r)/ *n.* 水库	a place where water is collected and stored for use	This ***reservoir*** is large enough to supply water to the entire city. 这水库大得足够供应全市的用水。

WORD	MEANING	TYPICAL USE
sod /sɒd/ *n.* 草皮	a piece or layer of the ground covered with grass; turf	He bought some ***sod*** to put in the bare spots of his lawn. 他买了些草皮种在庭院草坪的空地。
trash /træʃ/ *n.* 垃圾	anything of little or no worth; worthless stuff; rubbish	Rake up the ***trash*** in the yard and burn it. We will have some guests tonight. 把庭院里的垃圾耙拢烧掉。今晚我们有客人来访。
warehouse /ˈwɛəhaʊs/ *n.* 仓库	a place where goods are kept; depository; storehouse	The furniture will stay in the ***warehouse*** until they pay the storage cost. 那些家具会放在仓库中,直到他们付了保管费为止。

EXERCISE 16.4 从第四部分中选出最恰当的单词,填入空格内:

1. In spring these naked branches will put their graceful ______ on again.
2. The salmon makes a trip to the rivers or creeks for spawning. On the contrary the ______ of the eel is toward the sea.
3. We cut some ______ from a field and covered a bare spot in the lawn with it.
4. When the ______ indicates a rapid drop in air pressure, it means a storm is coming.
5. Some people go fishing to rivers; others go to ______ or lakes.

解答 1. foliage 2. hegira 3. sod 4. barometer 5. reservoirs

第五部分

WORD	MEANING	TYPICAL USE
belch /beltʃ/ *v.* 喷出	throw out gas through the mouth; eructate	The volcano ***belched*** a staggering amount of fire, smoke and ashes. 那火山喷出大量的火、烟和灰尘。
chore /tʃɔː(r)/ *n.* 琐事;困难而讨厌的事	small routine task; a difficult or disagreeable thing to do	It's such a ***chore*** to do the shopping every day. 每天购物是一件非常困难而讨厌的事。
crimson /ˈkrɪmzən/ *adj.* 深红色的	deep, slightly purplish color	When she was asked a sudden question, her face turned ***crimson*** in embarrassment. 当问她一个很突然的问题时,她困窘得脸红了。
fugitive /ˈfjuːdʒɪtɪv/ *n.* 逃亡者	a person escaping from the law, the police or danger	The ***fugitive*** had already packed and bought his ticket. 这逃亡者早就打好包,买好了票。

WORD	MEANING	TYPICAL USE
horde /hɔːd/ *n.* 群众;大群	a large number or crowd; swarm; multitude	Two women were quarrelling on the street, surrounded by a ***horde*** of people. 有两个女人在街上争吵,一大群人围观。
linguist /ˈlɪŋgwɪst/ *n.* 语言学家	a person who studies the science of language	Usually a ***linguist*** is skilled in a number of languages besides his own. 除了母语外,语言学家一般通晓许多种其他语言。
petroleum /pɪˈtrəʊlɪəm/ *n.* 石油	a natural oil found in the earth in certain parts of the world	The price of the ***petroleum*** has been raised too high during the last few years. 最近几年来,石油的价格猛涨。
rumple /ˈrʌmpl/ *v.* 使皱,起皱	crumple; crush; wrinkle	Mary ***rumpled*** her dress by sitting on the floor. 玛丽坐在地板上,把衣服弄皱了。
sneeze /sniːz/ *v.* 打喷嚏	let out the breath through the nose and mouth	People ***sneeze*** when they have a cold. 人感冒时会打喷嚏。

WORD	MEANING	TYPICAL USE
twine /twaɪn/ *v.* 盘曲;缠绕	wind or wrap around; twist together	She ***twined*** her arms around his neck and kissed him. 她把胳膊环在他脖子上亲吻他。
whirr /wɜː(r)/ *v.* 呼呼地转动	make a regular sound by something beating against the air	When we got inside the factory, we couldn't hear the guide explain because of the ***whirring*** of the motors. 当我们进入工厂时,因为马达呼呼地转动,我们听不见向导的解说。

EXERCISE 16.5 从第五部分中选出最恰当的单词,填入空格内:

1. Each morning she would get up, do the ______, then go next door for a talk with her neighbor.
2. The ______ crossed the border by night to escape arrest.
3. A(n) ______ collects and records utterances, and, comparing these with one another, abstracts the way of speaking.
4. The boy ______ his arms around his mother's leg and teased her for money to buy the toy.
5. ______ of Mongolians and Turks invaded Europe in the Middle Ages.

解答 1. chores 2. fugitive 3. linguist
4. twined 5. Hordes

效果检测

EXERCISE 16.6 从第二栏中选出第一栏各词的正确词意：

COLUMN Ⅰ	COLUMN Ⅱ
______ 1. lair	(A) full of tiny holes
______ 2. nightmare	(B) a spot on the skin
______ 3. mole	(C) a bunch of flowers
______ 4. belch	(D) to drink little by little
______ 5. upsurge	(E) to throw out gas through the mouth
______ 6. porous	(F) an unpleasant and terrible dream
______ 7. via	(G) a condition of misfortune or distress
______ 8. bouquet	(H) the resting place of a wild animal
______ 9. adversity	(I) an upward turn or trend; rise
______ 10. sip	(J) by way of; by means of

解答 1. H 2. F 3. B 4. E 5. I
6. A 7. J 8. C 9. G 10. D

EXERCISE 16.7 完整拼出下列句中所欠缺的单词，句后括号内为该词的词意：

1. Please take the basket of t______h to the garbage can. (*rubbish*)
2. Gasoline and other fuel oils are made from p______m. (*natural oil found in the earth*)
3. Lions and elephants are g______s; tigers are not. (*living in groups*)
4. When the knife slipped, it made a g______h in his thumb. (*deep wound*)
5. An a______e is arranged by agreement on all sides, often while a permanent peace is being arranged. (*temporary peace*)
6. With a b______r we can determine height above sea level and predict

probable changes in the weather. (*instrument for measuring the atmospheric pressure*)

7. Giving one's seat to a lady in a crowded bus is a sign of c______y. (*courtesy*)

8. The boys made a small s______k out of old boards in the backyard. (*roughly-built hut*)

9. Do not t______h the curtain aside; it may be torn off. (*pull with a sudden jerk*)

10. An open f______m on birth control was held in the hall last Tuesday evening. (*public discussion*)

解答			
	1. trash	2. petroleum	3. gregarious
	4. gash	5. armistice	6. barometer
	7. comity	8. shack	9. twitch
	10. forum		

EXERCISE 16.8 找出与其他三个不相关的词：

______ 1. (A) horde (B) swarm
(C) span (D) multitude

______ 2. (A) malice (B) courtesy
(C) civility (D) comity

______ 3. (A) indulge (B) insert
(C) interpose (D) interject

______ 4. (A) mushroom (B) fungus
(C) coral (D) toadstool

______ 5. (A) austere (B) placid
(C) severe (D) stern

______ 6. (A) dungeon (B) limbo

(C) jail (D) castle

______ 7. (A) turf (B) manure
(C) lawn (D) sod

______ 8. (A) coxcomb (B) fop
(C) dandy (D) mole

______ 9. (A) trash (B) litter
(C) rubbish (D) breach

______ 10. (A) rumple (B) crumple
(C) scramble (D) wrinkle

解答 1. C 2. A 3. A 4. C 5. B
6. D 7. B 8. D 9. D 10. C

EXERCISE 16.9 从下列单词中选出最恰当的词，填入空格内：

VOCABULARY LIST

impunity	whirr	smear	patent
crimson	incurred	petroleum	gym
rafts	clatter	twined	gregarious

1. The ______ came from the kitchen where pans were being washed.
2. They decided to build a large ______ for indoor athletic sports.
3. Be careful! If you touch the wall you will ______ the fresh paint.
4. The boatman ______ the rope around the post to prevent his boat from drifting down the river.
5. Before boats were invented, man first began to use ______ to cross rivers or streams.
6. The high price of ______ has driven many countries to develop new sources of energy.
7. A baby likes to play by himself, but as he grows older he becomes

______.

8. As what she said was proved to be a lie, her face turned ______ with shame.
9. If laws are not enforced, crimes are committed with ______.
10. She ______ great debts by buying a luxurious car which she could not afford.

解答 1. clatter 2. gym 3. smear 4. twined 5. rafts 6. petroleum 7. gregarious 8. crimson 9. impunity 10. incurred

LESSON 17

预备测验

选出最恰当的答案：

1. We watched the *astronauts*' journey to the ______ on television.

   （A） moon　　（B） Antarctic

2. Many criminals were ______ on the *gallows*.

   （A） hanged　　（B） shot to death

3. You need a ______ to take part in *masquerade*.

   （A） mask　　（B） uniform

4. The *phoenix* often symbolizes ______.

   （A） great victory　　（B） eternal life

5. He always felt that his father's ______ *stigmatized* both of them.

   （A） prison record　　（B） glorious death

解答 1. A 2. A 3. A 4. B 5. A

第一部分

WORD	MEANING	TYPICAL USE
alloy /ˈælɔɪ/ *n.* 合金	substance consisting of two or more metals and mixed together	An ***alloy*** is often harder, lighter and stronger than the pure metals of which it is composed. 合金通常较其成分金属要更硬、轻和牢固。

WORD	MEANING	TYPICAL USE
blackout /ˈblækˌaʊt/ *n.* 灯火管制	the action of turning off all lights as a protection against an air raid	The streets were not lighted at night during the ***blackout***. 在灯火管制的夜里，街道上没有灯。
cater /ˈkeɪtə(r)/ *v.* 备办食物	provide food and supplies; provide what is needed	Who is supposed to ***cater*** for your daughter's wedding next week? 谁将为你女儿下周的婚礼承办酒席?
cram /kræm/ *v.* 1. 仓促用功；(为应试)临时死记硬背	1. prepare oneself for an examination hastily	He is ***cramming*** facts and dates for his history examination tomorrow. 为了应付明天的历史考试，他正在死记硬背史实和日期。
2. 填塞；塞入	2. force or press into a small space; stuff	He ***crammed*** as many candy bars into his pockets as they would hold. 他尽量多地把棒棒糖塞进口袋，直到装不下为止。
fleece /fliːs/ *v.* 骗取；欺诈	rob by a trick or by charging too much money	If you paid $200 for the watch, you were ***fleeced***. I saw it in a department store for $70. 假若你花了200美元买那只表，那么你就被骗了。我在一家百货公司看到它只卖70美元。

WORD	MEANING	TYPICAL USE
habitat /ˈhæbɪtæt/ *n.* (动植物的)产地;栖息地	the natural home of a plant or animal	The jungle is the natural ***habitat*** of wild animals and plants. 丛林是野生动植物的栖息地。
locksmith /ˈlɒkˌsmɪθ/ *n.* 锁匠	a person who makes or repairs locks and keys	I lost my key to the door, and I went to the ***lock-smith*** to get a new one. 我把门钥匙弄丢了,于是就到锁匠那儿去配了一把新的。
pant /pænt/ *v.* 喘息;气喘吁吁地说话	breathe hard and quickly; speak with short quick breaths	He ***panted*** excitedly giving us the news as he had just heard it. 他气喘吁吁的,兴奋地告诉我们他刚刚听说的事。
rickety /ˈrɪkɪtɪ/ *adj.* 摇摇欲倒的	likely to fall or break down; shaky or weak; tottering	Don't use that old cart; it's ***rickety***. 不要用那辆旧马车,因为它摇摇晃晃的。
stigmatize /ˈstɪgmətaɪz/ *v.* 污辱;指责	set some mark of disgrace on; reproach	He has been ***stigmatized*** as a coward and liar. 他被指责为懦夫和说谎者。

WORD	MEANING	TYPICAL USE
unquenchable /ʌnˈkwentʃəbl/ *adj.* 难以抑制的；不能镇压的	not capable of being satisfied; not quenchable	Having been in the desert without water for two days, his thirst was ***unquenchable***. 他已经在沙漠中呆了两天没有水喝，口渴极了。

EXERCISE 17.1 从第一部分选出最恰当的单词，填入空格内：

1. Many students ______ for the final examination in the library all through the night.
2. The dog ______ along behind its master's horse.
3. A(n) ______ of gold and copper is harder and less costly than gold alone.
4. He runs a restaurant and also ______ for wedding and parties.
5. As to our white wine, they ______ it as a mere substitute for cider.

答案 1. crammed 2. panted 3. alloy 4. caters 5. stigmatized

第二部分

WORD	MEANING	TYPICAL USE
astronaut /ˈæstrənɔːt/ *n.* 宇航员	a pilot or member of the crew of a spacecraft; cosmonaut	The ***astronauts*** of the United States are returning to the earth from the moon. 美国宇航员正从月球返回地球。
bequeath /bɪˈkwɪːð/ *v.* 遗赠；遗留	give or pass on to others after death	One age ***bequeaths*** its knowledge to the next. 上一代将其知识传给下一代。
census /ˈsensəs/ *n.* 人口调查；人口普查	an official count of a country's total population	In the United States there is a ***census*** every ten years. 在美国，每 10 年有一次人口普查。
crusade /kruːˈseɪd/ *n.* 宗教上的圣战；反对某事的运动	the Christian expedition; a campaign or fight for a good cause	Everyone of the city was asked to join the ***crusade*** for better housing. 城市中的每个人都被要求去参加这个改善住房的活动。

WORD	MEANING	TYPICAL USE
ford /fɔːd/ *v.* 涉水	cross a river or stream by walking through the water	The stream was so deep that we could not ***ford*** it. 河水太深了,我们蹚不过去。
hover /ˈhʌvə(r)/ *v.* 守在近旁	stay in or near one place	The dog ***hovers*** around the kitchen door every mealtime. 每到吃饭时间,那只狗就守在厨房门边。
masquerade /ˌmæskəˈreɪd/ 1. *n.* 化装舞会 2. *v.* 乔装;伪装	1. a party or dance at which masks and fancy costumes are worn 2. disguise oneself; pretend to be	They were all dressed up to attend the ***masquerade***. 他们都盛装去参加那个化装舞会。 He got a free ticket to the play by ***masquerading*** as a friend of the actors. 他假扮成演员们的朋友而得到一张免费的戏票。
phoenix /ˈfiːnɪks/ *n.* 凤凰,长生鸟	an imaginary bird symbolizing eternal life	The ***phoenix*** is believed to live for 500 years and then burns itself to be born again from the ashes. 相传凤凰能活500年,然后就自焚,再从灰烬中重生。

WORD	MEANING	TYPICAL USE
rye /raɪ/ *n.* 黑麦	a plant with grain for making flour and as food for cattle	Some people prefer the dark bread made from ***rye*** to the white bread made from wheat. 有些人喜欢黑麦做的黑面包,而不喜欢小麦做的白面包。
stunt /stʌnt/ *n.* 惊人的技艺;引人注意的行动	a feat to attract attention; act showing boldness or skill	In the film he jumps off a running car and performs other dangerous ***stunts***. 在电影中,他跳下正在奔驰的汽车并表演了其他危险的惊人绝技。
versus /ˈvɜːsəs/ *prep.* 对	against	The most exciting game in hockey, was Havard ***versus*** Yale. 最刺激的一场曲棍球赛是哈佛对耶鲁的那一场。

EXERCISE 17.2 从第二部分中选出最恰当的单词,填入空格内:

1. The helicopter ______ over the spot where the lost men had been seen.
2. After the Second World War, many people joined in the ______ for the warless world.
3. The millionaire will ______ his colossal fortune to his only son.
4. The plane flew upside down, turned over twice, and did a few more ______

before landing.

5. The bridge is too far away from here. We'd better ______ the stream here.

答案 1. hovered 2. crusade 3. bequeath 4. stunts 5. ford

第三部分

WORD	MEANING	TYPICAL USE
artillery /ɑːˈtɪlərɪ/ *n.* 大炮	large, heavy guns moved on wheel carriers; cannon	Above all the ***artillery*** was the deciding factor in the battle. 在战争中，大炮是决定性因素。
bounty /ˈbaʊntɪ/ *n.*（政府施予的）奖金、津贴	money given by a government for some special act or service	In the early days of the West many states paid a ***bounty*** for captured criminals. 早期西方许多国家会施与被俘的罪犯一笔钱。
clench /klentʃ/ *v.* 紧握	close tightly together; grasp firmly	When he got a shot against typhus, the child ***clenched*** his teeth in pain. 当那小孩接受伤寒疫苗注射时，痛得紧紧咬着牙。

WORD	MEANING	TYPICAL USE
dirk /dɜːk/ *n.* 短剑；匕首	a short, pointed, two-edged knife used as a weapon	I saw a burglar, with a ***dirk*** in his hand, getting into the room where she was sleeping. 我看见一个小偷手里拿着匕首，进入她正在睡觉的房间。
gallows /ˈɡæləʊz/ *n.* 绞刑架；绞刑	a wooden frame with a rope from which criminals are hanged; punishment by hanging	The murderer entreated the judge for mercy, but was sentenced to the ***gallows***. 那个杀人犯恳求法官宽恕，但被判处绞刑。
inedible /ɪnˈedɪbl/ *adj.* 不可食的；不宜食用的	not suitable for eating; not edible	My steak, though delicious, was mostly fat and bones. Most of it was ***inedible***. 我的牛排虽然美味，但多半是肥肉和骨头，大部分都不能吃。
morale /mɒˈrɑːl/ *n.* 民心；士气	the state of mind with regard to pride or faith	The ***morale*** of the football team was very low after its defeat. 比赛失败后，这支足球队的士气非常低落。
prone /prəʊn/ *adj.* 1. 易于……的	1. inclined; liable; disposed; apt	We are more ***prone*** to make mistakes when we are tired. 我们疲倦的时候比较容易犯错。

WORD	MEANING	TYPICAL USE
2. 俯卧的	2. lying face down; lying flat; incumbent; prostrate	We fell ***prone*** to the ground and drank water from the spring. 我们俯卧在地上喝泉水。
scuttle /ˈskʌtl/ *v.* 疾走	run with quick, hurried steps; scurry	The robbers grasped the peril of their position and ***scuttled*** away. 抢劫者知道他们处境危险，于是很快就逃走了。
tack /tæk/ *n.* 大头钉	a short nail or pin with a flat head	The carpet was fastened to the floor with ***tacks***. 地毯用大头钉固定在地板上。
ward /wɔːd/ *n.* 被监护者	a person who is under legal protection	After his parents' death, the court made him a ***ward*** of his aunt. 他双亲去世后，法官让他的姑妈当监护人。

EXERCISE 17.3 从第三部分中选出最恰当的单词，填入空格内：

1. Some people hunt fugitives from the law or harmful animals to collect the ______ for their capture.
2. The children who had broken the window of the house ______ off when they saw a policeman.

3. We bought some ______ to fasten the small picture to the wall.
4. Trapped in the cave by a fall of rock, the men kept up their ______ by singing together.
5. While it was thundering, the little boy ______ his mother's arm in terror.

解答 1. bounty 2. scuttled 3. tacks 4. morale 5. clenched

第四部分

WORD	MEANING	TYPICAL USE
avalanche /ˈævəlɑːntʃ/ *n.* 雪崩	a large mass of snow crashing down the side of mountain	The terrible ***avalanche*** buried the whole village, and very few people survived it. 可怕的雪崩把整个村庄都掩埋了,只有少数幸存者。
briefcase /ˈbriːfkeɪs/ *n.* 公事包	a flat bag for carrying loose papers or books	I was so in a hurry that I left my ***briefcase*** at home. 我走得太匆忙了,以至于将公事包落在了家里。
commodious /kəˈməʊdjəs/ *adj.* 宽敞的	having plenty of room; spacious; roomy	The apartment is not ***commodious*** enough for his family to live in. 这公寓不够宽敞,无法住下他们全家。

WORD	MEANING	TYPICAL USE
dynasty /ˈdɪnəstɪ, ˈdaɪnɔstɪ/ *n.* 王朝	a series of rulers who belong to the same family	The Bourbon ***dynasty*** ruled France for more than two hundred years. 波旁王朝统治法国两百多年。
gibberish /ˈdʒɪbərɪʃ/ *n.* 乱语	senseless chatter; confused meaningless talk; jargon; gabble	After he got out of the bar, he suddenly began to yell drunken ***gibberish*** on the sidewalk. 他走出酒吧后，突然在人行道上开始大声说醉话。
invoke /ɪnˈvəuk/ *v.* 恳求；祈求	ask earnestly; request or beg for	I ***invoked*** his forgiveness many times, but failed to move him. 我好几次请求他的原谅，但没有打动他。
myriad /ˈmɪrɪəd/ *n.* 无数；一万	a very great number; ten thousand	There are ***myriads*** of stars in the sky at night; we can-not count them. 夜晚的天空中有无数的星星，我们无法计算它们的数量。

WORD	MEANING	TYPICAL USE
quarry /ˈkwɒrɪ/ *n.* 采石场	a place from which stone, sand, etc. are dug out	Thousands of men and women are working in the ***quarry*** to get stones for use in building the castle. 数以千计的男人和女人们在采石场掘取建筑城堡用的石头。
slum /slʌm/ *n.* 贫民区	a city area of poor living conditions and dirty buildings	Poverty and disease are common in the ***slums***. 在贫民区里,贫困和疾病是很普遍的。
tinkle /ˈtɪŋkl/ *v.* 使发丁当声	make short, light, ringing sounds	He ***tinkled*** his coins together in his pocket. 他使口袋中的硬币碰在一起发出丁当声。
whirlpool /ˈwɜːlˌpuːl/ *n.* 漩涡	a place with circular currents of water	The swimmer caught in the ***whirlpool*** struggled to keep from drowning. 被卷进漩涡的游泳者,挣扎着以免溺水。

EXERCISE 17.4 从第四部分中选出最恰当的单词,填入空格内:

1. History shows that China was in a prosperous condition under the Ming ______.

2. The government is tearing down the ______ and building new houses.
3. When you swim, do not get close to the ______; you may be drowned.
4. Even during change of classes there is no crowding because the halls and stairways are ______.
5. The country faced with famine is expected to ______ the help of its more fortunate neighbors.

答案 1. Dynasty 2. slums 3. whirlpool 4. commodious 5. invoke

第五部分

WORD	MEANING	TYPICAL USE
blockade /blɒˈkeɪd/ *n.* 封锁	the shutting up of a place by police or soldiers	We ended our ***blockade*** of the enemy's port when peace was established. 当和平建立时，我们结束了对敌人港口的封锁。
burrow /ˈbɜːrəʊ/ *n.* 动物所掘的地洞；洞穴	a hole dug in the ground by an animal for refuge	The fox likes to live in a ***burrow***; it's warm in winter and cool in summer. 狐狸喜欢住在洞穴里，因为它冬暖夏凉。
corollary /ˈkɒrəˌlərɪ/ *n.* 自然的结果	natural consequence or result	Destruction and suffering are ***corollaries*** of war. 破坏和苦难是战争的自然结果。

WORD	MEANING	TYPICAL USE
fawn /fɔːn/ *v.* 巴结；奉承	try to get favor by acting on a flattering way	Many flattering relatives ***fawned*** on the rich old man. 许多谄媚的亲戚都去巴结那个富有的老人。
grope /grəʊp/ *v.* 摸索	feel about with the hands	He ***groped*** for the light switch in the dark basement. 在黑暗的地下室里，他摸索着电灯的开关。
latch /lætʃ/ *n.* 门锁	a simple fastening for a door or gate	He turned the ***latch*** of the door and opened it so gently. 他转开门锁轻轻地把门打开。
nostalgia /nɒsˈtældʒɪə/ *n.* 乡愁；思乡病	a painful yearning for one's home; yearning for something in the past	The soldiers were filled with ***nostalgia*** by hearing my old favorite song. 士兵们听我唱了大家爱听的老歌后，心中充满了乡愁。
resound /rɪˈzaʊnd/ *v.* (声音)巨响；发出回响	be loudly and clearly heard; give back sound	The notes of the hunting horn ***resounded*** through the forest. 打猎的号角声在森林里回荡。

WORD	MEANING	TYPICAL USE
splinter /ˈsplɪntə(r)/ 1. *v.* 碎裂	1. split or break into small pieces	The fireman ***splintered*** the locked door with an ax to save the boy in the room. 消防队员用斧头将紧锁的门劈开，以解救屋里的小孩。
2. *n.* 碎片	2. a sharp pointed piece broken off hard material	No one in the plane survived the crash; it crashed down into ***splinters***. 这次空难事件无人幸免，因为飞机坠毁成碎片了。
truce /truːs/ *n.* 休战；停战	the act of stopping fighting; peace for a short time; armistice	A ***truce*** was declared at Christmas between the two armies. 在圣诞节当天双方军队宣布停战。
vernacular /vəˈnækjʊlə(r)/ *n.* 本国语；土语	the language spoken by the members of a certain country or place	There is not a single grammar book on the ***vernacular*** of this African tribe. 关于这个非洲部落的土语是没有语法书的。

EXERCISE 17.5 从第五部分中选出最恰当的单词，填入空格：

1. Before you open the window you have to turn its ______.
2. He ______ on her only to borrow money; in fact he does not like her so

much.

3. The blind man ______ his way to the door of the room.

4. A five-day ______ was declared between the two armies on New Year's Day.

5. The name of the new champion ______ all over the world.

解答 1. latch 2. fawns 3. groped 4. truce 5. resounded

效果检测

EXERCISE 17.6 从第二栏中选出第一栏各词的正确词意：

	COLUMN Ⅰ	COLUMN Ⅱ
______	1. clench	(A) the area of poor living conditions
______	2. invoke	(B) to give to others after death
______	3. slum	(C) a feat to attract attention
______	4. artillery	(D) to rob by a trick
______	5. latch	(E) to ask earnestly; beg for
______	6. fleece	(F) large heavy guns
______	7. stunt	(G) to grasp firmly
______	8. bequeath	(H) a simple fastening for a door
______	9. splinter	(I) to stay near one place
______	10. hover	(J) to break into small pieces

解答 1. G 2. E 3. A 4. F 5. H
6. D 7. C 8. B 9. J 10. I

EXERCISE 17.7 完整拼出下列句中所欠缺的单词,句后括号内为该词的词意:

1. She could put all her clothes in one c______s drawer. (*spacious*)
2. An a______e often carries with it thousands of tons of rock, and sometimes destroys houses and roads. (*large mass of snow*)
3. Good health is a c______y of good nutrition. (*natural consequence*)
4. Terribly drunken men are apt to quarrel with others or yell g______h on the street. (*confused meaningless talk*)
5. The poisonous mushrooms are not suitable for eating; they are i______e. (*not eatable*)
6. One who has to spend so much of his life in foreign countries always feels n______a. (*painful yearning for one's home*)
7. He hammered a t______k into the wall and hung the picture from it. (*short nail with a flat head*)
8. Two robbers sneaked into the room and one of them pointed his d______k toward the old man's neck. (*short knife as a weapon*)
9. A m______d of thoughts passed through her mind. (*great number*)
10. We are p______e to think evil of people whom we do not like. (*apt*)

解答

1. commodious	2. avalanche	3. corollary
4. gibberish	5. inedible	6. nostalgia
7. tack	8. dirk	9. myriad
10. prone		

EXERCISE 17.8 选出最符合句意的单词:

1. Many teenagers have a(n) ______ thirst for adventure stories; they read

one after another.

(A) commodious (B) unquenchable

2. A ______ of all the harbors would require thousands of warships.

(A) blockade (B) truce

3. I ______ my way to the seat in the dark theater.

(A) groped (B) scuttled

4. There are many strange words in the ______ speech of lawyers.

(A) crusade (B) vernacular

5. Don't take a seat on the ______ chair; it might be broken down.

(A) rickety (B) sturdy

解答 1. B 2. A 3. A 4. B 5. A

EXERCISE 17.9 从下列单词中选出最恰当的词,填入空格内:

VOCABULARY LIST

habitat	blackout	locksmith	blockade
alloy	versus	fleeced	vernacular
stigmatized	resounded	forded	masqueraded

1. They ______ their political opponent as a liar so as to make him unpopular.
2. The prince who ______ as a peasant walked into the town, and no one recognized him.
3. If you paid $1,000 for the used car, you were ______. The mechanic says it's worth no more than $500.
4. Brass is a(n) ______ of copper and zinc.
5. After the earthquake the police set up a(n) ______ into the town to prevent looting.
6. If you lose the key to your apartment, you can get a new one from the ______.

7. The noise of laughter and whistles ______ through the empty corridor.
8. The big cricket match is starting today; it's England ______ Australia.
9. During the enemy's air raid we have to turn off or conceal all the lights for a perfect ______.
10. Having lived in the United States for a long time, he had gotten used to speaking English. But when he returned home to Korea he soon lapsed into his ______.

解答 1. stigmatized 2. masqueraded 3. fleeced
4. alloy 5. blockade 6. locksmith
7. resounded 8. versus 9. blackout
10. vernacular

LESSON 18

预备测验

选出最恰当的答案：

1. Most *anesthetics* put the patients to ______.

   (A) pain　　(B) delight　　(C) sleep

2. They found a *cavern* on the side of the ______.

   (A) mountain　　(B) building　　(C) cabinet

3. *Chisels* are used to ______ wood, stone or metal.

   (A) cut　　(B) melt　　(C) decorate

4. *Gruel* is often given to those who are ______.

   (A) diligent, sincere or excellent

   (B) deserved to be punished

   (C) sick or very old

5. *Soot* usually collects ______.

   (A) in the shallow, warm stream

   (B) under the branches of a tree

   (C) on the inside of chimneys

解答 1. C 2. A 3. A 4. C 5. C

第一部分

WORD	MEANING	TYPICAL USE
anesthetic /ˌænɪsˈθetɪk/ *n.* 麻醉剂;麻药	substance that produce inability to feel pain	The use of ***anesthetics*** is less than a hundred years old. 麻醉剂的使用还不到100年。
beacon /ˈbiːkən/ *n.* 烽火;信号	a light or fire used as a signal to guide or warm	The fire on the hill was a ***beacon*** to the villagers that the enemy was coming. 山丘上的火是通知村民敌人来了的信号。
coroner /ˈkɒrənə(r)/ *n.* 验尸官	an official who investigates the cause of death	The ***coroner*** concluded that the death of the old woman was accidental. 验尸官断定那个老妇人是意外死亡。
duel /ˈdjʊ(uː)əl/ *n.* 决斗;相斗	a formal fight to settle a quarrel or avenge an insult	They decided to settle their qurrel by a ***duel***. 他们决定以决斗来解决他们的纷争。
graft /grɑːft/ *v.* 嫁接	put a shoot from one tree into a slit in another tree	Peach trees can be ***grafted*** on plum trees. 桃树可以嫁接到李子树上。

WORD	MEANING	TYPICAL USE
impersonal /ɪmˈpɜːsənəl/ *adj.* 一般人称的	not influenced by personal feeling	"First come, first served" is an ***impersonal*** remark. "先到先得"是不以特定人为对象的语句。
loom /luːm/ *v.* 隐现；隐约可现	appear dimly or vaguely	A large iceberg ***loomed*** through the thick, gray fog. 从灰蒙蒙的浓雾中隐约可见一座大冰山。
peal /piːl/ *n.* 洪亮的响声；洪亮的钟声	a loud, long sound; the loud ringing of bells	As the speaker made a funny joke, ***peals*** of laughter rang through the auditorium. 当演说者讲了一个有趣的笑话时，响亮的笑声传遍了礼堂。
roundup /ˈraʊndˌʌp/ *n.* (把牲口)赶拢；聚拢	bring cattle together; a gathering	The missing cattle is discovered in the annual ***roundup***. 那头遗失的牛在一年一度的围捕中被发现。
straggle /ˈstrægl/ *v.* 散开；迷途	wander in a scattered fashion; roam; stray from the rest	The cowboys worked all night to gather the cattle that had ***straggled*** behind the rest of the herd. 牧童们工作了一整夜，聚拢那些离了群落落在后面的牛群。

WORD	MEANING	TYPICAL USE
ulterior /ʌlˈtɪərɪə(r)/ *adj.* 隐密的；未揭露的	beyond what is seen or expressed; hidden or kept secret	He was suspected of having ***ulterior*** motives for making his generous offer, but in fact his offer was from the bottom of his heart. 他的慷慨奉献被怀疑是出于不为人知的动机，但是事实上他是发自内心的。

EXERCISE 18.1 从第一部分中选出最恰当的单词，填入空格内：

1. We ______ a branch of a tree on another tree so that it will grow there permanently.
2. He was very tired, and he fell asleep in spite of ______ of thunder.
3. As the children walked along the street, they ______ behind their parents.
4. The answers from a(n) ______ of scholars and business leaders helped the President set up his policies.
5. History should be written from a(n) ______ point of view.

解答 1. graft 2. peals 3. straggled 4. roundup 5. impersonal

第二部分

WORD	MEANING	TYPICAL USE
auction /ˈɔːkʃən/ *n.* 拍卖	public sale of goods to the person who offers the most money	The old Chippendale chair was sold at a good price at the ***auction***. 那把奇彭代尔式的旧椅子在拍卖时卖了个好价钱。
calligraphy /kəˈlɪgrəfɪ/ *n.* 书法	beautiful writing by hand	The old man is famous for superb ***calligraphy***. 那个老人以出色的书法著名。
cope /kəʊp/ *v.* 应付	fight with some degree of success; get on successfully	Jean felt unable to ***cope*** with driving in heavy traffic after her accident. 琼出了车祸后，在交通拥挤时她总觉得无法顺利驾驶。
cucumber /ˈkjuːkʌmbə(r)/ *n.* 黄瓜	a long green vegetable with firm flesh seeds inside	Please get some ***cucumbers*** in the vegetable section; I'll make pickles. 请在蔬菜区买些黄瓜，我想做腌菜。

WORD	MEANING	TYPICAL USE
gruel /grʊəl/ *n.* 粥	a nearly liquid food	Her grandfather is 90 years old, and every mealtime she has to prepare ***gruel*** for him by boiling oatmeal in water. 她的祖父现年90岁高龄，每餐她都必须为他煮燕麦粥。
hustle /ˈhʌsl/ *v.* 驱赶	push or shove roughly; bustle; jostle	She ***hustled*** off her children to school and started working. 她把孩子赶去上学，然后开始工作。
maneuver /məˈnuːvə(r)/ 1. *n.* 调遣；策略；演习	1. planned movement of the armed forces; skillful plan or movement	Every year the army and the navy hold ***maneuvers*** for practice. 每年陆军和海军都进行防空演习。
2. *v.* 调遣；操纵	2. move skillfully, get by clear tricks	She ***maneuvered*** her car into a narrow parking space with ease. 她熟练地驾驶着车，开进狭窄的停车场。
plight /plaɪt/ *n.* (恶劣的)情势；苦境	a bad or dangerous situation; predicament	He was in a terrible ***plight***, trapped at the back of the cave. 他正处于恶劣的境地，被诱入洞穴的后面。

WORD	MEANING	TYPICAL USE
scoff /skɒf/ *v.* 嘲笑;嘲弄	speak or act disrespectfully; laugh at; sneer; jeer	I came to the meeting to ***scoff***, but the speaker persuaded me. 我本是来嘲弄这个会议,但被演说者劝阻了。
stun /stʌn/ *v.* 使昏迷;使目瞪口呆	knock unconscious; make senseless	She was ***stunned*** by the news of her mother's death. 她听到母亲去世的消息后惊呆了。
vulture /ˈvʌltʃə(r)/ *n.* 兀鹰	a large bird related to the eagle	A ***vulture*** usually lives on the flesh of dead animals. 兀鹰靠吃死去的动物的肉来维生。

EXERCISE 18.2 从第二部分中选出最恰当的单词,填入空格内:

1. Many people at the ______ bid on the old furniture, but he was given the contract for it.
2. Mother could not ______ with all the housework and two sick children.
3. The policemen caught the thief on the street and ______ him into their van.
4. She was in a sad ______ when her husband got ill and she had quite inadequate money for his medical expenses.
5. When we refused to use his idea, he tried to force it on us by a series of ______.

答案 1. auction 2. cope 3. hustled 4. plight 5. maneuvers

第三部分

WORD	MEANING	TYPICAL USE
bankrupt /ˈbæŋkrʌpt/ *n.* 破产者；无还债能力者	a person who is unable to pay his/her debts	After his store burned, the storekeeper became a ***bankrupt***. 商店被烧毁后，店主就破产了。
cavern /ˈkævən/ *n.* (尤指大的)洞穴；山洞	a large deep cave	It suddenly began to shower, and we took refuge in the ***cavern***. 突然下起阵雨来，我们进洞躲雨。
chrysanthemum /krɪˈsænθəməm/ *n.* 菊花	any of various types of garden plant with round flower	***Chrysanthemum*** usually bloom in fall and show great varieties in the size and color of its flower. 菊花通常在秋天开花，花的大小和颜色各不相同。
fishery /ˈfɪʃərɪ/ *n.* 渔业；渔场	the occupation of catching fish; a place for catching or breeding fish	The inhabitants of the port are occupied mainly with ***fishery***. 港口的居民们主要从事渔业。

WORD	MEANING	TYPICAL USE
gust /gʌst/ *n.* 一阵强风;(怒、笑等的)爆发	a sudden, violent rush of wind; a short outflow of feeling	In a ***gust*** of uncontrollable anger he broke the picture into pieces. 在忍无可忍的怒气中,他将图画撕成碎片。
ingratiate /ɪnˈɡreɪʃɪeɪt/ *v.* 逢迎;讨好	make (oneself) very pleasant to someone in order to gain favor	She tried to ***ingratiate*** herself with the teacher by offering some precious gifts. 她试着用珍贵的礼物来讨好老师。
munition /mjʊ(uː)ˈnɪʃən/ *n.* 军火;军需品	material used in war such as guns, shells, bombs, etc.	The reason why we lost the war was not just because of a shortage of ***munitions***. 我们打败仗的原因并不只是因为军火短缺。
prostrate /ˈprɒstreɪt/ *v.* 平卧;卧倒	lay down flat; cast down	The wretched slaves ***prostrated*** themselves before their master. 可怜的奴隶卧倒在他们的主人面前。
smolder /ˈsməʊldə(r)/ *v.* (无火苗地)阴燃;郁积	burn and smoke without flame; continue in a suppressed condition	The campfire ***smoldered*** for several hours after the blaze died down. 火焰渐熄后,营火闷燃了好几个小时。

WORD	MEANING	TYPICAL USE
tattoo /tæˈtuː/ *n.* 连续的轻敲	a series of taps or raps; beating of drums or bugles	The hail beat a loud ***tattoo*** on the windowpane. 冰雹打在窗户的玻璃上，发出乒乒乓乓的声音。
wield /wiːld/ *v.* 支配；控制	use or control skillfully; manage; control	In a democratic system it is the people that ***wield*** the power. 在民主体制中，人民掌握着权力。

EXERCISE 18.3 从第三部分中选出最恰当的单词，填入空格内：

1. He was beating a(n) ______ on the table with his fingers while singing a pop song.
2. The people's discontent ______ for years before it broke out into open rebellion.
3. While he was walking down the street, a(n) ______ of chilly wind blew his hat off.
4. We have to save our ______ to meet the enemy's attack in the near future.
5. All the captives except him ______ themselves before the conqueror.

解答 1. tatoo 2. smoldered 3. gust 4. munitions 5. prostrated

第四部分

WORD	MEANING	TYPICAL USE
allude /əˈljuːd/ *v.* 暗指;提及	refer indirectly; mention slightly; insinuate	In his letter he ***alluded*** to me a matter which I had completely forgotten. 他在信中向我提及一件我已经完全忘记了的事。
chisel /ˈtʃɪzl/ *n.* 凿子;錾子	a tool with a sharp cutting edge at the end of a strong blade	A ***chisel*** and a hammer are indispensable tools for a sculptor. 对于一个雕刻家来说,錾子和铁锤是不可缺少的工具。
cricket /ˈkrɪkɪt/ *n.* 蟋蟀	a small brown insect related to the grasshopper	Male ***crickets*** make a chirping noise by rubbing their front wings together. 雄蟋蟀凭借前翅的磨擦发出唧唧声。
flit /flɪt/ *v.* 飞跃;轻快地飞	fly or move lightly and swiftly; flutter	As we stepped into the bush, birds ***flitted*** from tree to tree. 我们走进灌木丛时,鸟儿在树间轻快地飞。

WORD	MEANING	TYPICAL USE
high-handed /ˈhaɪˈhændɪd/ *adj.* 专横的；高压的	using one's power too forcefully; domineering; autocratic	It was rather ***high-handed*** to punish the child for the accident. 为了这起意外事件而处罚孩子，真是专横。
lag /læg/ *v.* 落后；慢慢地走	fall behind; move too slowly	The child ***lagged*** behind others because he was very tired. 这个孩子因为非常疲倦而落在其他小孩后面。
naughty /ˈnɔːtɪ/ *adj.* 顽皮的；淘气的	not obedient; bad in behavior; mischievous	You ***naughty*** boy! I told you not to play on the road. 你这个顽皮的孩子！我告诉过你不要在马路上玩。
rattle /ˈrætl/ *n.* 连续短促的尖利声；碰撞声	a number of short, sharp sound	We used to hear the ***rattle*** of the milk bottles in the early morning. 我们过去常在清早听牛奶瓶乒乒乓乓的碰撞声。
soot /sʊt/ *n.* 煤烟；油烟	a black substance in the smoke	***Soot*** is caused by incomplete burning and makes smoke dark. 煤烟是由于不完全燃烧而使烟变黑造成的。

WORD	MEANING	TYPICAL USE
tributary /ˈtrɪbjʊtərɪ/ *n.* 支流；纳贡国	a stream or river that flows into a large one; a nation that pays tribute to another	The Ohio River is one of the ***tributaries*** of the Mississippi River. 俄亥俄河是密西西比河的一条支流。
undo /ˌʌnˈduː/ *v.* 1. 废弃；打消	1. cause to be as if never done; cancel or reverse; rescind	The workmen mended the road, but a heavy storm ***undid*** their work. 一场暴风雨破坏了工人们已修补好的道路。
2. 解开	2. unfasten, untie or open	The children began to ***undo*** the string round the parcel to see what was in it. 小孩们开始解开绑包裹的绳子，看看里面到底是什么东西。

EXERCISE 18.4 从第四部分中选出最恰当的单词，填入空格内：

1. We found it hard to like the new boy because of his ______ manners.
2. She did not say Mr. Smith's name, but it was clear she was ______ to him.
3. The country still ______ far behind that country in the exploration of the space.
4. The Roman Empire had many ______ around it at its golden age.
5. The teacher punished the ______ girl; she had been disobedient to her teacher.

答案 1. high-handed 2. alluding 3. lags 4. tributaries 5. naughty

第五部分

WORD	MEANING	TYPICAL USE
belabor /bɪˈleɪbə(r)/ *v.* 重打；痛击	beat vigorously; thrash	The rider ***belabored*** his tired horse with a stick. 骑马的人用鞭子狠狠地抽打那匹倦马。
circumference /səˈkʌmfərəns/ *n.* 圆周；周围	the boundary line of a circle or of certain other surfaces	After dinner they walked around the ***circumference*** of the lake. 晚饭后他们沿着湖周围散步。
devolve /dɪˈvɒlv/ *v.* 传下；授与	be handed down to someone else; be transferred	In case of failure of direct descendants, the throne ***devolves*** upon the nearest prince. 如果没有直系子孙，王位就传给最亲近的王子。
fret /fret/ *v.* 烦躁；激怒	(cause to) be continually worried and anxious	Don't ***fret*** too much; everything will be all right. 不要烦躁不安，一切都会顺利的。

WORD	MEANING	TYPICAL USE
honk /hɒŋk/ *v.* (雁)鸣叫	make the cry of wild goose	The wild geese ***honked*** high in the autumn sky. 秋日的天空中,大雁在鸣叫。
levy /ˈlevɪ/ *v.* 征集;征税	collect by authority or force	The government decided to ***levy*** a tax on tobacco; it had been free from tax. 政府决定征收烟草税,这向来是不征税的。
override /ˌəʊvəˈraɪd/ *v.* 不顾;藐视	prevail over; take no notice of	The new rule ***overrides*** all the previous ones. 新的法规不顾所有旧的规定。
rally /ˈrælɪ/ *v.* 重整;重振;集合	bring together again; come together again	The scattered soldiers were ***rallied*** in the vale for the next attack. 为了下次的出击,分散的士兵被集合在山谷中。
sprawl /ˈsprɔːl/ *v.* 仰卧;伸开四肢躺	stretch out oneself or one's limbs	Many people ***sprawled*** on the beach in their bathing suits. 许多人穿着泳衣躺在海滨。
trudge /trʌdʒ/ *v.* 跋涉;吃力地走	walk heavily, wearily or with effort	The old man ***trudged*** through the deep snow back towards home. 老人在厚厚的积雪中向家里跋涉。

EXERCISE 18.5 从第五部分中选出最恰当的单词，填入空格内：

1. The girl at the camp ______ to get the meals when the cook was sick.
2. Every point on the ______ of a circle is at the same distance from the center.
3. You must not ______ other's happiness in pursuit of your own.
4. If the president is unable to handle his duties, they ______ upon the vice-president.
5. The man concerned with his responsibilities will not be ______ about the matter of his privileges.

解答 1. rallied 2. circumference 3. override 4. devolve 5. fretted

效果检测

EXERCISE 18.6 从第二栏中选出第一栏各词的正确词意：

COLUMN I	COLUMN II
______ 1. gruel	(A) to fall behind; move too slowly
______ 2. levy	(B) a light or fire used as a signal
______ 3. munition	(C) a nearly liquid food
______ 4. lag	(D) to fight with some degree of success
______ 5. beacon	(E) to prevail over
______ 6. override	(F) the planned movement of the armed forces
______ 7. cope	(G) material used in war
______ 8. stun	(H) to bring together again
______ 9. rally	(I) to make unconscious
______ 10. maneuver	(J) to collect by authority or force

解答 1. C　2. J　3. G　4. A　5. B
6. E　7. D　8. I　9. H　10. F

EXERCISE 18.7 完整拼出下列句中所欠缺的单词,句后括号内为该词的词意:

1. When the commander is unable to handle his duties, they d______e upon the next-ranking officer. (*are handed down*)
2. He is almost exhausted now; he had to t______e about 20 miles along the rugged road. (*walk heavily and wearily*)
3. In China, c______y is a higher accomplishment than painting. (*beautiful writing by hand*)
4. When a person is declared to be a b______t by the court of law, his property is distributed among the people to whom he owes money. (*person unable to pay his debts*)
5. A c______n has three zones: the open area just inside the entrance, a twilight region and the perfectly dark interior. (*large deep cave*)
6. At the f______y we saw long trays of fish eggs under water that would turn into trouts later. (*a place for breeding fish*)
7. He is rather unfamiliar to me, but frequently calls on me with expensive gifts. I can't understand his u______r purpose for doing so. (*hidden*)
8. C______r is eaten usually in thin slices in a salad, or used to make pickles. (*long green vegetable*)
9. He insulted me in public, and I challenged him to a d______l. (*formal fight*)
10. One of the old lady's eyes resembled that of a v______e. (*large bird related to be eagle*)

解答 1. devolve 2. trudge 3. calligraphy
4. bankrupt 5. cavern 6. fishery
7. ulterior 8. Cucumber 9. duel
10. vulture

EXERCISE 18.8 找出与其他三个不相关的词：

______ 1. (A) hustle (B) bustle
(C) jostle (D) castle

______ 2. (A) disobedient (B) naughty
(C) tributary (D) mischievous

______ 3. (A) belabor (B) thrash
(C) beat (D) devolve

______ 4. (A) tatoo (B) plight
(C) adversity (D) predicament

______ 5. (A) scoff (B) loom
(C) sneer (D) jeer

______ 6. (A) insinuate (B) trudge
(C) allude (D) imply

______ 7. (A) levy (B) straggle
(C) roam (D) wander

______ 8. (A) domineering (B) autocratic
(C) ulterior (D) high-handed

______ 9. (A) undo (B) stun
(C) cancel (D) reverse

______ 10. (A) fly (B) flutter
(C) flit (D) fret

解答 1. D　2. C　3. D　4. A　5. B
6. B　7. A　8. C　9. B　10. D

EXERCISE 18.9 从下列单词中选出最恰当的词,填入空格内:

VOCABULARY LIST

gust	circumference	auction	anesthetics
rattle	ingratiate	graft	allude
fret	belabored	prostrated	scoffed

1. At a(n) ______ each thing is sold to the person who offers the most money for it.
2. The ______ of the earth is nearly 25,000 miles at the equator.
3. Some politicians tried to ______ rich or influential people so as to get more supporters.
4. After the terrible hurricane, we saw many trees ______ on the sidewalk.
5. The girl ______ at his proposal of marriage, but she married him later.
6. No one has been able to ______ together trees belonging to quite distant families.
7. Do not ______ at the train's delay; it will arrive here soon.
8. As his poor donkey became exhausted under the heavy load, the man ______ him soundly.
9. Doctors often use ______ before performing surgical operations so that patients will not feel pain.
10. Do not ask him about his failure; do not even ______ to it.

解答 1. auction　2. circumference　3. ingratiate
4. prostrated　5. scoffed　6. graft
7. fret　8. belabored　9. anesthetics
10. allude

LESSON 19

预备测验

选出最恰当的答案：

1. We can seldom see the *cavalry* in modern battlefields. It has been replaced by the ______.

   (A) infantry　　(B) armor　　(C) artillery

2. He ______ three candles with a single *puff*.

   (A) picked up　　(B) took away　　(C) blew out

3. The *surname* of John W. Smith is ______.

   (A) John　　(B) W.　　(C) Smith

4. The actress wore a black *wig* ______.

   (A) over her blond hair　　(B) around her slender waist

   (C) over her shoulders

5. The boys made *snares* to ______.

   (A) collect stamps　　(B) catch rabbits

   (C) cross the river

解答 1. B 2. C 3. C 4. A 5. B

第一部分

WORD	MEANING	TYPICAL USE
ambush /ˈæmbʊʃ/ 1. *n.* 伏兵	1. a surprise attack from a place of hiding	The soldiers lay in ***ambush***, waiting for the signal to open fire. 士兵们布下伏兵,等待开火的信号。
2. *v.* 埋伏	2. put soldiers in hiding for a surprise attack	The major ***ambushed*** his troops in the woods on both sides of the road. 少校把他的部队埋伏在马路两旁的树丛中。
brag /bræg/ *v.* 夸大;吹牛	praise oneself or what one has; boast; vaunt	He is always ***bragging*** about what he can do with a car. 他总是吹牛自己对车子有多在行。
cleanse /klenz/ *v.* 使清洁	make clean by chemical or other technical processes	Be sure that you ***cleanse*** the wound before bandaging it. 在你包扎伤口之前,要确定已消毒清洁好了。
discourse /dɪsˈkɔːs/ *n.* 演讲;论文	an orderly expression of ideas in speech or writing	The professor will deliver a ***discourse*** on the poetic style of John Keats. 那位教授将做一次有关济慈诗风的演讲。

WORD	MEANING	TYPICAL USE
foxhole /ˈfɒksˌhəʊl/ *n.* (军)散兵坑	a hole in the ground from which one or two soldiers fire at the enemy	In World War Ⅱ the general made it a point of pride to dig his own ***foxhole***. 第二次世界大战时，那位将军骄傲地强调他自己挖散兵坑。
inflammation /ˌɪnfləˈmeɪʃən/ *n.* 发炎；炎症	a painful, hot, red swelling of some part of the body	The ***inflammation*** of his knee made it difficult for him to walk. 他膝盖发炎，走路都困难。
lever /ˈliːvə; ˈlevə(r)/ *n.* 杠杆	a bar used for lifting something heavy	The huge stone is so heavy that we cannot move it without a ***lever***. 那块巨石很重，我们如果不用杠杆就无法移动。
notation /nəʊˈteɪʃən/ *n.* 科学或艺术方面所使用的一套符号	a system of signs and symbols used in the sciences or arts	In arithmetic we use the Arabic ***notation*** (1, 2, 3 and so on) or sometimes the Roman ***notation*** (Ⅰ, Ⅱ, Ⅲ and so on). 在算术方面我们用阿拉伯数字(1,2,3 等)，或有时也用罗马数字(Ⅰ,Ⅱ,Ⅲ等)。

WORD	MEANING	TYPICAL USE
ransom /ˈrænsəm/ *n.* 赎金;赎回	a price paid or demanded before a captive is set free	A large ***ransom*** was asked for the safe return of the child. 需交纳一笔巨额的赎金,小孩才能安全地赎回。
sop /sɒp/ *v.* 浸于液体中	dip or soak	He ***sopped*** a piece of bread in milk; it was too crisp to eat. 他把一片面包浸于牛奶中;它太干了没法吃。
tingle /ˈtɪŋgl/ *v.* 有刺痛之感	have a pricking, stinging feeling	His cheek ***tingled*** from the slap she had given him. 她给了他一个耳光,他脸上火辣辣的。

EXERCISE 19.1 从第一部分中选出最恰当的单词,填入空格内:

1. The priest delivered a long ______ upon the evils of untrustfulness.
2. The two scientists use different ______ for the same objects.
3. The room is too dirty. Please ______ the room with soap and water.
4. As the enemy's artillery began to fire, the soldiers jumped into their ______.
5. Her ears were ______ with cold after ice-skating for an hour.

解答 1. discourse 2. notations 3. cleanse 4. foxholes 5. tingling

第二部分

WORD	MEANING	TYPICAL USE
armament /ˈɑːməmənt/ *n.* 兵力;军势	war equipment and supplies; equipment of the armed forces	A large percentage of the budget is for ***armaments***. 大部分预算是用于国防。
brunch /brʌntʃ/ *n.* 早午餐	a combination of breakfast and lunch	On Sunday she gets up late in the morning and has a ***brunch*** around 10:30. 星期天她起得很晚,10:30左右吃早午餐。
coffin /ˈkɒfɪn/ *n.* 棺;柩	a box into which a dead person is put to be buried; casket	His ***coffin*** was laid to rest in a deep grave. 他的棺柩被安放在一个深深的墓穴中。
envision /ɪnˈvɪʒən/ *v.* 预想;想象	see in the mind as a future possibility; envisage	The mother ***envisioned*** her little girl as a prima ballerina. 那母亲想象她的小女儿是一个芭蕾舞团的首席女星。

WORD	MEANING	TYPICAL USE
gangster /ˈgæŋstə(r)/ *n.* 歹徒;匪盗	a member of a gang of criminals or rogues	The ***gangster*** who had taken part in the robbery was arrested by the police. 参加抢劫的盗匪被警方逮捕了。
illegible /ɪˈledʒəbl/ *adj.* (字迹)难读的	very hard or impossible to read; not legible	The ink had faded so that many words were ***illegible***. 墨水褪色了,所以许多词不易辨认。
malcontent /ˈmælkənˌtent/ *n.* 不平者;不满者	a discontented or rebellious person	The rebellion was started by some ***malcontents*** who had been dissatisfied with the policy. 叛乱是一些向来对政策不满的人发动的。
pavilion /pəˈvɪljən/ *n.* (运动会的)休息处;亭子	a large tent or a light building used for shelter or pleasure	We will take a rest in the ***pavilion*** until the game starts. 比赛开始之前我们在休息处休息一下。
shroud /ʃraʊd/ *n.* 遮蔽物;幕;寿衣	something that covers or conceals; a cloth to be wrapped	The prisoners escaped out of the jail under the ***shroud*** of night. 在夜色的掩护下,囚犯逃离了监狱。

WORD	MEANING	TYPICAL USE
spurt /spɜːt/ *v.* 喷出；涌出	flow out suddenly or violently; gush; spout; squirt	The room soon filled with the water ***spurting*** from the broken pipe. 水管破裂后房间内顿时充满了水。
varnish /ˈvɑːnɪʃ/ *n.* 油漆	liquid which gives a clear, hard, shiny surface	He put ***varnish*** on the table top to protect it, but somebody has scratched it. 他在桌面上漆上油漆以保护它，但有人在上面乱划。

EXERCISE 19.2 从第二部分中选出最恰当的单词，填入空格内：

1. The architect looked at the plans and ______ the finished house.
2. They prayed to God for the dead before lowering the ______ into the grave.
3. The strike was caused by a few ______ who felt they had been ignored when the promotions were made.
4. Do not put the hot plate on the table; it may spoil the ______ on it.
5. Blood will ______ out from the wound when the artery is cut off.

解答 1. envisioned 2. coffin 3. malcontents 4. varnish 5. spurt

第三部分

WORD	MEANING	TYPICAL USE
ballad /ˈbæləd/ *n.* 民歌；民谣	a poem or song that tells a story; a popular love song	Many old ***ballads*** are sung to new words. 许多古老的民歌配上了新词。
butt /bʌt/ 1. *n.* 粗大的一头；残端	1. the thicker end of anything; the end that is left	The ***butt*** of pipe stuck out from the wall where the sink had been removed. 水管粗大的一端从水槽给移走了的那片墙突出来。
2. *v.* 撞；以头或角撞	2. push or hit with the head or horns	The goat ***butted*** the boy and knocked him down. 山羊用角撞那男孩，把他撞倒了。
consul /ˈkɒnsəl/ *n.* 领事	an official who protects or helps his/her citizen in a foreign country	You will have to call the ***consul*** before your passport is expired. 在你的护照期满之前得打电话给领事。
enshrine /ɪnˈʃraɪn/ *v.* 铭记	enclose in a shrine; keep sacred; cherish	Memories of happier days were ***enshrined*** in the old man's heart. 老人心中铭记着快乐的时光。

WORD	MEANING	TYPICAL USE
gobble /ˈgɒbl/ *v.* 狼吞虎咽	eat fast and greedily; gulp; devour	He ***gobbled*** the ice cream so fast that he got a headache. 他狼吞虎咽地吃冰淇淋,结果头痛了起来。
harangue /həˈræŋ/ *n.* 长篇激烈的演说	a loud or long speech; a noisy speech; tirade	We had to listen to a long ***harangue*** about our own shortcomings. 我们必须去听有关我们缺点的长篇大论。
mow /məʊ; maʊ/ *v.* 割	cut down with a machine or a scythe	He spent the whole afternoon ***mowing*** the grass in the back-yard. 他花了整个下午的时间来割后院的草坪。
pilgrim /ˈpɪlgrɪm/ *n.* 朝圣者	one who travels to a holy place for religious purpose	In the Middle Ages, many people used to go as ***pilgrims*** to Jerusalem and to other holy places in Europe. 在中世纪,许多人常到耶路撒冷或其他欧洲宗教圣地去朝拜。
shear /ʃɪə(r)/ *v.* 修剪	remove from by cutting; cut off	The farmers ***sheared*** the wool from the sheep. 农夫从羊身上剪羊毛。

WORD	MEANING	TYPICAL USE
strangle /ˈstræŋgl/ *v.* 扼杀；勒死	killed by pressing the throat; choke; stifle	He ***strangled*** her to death by a cord put around her neck. 他用细绳绕在她的脖子上，将她勒死了。
walnut /ˈwɔːlnət/ *n.* 核桃	a large, round, eatable nut	The kernel of the ***walnut*** is eaten by itself or used in cakes or cookies. 核桃仁可以直接食用，也可以掺进蛋糕、饼干中食用。

EXERCISE 19.3 从第三部分中选出最恰当的单词，填入空格内：

1. The ______ who came from various countries in Europe entered the church to pray.
2. Let me show you how to strike the enemy with the ______ of your rifle.
3. The old man sang ______ of the clan's heroes, often to the tune of a folk song.
4. He joined the army two months ago. When I met him yesterday he looked very strange with his closely ______ head.
5. His high, stiff collar was so tight that it was almost ______ his neck.

解答 1. pilgrims 2. butt 3. ballads 4. sheared (shorn) 5. strangling

第四部分

WORD	MEANING	TYPICAL USE
beaver /ˈbiːvə(r)/ *n.* 海狸	an animal with soft fur and feet adapted to swimming	***Beavers*** are noted for their skill in building dams across streams. 海狸以会在溪流中筑水坝而闻名。
cavalry /ˈkævəlrɪ/ *n.* 骑兵	soldiers who fight on horseback	The ***cavalry*** is much superior in mobility to the infantry. 骑兵的机动性远远优于步兵。
creak /kriːk/ *v.* 嘎吱嘎吱作响	make a sharp, high sound; squeak; grate	The floor ***creaked*** as he stepped on a loose board. 当他踩到了一块松动的板子时，地板吱吱作响。
fir /fɜː(r)/ *n.* 冷杉；枞树	an evergreen tree belonging to the pine family	The ***fir*** remains green all year and its needles are distributed evenly around the branch. 枞树终年常绿，它的针状树叶均匀地分布在树枝上。
hangar /ˈhæŋə(r)/ *n.* 飞机棚；飞机库	a garage for airplanes	During the heavy storm, airplanes should be kept in the ***hangar***. 暴风雨来临时，飞机应被存放在机库中。

WORD	MEANING	TYPICAL USE
kernel /ˈkɜːnəl/ *n.* 中心;要点;核仁	the soft part of a seed; core; nucleus	The ***kernel*** of the argument is who discovered the islands first. 争执的要点是谁最先发现了那些岛屿。
measles /ˈmiːzlz/ *n.* 麻疹	a contagious disease of infants caused by virus	What seems to be a cold often turns out to be the beginning of ***measles***. 看似感冒的症状结果常常是麻疹的开始。
puff /pʌf/ *n.* 吹;喷	a short, quick blast of air, smoke, etc.	With a huge ***puff*** the balloon was blown up and then suddenly burst. 猛地吹了一大口气后,汽球膨胀起来,然后突然爆了。
sleet /sliːt/ *n.* 霰	partly frozen rain; snow mixed with rain	***Sleet*** forms when rain falls through a layer of cold air. 雨穿过一层冷空气便形成了霰。
surname /ˈsɜːneɪm/ *n.* 姓	a last name; family name	Smith is a very common English ***surname***. 史密斯是一个很普通的英国姓氏。

WORD	MEANING	TYPICAL USE
wig /wɪɡ/ *n.* 假发	head-covering of false hair	Women often wear ***wigs*** over their real hair for beauty or fashion. 女人常为了漂亮或赶时髦而戴假发。

EXERCISE 19.4 从第四部分中选出最恰当的单词,填入空格内:

1. Would you please repair the door? It always ______ whenever I open it.
2. This beautiful Christmas tree was made of a small ______.
3. The ______ of his religious teaching is love for all men.
4. It is very dangerous to drive a car as the road is covered with ______.
5. ______ is much more common in children than in grown-ups.

答案 1. creaks 2. fir 3. kernel
4. sleet 5. Measles

第五部分

WORD	MEANING	TYPICAL USE
bleach /bliːtʃ/ *v.* 去色;漂白	make white by using chemicals or exposing to sunlight	***Bleached*** bones lay on the hot sands of the desert. 白骨曝在炎热的沙漠中。

WORD	MEANING	TYPICAL USE
chariot /ˈtʃærɪət/ *n.* 两轮马车	a two-wheeled carriage pulled by horses	***Chariots*** were used in ancient times for fighting, racing and in processions. 古时候两轮马车用于打仗、赛马和行列。
crutch /krʌtʃ/ *n.* 拐杖	a support to help a lame person walk	He has been crippled since he broke his leg. Now he can't walk without a pair of ***crutches***. 他腿断了之后脚就跛了，现在走路一定要用拐杖。
flirt /flɜːt/ *v.* 调情；玩弄	play at love; make love without meaning it	She ***flirted*** with many men but loved only one. 她和许多男子调情，却只爱一个。
gull /gʌl/ *n.* 鸥	a graceful seabird living on or near sea	They were very pleased to see some ***gulls*** flying in the sky, full of hope that they would soon get ashore. 他们看到天空中飞翔的海鸥很高兴，心里充满了能够在不久之后靠岸的希望。

WORD	MEANING	TYPICAL USE
kit /kɪt/ *n.* 装备	a set of tools, instruments, supplies, etc.	When I bought a new car, a ***kit*** of tools came with it. 我买了一辆新车，该车附带一套工具箱。
morsel /ˈmɔːsəl/ *n.* 一口；少量	a small bite; a small quantity; fragment; bit	The hungry children did not leave a ***morsel*** of food on their plates. 饥肠辘辘的孩子们把盘里的食物吃得精光。
prototype /ˈprəʊtətaɪp/ *n.* 原型	the first or primary type of anything; original or model	The strange mechanical device is the ***prototype*** of modern cars. 这奇怪的机械装置就是现代汽车的原型。
snare /snɛə/ *n.* 陷阱	a trap for catching an animal	They set a ***snare*** for rabbits on the hill, but unfortunately a wild cat was caught by it. 他们在山上设了一个陷阱抓野兔，却不幸地抓到了一只野猫。
trigger /ˈtrɪɡə(r)/ 1. *n.* 扳机	1. a device which, when pressed, starts an action	When you squeeze the ***trigger***, a round or rounds of ammunition are fired. 当你扣动扳机时，一发或几发子弹就射出了。

WORD	MEANING	TYPICAL USE
2. *v.* 引起；促使	2. set off; start; initiate	When the burglar tripped the wire it ***triggered*** an alarm. 窃贼绊到了铁丝网，引起警铃大作。
weir /wɪə(r)/ *n.* 堰；水坝	a small dam or wall erected across a river	The ***weir*** across the river stops or controls the flow of the river above it. 河上的水坝可以制止或控制上面河水的流量。

EXERCISE 19.5 从第五部分中选出最恰当的一个单词，填入空格内：

1. The hollowed log used by primitive people is the ______ of the modern ship.
2. The girl was very hungry, and consumed the oatmeal to the last ______.
3. She doesn't like going to parties because her husband always ______ with every girl in the room.
4. The sun will ______ the cloth and make it whiter.
5. Hold your breath while squeezing the ______, or you cannot hit the target.

答案 1. prototype 2. morsel 3. flirts 4. bleach 5. trigger

效果检测

EXERCISE 19.6 从第二栏中选出第一栏各词的正确词意：

COLUMN I	COLUMN II
______ 1. consul	(A) a support to help a lame person walk
______ 2. mow	(B) snow mixed with rain
______ 3. chariot	(C) a combination of breakfast and lunch
______ 4. hangar	(D) to eat fast and greedily
______ 5. sleet	(E) a graceful seabird
______ 6. armament	(F) a two-wheeled carriage pulled by horses
______ 7. gull	(G) to cut down with a machine
______ 8. crutch	(H) war equipment and supplies
______ 9. brunch	(I) a garage for airplanes
______ 10. gobble	(J) an official who protects or helps his citizens in a foreign country

解答 1. J　2. G　3. F　4. I　5. B
6. H　7. E　8. A　9. C　10. D

EXERCISE 19.7 完整拼出下列句中所欠缺的单词，句后括号内为该词的词意：

1. You can move the huge stone by using only a short l______r. (*bar used for lifting something heavy*)
2. It is unpleasant to hear one b______g about his own abilities, achievements or possessions. (*praise oneself*)
3. The hinges on the door c______k; they need oiling. (*make a sharp, high sound*)

4. The angry senator arose and delivered a h______e. (*long*, *loud speech*)
5. He wouldn't do such silly things if he had a m______l of sense. (*small quantity*; *bit*)
6. The detective used marked money as a s______e for the thief. (*trap*)
7. They built a w______r in order to convey the stream to the mill. (*small dam*)
8. The soldier slowly pressed the t______r to shoot the rifle. (*device which*, *when pressed*, *causes firing*)
9. The boy's handwriting was so bad that his letter to his mother was i______e. (*impossible to read*)
10. The i______n of her elbow made it impossible for her to swim. (*painful*, *hot red swelling*)

解答 1. lever 2. brag 3. creak 4. harangue
5. morsel 6. snare 7. weir 8. trigger
9. illegible 10. inflammation

EXERCISE 19.8 找出与其他三个不相关的词:

______ 1. (A) gobble (B) bleach
(C) devour (D) gulp

______ 2. (A) weir (B) core
(C) nucleus (D) kernel

______ 3. (A) clarify (B) cleanse
(C) purify (D) pledge

______ 4. (A) drag (B) sop
(C) dip (D) soak

______ 5. (A) stifle (B) choke
(C) flirt (D) strangle

_____ 6. (A) brag (B) vaunt
(C) fawn (D) boast

_____ 7. (A) tingle (B) shear
(C) prick (D) sting

_____ 8. (A) creak (B) squeak
(C) grate (D) allot

_____ 9. (A) spout (B) squat
(C) squirt (D) spurt

_____ 10. (A) rogue (B) gangster
(C) villain (D) ballad

解答					
	1. B	2. A	3. D	4. A	5. C
	6. C	7. B	8. D	9. B	10. D

EXERCISE 19.9 从下列单词中选出最适当的词，填入空格内：

VOCABULARY LIST

ransom	measles	butt	ambush
prototype	notation	shroud	enshrined
levied	strangled	honked	envisioned

1. The crude craft which the Wright brothers made in 1903 was the _____ of the modern airplane.
2. The basic human rights are _____ in the constitution.
3. Many people went to America because they _____ a better future there for themselves and their children.
4. Indians often trapped their enemies by _____, instead of meeting them in open battle.
5. After smoking do not throw away the _____ on the street; you will be heavily fined.

6. Music has a special system of ______, and so does chemistry.
7. The sufferer of ______ usually has a high fever and small red spots on the skin.
8. She was almost ______ on a piece of meat that caught in her throat.
9. The kidnappers asked a large ______ for the return of the little girl.
10. The enemy seems to attack our defense positions tonight under the ______ of darkness.

解答 1. prototype 2. enshrined 3. envisioned
4. ambush 5. butt 6. notation
7. measles 8. strangled 9. ransom
10. shroud

LESSON 20

预备测验

选出最恰当的答案：

1. The court *annulled* the marriage because it was ______.
   (A) legitimate (B) illegal (C) incomplete
2. The *excess* of imports over exports will ______ the national economy.
   (A) harm (B) stabilize (C) boost
3. It is considered to be ______ to read somebody else's *diary*.
   (A) generous (B) impolite (C) dangerous
4. He *augmented* his wages by ______ his free time.
   (A) wasting (B) enlarging (C) working in
5. ______ persons are *averse* to punishing people.
   (A) Critical (B) Indifferent (C) Generous

解答 1. B 2. A 3. B 4. C 5. C

第一部分

WORD	MEANING	TYPICAL USE
access /ˈækses/ *n.* 接近权；享用权；通道；接近	the right or privilege to approach, enter or use; entrance; approach	The students have ***access*** to the library only in the afternoon. 学生们只能在下午使用图书馆。

WORD	MEANING	TYPICAL USE
excess /ˈekses/ *n.* 过量	more than enough; surplus; overabundance	Last year we had several floods; we had an ***excess*** of rain. 去年发了几次洪水，我们的雨水过多了。
adapt /əˈdæpt/ *v.* 使适合；使适应	make suitable; adjust; fit	Long ago Eskimos learned how to ***adapt*** to the cold to live in the Arctic Region. 很久以前，爱斯基摩人为了住在北极地区便去学习如何适应严寒。
adopt /əˈdɒpt/ *v.* 采用；采纳	take as one's own; accept formally	The club ***adopted*** a new set of rules concerning its membership. 那俱乐部采用一套新的会员资格规定。
adverse /ədˈvɜːs, ˈædvɜːs/ *adj.* 有敌意的；敌对的	unfriendly in purpose; hostile; injurious	His ***adverse*** criticism didn't upset me, but encouraged me. 他恶意的批评并未使我气馁，反而激励了我。
averse /əˈvɜːs/ *adj.* 不愿意的；反对的	not liking; opposed; unwilling	My parents are ***averse*** to our picnic plan; they don't approve of it. 我的父母反对我们的野餐计划；他们不同意这计划。

WORD	MEANING	TYPICAL USE
affect /əˈfekt/ *v.* 影响	have an effect upon; influence; change	The government decision whether to continue the project will ***affect*** the future of our national economy. 政府是否继续进行该项计划的决定会影响我国未来的经济。
effect /ɪˈfekt/ *n.* 结果	something made to happen by a person or thing; result; consequence	I have warned him to drive slowly several times, but it doesn't have any ***effect*** at all. 我好几次警告他开慢一点,可是一点用也没有。
affectation /ˌæfekˈteɪʃən/ *n.* 虚饰;假装	an artificial way of talking or acting; show; pretense	The new secretary is sincere and quiet without ***affectation***. 那位新秘书真诚、安静,且不做作。
affection /əˈfekʃən/ *n.* 爱	gentle, lasting love as of a parent's for its child; fondness; tenderness	His gentleness and kind ways increased his colleagues' ***affection*** for him. 他温和且慈祥的态度增加了同事们对他的好感。

EXERCISE 20.1 从第一部分中选出最恰当的单词,填入空格内:

1. The ______ of losses over profits will ruin the business.
   (A) access (B) excess
2. The man ______ an old car engine to drive his boat.
   (A) adapted (B) adopted
3. An unbalanced diet has an ______ effect upon health.
   (A) adverse (B) averse
4. This medicine will have a miraculous ______ on you.
   (A) affect (B) effect
5. Nothing is greater than mothers' ______ for their children.
   (A) affectation (B) affection

解答 1. B 2. B 3. A 4. B 5. B

第二部分

WORD	MEANING	TYPICAL USE
allusion /əˈljuːʒən/ *n.* 间接提及;暗示	indirect reference; hint; suggestion; insinuation	The preacher likes to make an ***allusion*** to Homer while preaching. 那牧师在传道时喜欢间接提到荷马。
illusion /ɪˈljuːʒən/ *n.* 错觉;幻影	a false impression; misleading appearance	The white walls create the ***illusion*** that the room is very large. 白色的墙壁产生一种错觉,好像这房间很大。

WORD	MEANING	TYPICAL USE
annual /ˈænjʊəl/ *adj.* 一年一次的	coming once a year; living only one year or season	My birthday party is the biggest ***annual*** event of my family. 我的生日聚会是我家一年一度最盛大的事。
annul /əˈnʌl/ *v.* 取消；宣告作废	make void; cancel; nullify	The judge ***annulled*** the contract because one of the signers was too young. 由于签署人中有一位年纪太轻，法官宣告这个合同无效。
appraise /əˈpreɪz/ *v.* 估价；评价	estimate the value, amount, quality or merit of; judge; rate	The couple ***appraised*** the house carefully before offering to buy it. 那对夫妻在出价买那房子之前仔细地估过价。
apprise /əˈpraɪz/ *v.* 报告；通知	give notice to; inform; notify	The club members were immediately ***apprised*** of his change of plans. 很快，俱乐部的会员们被告知他改变了计划。

WORD	MEANING	TYPICAL USE
argument /ˈɑːgjuːmənt/ *n.* 辩论；争论	a discussion by persons who disagree; dispute; debate	We should try to settle the matter by ***argument***, not by fighting. 我们该试着用辩论来解决这件事，而不是打架。
augment /ɔːgˈment/ *v.* 增大；增加	make greater in size, number, amount or degree; enlarge; increase	The king ***augmented*** his power by taking over rights that had belonged to the nobles. 国王接管了贵族们的权力，以扩张自己的势力。
assure /əˈʃʊə(r)/ *v.* 使相信，使确信	tell positively or confidently; guarantee; convince	The man ***assured*** himself that the bridge was safe before crossing it. 在过桥前那人先确定那座桥是安全的。
insure /ɪnˈʃʊə(r)/ *v.* 1. 投保	1. guard against loss or harm	He ***insured*** his car against accident, theft, and fire. 他给车子投了意外险、失窃险和火险。
2. 使确实	2. make sure; ensure	Don't forget to check your work to ***insure*** its accuracy. 不要忘记检查你的工作，以确认无误。

EXERCISE 20.2 从第二部分中选出最恰当的单词,填入空格内:

1. It was an ______ caused by the dim lights that made me think I saw a man in the shadows.
   (A) allusion (B) illusion
2. An ______ plant lives only one year or season.
   (A) annual (B) annul
3. We were ______ that they would arrive before noon.
   (A) appraised (B) apprised
4. His strong ______ persuaded us to accept his conclusions.
   (A) arguments (B) augments
5. After the fire, the captain of the ship ______ the passengers that there was no more danger.
   (A) assured (B) insured

解答 1. B 2. A 3. B 4. A 5. A

第三部分

WORD	MEANING	TYPICAL USE
bandage /ˈbændɪdʒ/ *n.* 绷带	a strip of cloth used in binding up and dressing a wound	The doctor tied up the patient's broken ankle with a ***bandage***. 医生用绷带把病人摔折的脚脖子包起来。

WORD	MEANING	TYPICAL USE
bondage /ˈbɒndɪdʒ/ *n.* 奴役;囚禁	lack of freedom; slavery; servitude	They seem to love ***bondage*** more than liberty. 他们好像爱奴役胜过爱自由。
carton /ˈkɑːtən/ *n.* 纸盒	a box made of cardboard or pasteboard	Pack the books in a small ***carton*** to carry it easily. 为了便于携带,要把书用小纸盒包起来。
cartoon /kɑːˈtuːn/ *n.* 漫画	a drawing of persons, things or events in an amusing way	Political ***cartoons*** often represent the U. S. as a tall man with chin whiskers, called Uncle Sam. 政治性的漫画通常用一个高大、有胡子的山姆大叔形象来代表美国。
censor /ˈsensə(r)/ 1. *n.* 检查员(检查新闻、书籍、戏剧、电影、广播等)	1. a person who examines books, plays, letters, etc, to prohibit what seems objectionable	The novel was banned by the ***censor*** as likely to stir up suspicion of the government among the readers. 审查员查禁了那本小说,因为它会煽动读者对政府产生怀疑。
2. *v.* 审查;检查	2. prohibit, suppress or remove allegedly objectionable material	All news is being rigorously ***censored***. 所有新闻正在接受严格审查。

WORD	MEANING	TYPICAL USE
censure /ˈsenʃə(r)/ *v.* 责难；非难	reprimand; blame; denounce	The principal of the school ***censured*** the students for their rude behavior. 校长指责学生们无礼的行为。
collision /kəˈlɪʒən/ *n.* 猛烈相撞	a vident rushing against; clash; conflict	Many people were killed in the ***collision*** between the bus and the car. 公共汽车和汽车相撞，许多人丧生了。
collusion /kəˈluːʒən/ *n.* 共谋；串骗；勾结	a secret agreement or some wrong or harmul purpose; conspiracy	The leaders of the ***collusion*** against the government were caught and punished. 阴谋反对政府的领导者被抓住且被惩罚。
confidant /ˌkɒnfɪˈdænt/ *n.* 密友，知己	a close friend	I have only one ***confidant*** to whom I can tell my secrets. 我只有一个可以诉说秘密的知己。
confident /ˈkɒnfɪdənt/ *adj.* 确信的；确定的	firmly believing; certain; sure	The doctor felt ***confident*** that his patient would recover from pneumonia. 那医生确信他的病人的肺炎会痊愈。

EXERCISE 20.3 从第三部分中选出最恰当的单词,填入空格内:

1. According to the Bible, Moses led Israelites out of ______ from Egypt.
   (A) bandage (B) bondage
2. Sir Max Beerborn made ______ of many prominent politicians, artists and writers.
   (A) cartons (B) cartoons
3. The employer ______ him for neglecting his work.
   (A) censored (B) censured
4. There was a ______ of interests on how to spend the club's money.
   (A) collision (B) collusion
5. The politician spoke to the voters in a ______ voice.
   (A) confidant (B) confident

解答 1. B 2. B 3. B 4. A 5. B

第四部分

WORD	MEANING	TYPICAL USE
consul /ˈkɒnsəl/ *n.* 领事	a foreign-based government official below the rank of ambassador	I am Swedish. Is there a Swedish ***consul*** in Omaha? 我是瑞典人。奥马哈有没有瑞典领事?

WORD	MEANING	TYPICAL USE
council /ˈkaʊnsəl/ *n.* 会议	a group of people organized to deliberate or rule; meeting; conference; assembly	The ***council*** of ministers advised the king to dismiss the general. 内阁建议国王将那个将军免职。
counsel /ˈkaʊnsəl/ *n.* 1. 劝告;忠告	1. advice; recommendation; opinion	The young man refused to listen to the old man's ***counsel***. 年轻人拒绝听从那老人的忠告。
2. 律师或法律顾问	2. a lawyer or adviser	The murder suspect refused to answer the questions on the advice of his ***counsel***. 谋杀案的嫌疑犯因其律师的建议而拒绝回答问题。
dairy /ˈdɛərɪ/ *n.* 乳牛场	a farm or barn where milk cows are kept; a place where milk and milk products are prepared and sold	The Hopkinses run the biggest ***dairy*** farm in the state of Arizona. 霍普金斯家族经营着亚利桑那州最大的乳牛场。
diary /ˈdaɪərɪ/ *n.* 日记	a daily record or jounal	It is very rewarding to keep a ***diary*** of daily happenings. 写日记记下每天发生的事是很有用的。

WORD	MEANING	TYPICAL USE
decease /dɪˈsiːs/ *n.* 死亡	an act or fact of dying; death	Upon his ***decease*** all his properties passed to his wife. 他死后所有的财产都遗留给了太太。
disease /dɪˈziːz/ *n.* 疾病	sickness; illness	Measles and chicken pox are two ***diseases*** of childhood. 麻疹和水痘是两种儿童疾病。
decent /ˈdiːsənt/ *adj.* 适合的;得体的	suitable; respectable; socially acceptable	It is not ***decent*** to laugh at a crippled person. 嘲笑一个跛脚的人是不对的。
descent /dɪˈsent/ *n.* 降下;降落	coming down from a higher to a lower place	The road makes a sharp ***descent*** just around the corner. 那条路在转角处形成一个陡峭的斜坡。
dissent /dɪˈsent/ 1. *v.* 不同意	1. differ; disagree	The three justices ***dissented*** from the Supreme Court's decision. 那三位法官不同意最高法庭的判决。

WORD	MEANING	TYPICAL USE
2. *n.* 异议	2. difference of opinion; disagreement	***Dissent*** among the senior members was the main cause of the disintegration of the club. 资深会员间的分歧是造成俱乐部分裂的主要原因。

EXERCISE 20.4 从第四部分中选出最恰当的单词,填入空格内:

1. A ______ looks after the business interests of his own country and protects citizens of his country who are traveling or living there.
   (A) counsel　(B) consul　(C) council
2. My family buys milk and ice cream at a local ______.
   (A) dairy　(B) diary
3. Many ______ are caused by bacteria; cleanliness helps prevent them.
   (A) deceases　(B) diseases
4. The ______ of the balloon was more rapid than its rise had been.
   (A) decent　(B) descent　(C) dissent

解答　1. B　2. A　3. B　4. B

效果检测

EXERCISE 20.5 从第二栏中选出第一栏各词的正确词意：

COLUMN Ⅰ	COLUMN Ⅱ
______ 1. access	(A) coming down from a higher to a lower place
______ 2. excess	(B) the right to enter
______ 3. adverse	(C) prohibit allegedly objectionable material
______ 4. averse	(D) more than enough
______ 5. appraise	(E) estimate the value of
______ 6. apprise	(F) not liking
______ 7. censor	(G) unfriendly in purpose; injurious
______ 8. censure	(H) reprimand; blame
______ 9. descent	(I) difference of opinion
______ 10. dissent	(J) give notice to

解答 1. B　2. D　3. G　4. F　5. E
6. J　7. C　8. H　9. A　10. I

EXERCISE 20.6 读下面的句子，选出句中斜体词所代表的意义：

______ 1. Most animals easily *adjust* themselves to the weather and surroundings.

(A) adapt　　(B) adopt

______ 2. The disease *influenced* his mind so that he lost his memory completely.

(A) affected　　(B) effected

______ 3. It's not good to make a personal *insinuation* to anyone.

(A) allusion　　(B) illusion

______ 4. A teacher should be able to *estimate* ability and achievement in students.

(A) appraise (B) apprise

______ 5. It is quite certain that a *clash* with congress will ruin the government's plans.

(A) collision (B) collusion

解答 1. A 2. A 3. A 4. A 5. A

EXERCISE 20.7 找出与斜体词的意义最接近的单词:

______ 1. cause and *effect*

(A) reason (B) consequence

(C) condition (D) influence

______ 2. *decent* suit

(A) respectable (B) tight

(C) loose (D) untidy

______ 3. the Chinese *consul*

(A) resident (B) close friend

(C) lawyer (D) foreign-based official

______ 4. plaintiff's *counsel*

(A) witness (B) lawyer

(C) judge (D) prosecutor

______ 5. *confident* voice

(A) faint (B) loud

(C) certain (D) clear

______ 6. candy *carton*

(A) box (B) drawing

(C) taste (D) sweetness

______ 7. *adopt* children

(A) educate (B) take as one's own

(C) adjust (D) control the number of

______ 8. *adverse* conditions

(A) unfavorable (B) suitable

(C) acceptable (D) regretful

______ 9. mother's *affection*

(A) prejudice (B) fondness

(C) chore (D) understanding

______ 10. optical *illusion*

(A) indirect suggestion (B) distant view

(C) sudden disturbance (D) false impression

解答 1. B 2. A 3. D 4. B 5. C
6. A 7. B 8. A 9. B 10. D

EXERCISE 20.8 从下列单词中选出最恰当的词,填入空格内:

VOCABULARY LIST

collusion	adapt	argument	illusion
access	decease	consul	affectation
insure	confidant	adverse	apprised

1. The general's sudden ______ left the army without a leader.
2. It's not easy to approach the building. The only ______ to that building is along that muddy track.
3. One of the striking facts of nature is the ability of living things to ______ themselves to any environment on earth.
4. I believe the judge is biased against us. He gave us a(n) ______ decision on the case.

5. Her roughness is but a(n) ______; she is really a quiet, gentle girl.
6. John told me that the teacher had ______ us there would be a test on Monday.
7. He won the ______ against the other members of the association by producing figures to prove his point.
8. When you mail a package with valuable items, it is safe to ______ it against theft and damage.
9. The two men made the ______ to steal the jewels and sell them to a jeweler in another country.
10. John talked about his personal matters with his ______.

解答 1. decease 2. access 3. adapt
4. adverse 5. affectation 6. apprised
7. argument 8. insure 9. collusion
10. confidant

LESSON 21

预备测验

选出最恰当的答案：

1. The mechanic *disassembled* the car to ______ it.
   (A) buy (B) sell (C) repair
2. A *drought* of three months ______ the wheat.
   (A) ruined (B) helped (C) ripened
3. The boy gave an *ingenuous* account of his acts, ______ nothing.
   (A) discarding (B) telling (C) concealing
4. The abolitionists felt a *moral* responsibility to ______ the slaves.
   (A) capture (B) free (C) trade
5. The driver was *prosecuted* for his ______ driving.
   (A) skillful (B) careful (C) reckless

解答 1. C 2. A 3. C 4. B 5. C

第一部分

WORD	MEANING	TYPICAL USE
desert 1. /ˈdezət/ *n.* 沙漠	1. an arid area	Lawrence rode a camel across the ***desert*** on an exploring expedition. 劳伦斯骑着骆驼横穿沙漠，从事探险。

WORD	MEANING	TYPICAL USE
2. /dɪˈzɜːt/ *v.* 遗弃	2. abandon; forsake	He had intended to ***desert*** his wife and children, but changed his mind. 他原来想遗弃妻子和孩子们，但是又改变了主意。
dessert /dɪˈzɜːt/ *n.* 餐后的甜点心	a sweet course at the end of a meal	Strawberry pie is one of my most favorite ***desserts***. 草莓派是我最喜爱的餐后甜点之一。
disassemble /ˌdɪsəˈsembl/ *v.* 分解	take apart; take to pieces	Many students know how to ***disassemble*** the radio, but few know how to put it together. 很多学生知道如何拆开收音机，却很少有人知道如何把它组装起来。
dissemble /dɪˈsembl/ *v.* 隐藏；伪装	hide (one's true feelings, intentions, etc.); disguise	She tried to ***dissemble*** her anger with a smile on her face. 她试图用微笑来掩盖怒火。

WORD	MEANING	TYPICAL USE
draught, draft /drɑːft/ *n.* 草稿	the first rough written form of anything; a rough plan	I've made a first ***draught*** of my speech for Friday, but it still needs a lot of work. 我已经拟好星期五的演说草稿，但它仍需要进行大量修改。
drought /draʊt/ *n.* 久旱	a long period of dry weather; continued lack of rain; dryness	The long ***drought*** has killed most of the crops in the fields. 久旱已使田里的大部分农作物枯死。
eligible /ˈelɪdʒəbl/ *adj.* 合适的；合格的	suitable to be chosen; desirable; qualified	She knows a lot of ***eligible*** young men who are all rich and attractive. 她认识很多合适的青年，都既富有又吸引人。
illegible /ɪˈledʒəbl/ *adj.* 难读的	very hard or impossible to read; not legible	The ink had faded so that many words were ***illegible***. 墨水褪色了，所以许多字迹都难以辨认。
eminent /ˈemɪnənt/ *adj.* 闻名的；显赫的	highly respected; well-known; distinguished; outstanding	Washington was ***eminent*** both as general and as president. 不管是作为将军还是总统，华盛顿都很有名。

WORD	MEANING	TYPICAL USE
imminent /ˈɪmɪnənt/ *adj.* 迫近的	about to happen; impending	The scientist predicted that an earthquake was ***imminent*** in Tokyo area. 科学家预言,东京地区即将发生地震。

EXERCISE 21.1 从第一部分中选出最恰当的单词,填入空格内:

1. Great sections of ______ in Arizona and California have been made into farmland by irrigation.

   (A) desert　　(B) dessert

2. Somehow he was able to ______ the radio but failed to reassemble it.

   (A) disassemble　　(B) dissemble

3. He made three different ______ of his report before he handed it in final form.

   (A) draughts　　(B) droughts

4. The old professor was looking for an ______ young man for his daughter.

   (A) eligible　　(B) illegible

5. Censure is the tax a man pays to the public for being ______.

   (A) eminent　　(B) imminent

解答　1. A　2. A　3. A　4. A　5. A

第二部分

WORD	MEANING	TYPICAL USE
exalt /ɪɡˈzɔːlt, eɡˈzɔːlt/ *v.* 提升	raise a person to a high position; elevate; promote	The members ***exalted*** Mr. Smith when they elected him president of the association. 会员提拔史密斯先生,选他为协会的会长。
exult /ɪɡˈzʌlt/ *v.* 欢腾	rejoice greatly; show delight; be very glad	All the people ***exulted*** to find that our national team won the gold medal in the International Basketball Tournament. 当得知我们的国家代表队在国际篮球赛中赢得了金牌时,全民欢腾了。
ingenious /ɪnˈdʒiːnjəs/ *adj.* 设计精巧的	skillful; clever; inventive; cleverly made	The trap made of an old tin can and some wire is an ***ingenious*** device. 这个用旧罐头盒和金属丝做成的捕捉器是一件精巧的设计。

WORD	MEANING	TYPICAL USE
ingenuous /ɪnˈdʒenjʊəs/ *adj.* 天真的；老实的	frank and open; sincere; simple	The ***ingenuous*** person had never thought of being suspicious of what others told him. 天真的人从来不会怀疑别人告诉他的话。
jealous /ˈdʒeləs/ *adj.* 嫉妒的	fearful that a person one loves may love someone else; possessive; envious	When my little brother sees mother holding the new baby, he becomes ***jealous***. 看到妈妈抱着刚出生的婴儿，我的小弟嫉妒了。
zealous /ˈzeləs/ *adj.* 热心的	actively enthusiastic; eager; earnest; ardent; fervent	The clerk in the toy section of the department seems very ***zealous*** in pleasing the customers. 百货公司玩具部的售货员似乎非常热情地取悦顾客。
material /məˈtɪərɪəl/ *n.* 材料	anything of which something can be made	The dress that Miss Lee was wearing at the party was made of synthetic ***material***. 李小姐在舞会上穿的那套礼服是合成材料做成的。

WORD	MEANING	TYPICAL USE
materiel /məˌtɪərɪˈel/ *n.* (军队的)装备;设备	military supplies; equipment	The statesman said the Iron Curtain countries had vast resources in man-power and ***materiel***. 政治家说铁幕内的国家在人力和军备上均有大量资源。
moral /ˈmɒrəl/ *adj.* 品行端正的	good in character or conduct; right; just	George Washington is known to be a ***moral*** and just man. 乔治・华盛顿以品行端正和公正闻名。
morale /mɔːˈrɑːl/ *n.* 士气	a state of mind in terms of confidence and courage	I am sure that we will win the battle; the ***morale*** of our troops is very high. 我相信我们会赢得这场战役,我们的士气非常高昂。

EXERCISE 21.2 从第二部分中选出最恰当的单词,填入空格内:

1. He was ______ to the most eminent position in the government.
   (A) exalted　　(B) exulted
2. The ______ boy made a radio set for himself after reading the manual.
   (A) ingenious　　(B) ingenuous
3. The boys and girls made ______ efforts to clean up house for the party.
   (A) jealous　　(B) zealous

4. The general needs more troops and ______ to win the victory.

(A) material (B) materiel

5. The ______ of the team is low after its seven consecutive defeats.

(A) moral (B) morale

解答 1. A 2. A 3. B 4. B 5. B

第三部分

WORD	MEANING	TYPICAL USE
ordinance /ˈɔːdɪnəns/ *n.* 法令	a rule or law made by authority; regulation; canon	Freedom of religious worship was guaranteed to all settlers in the Northwest Territory by the ***ordinance*** of 1787. 1787 年的法令保证西北领地居民的宗教信仰自由。
ordnance /ˈɔːdnəns/ *n.* 炮;军械	cannon or artillery; arms; armament	The pirate ships in the West Indies were armed with heavy ***ordnance***. 西印度群岛的海盗船装有大量军火。

WORD	MEANING	TYPICAL USE
parish /ˈpærɪʃ/ *n.* 教区	a district that has its own church and clergyman	The minister worked very hard to make the rounds of his ***parish*** and visit the homes of the sick. 牧师卖力地巡查他的教区，拜访病人的家。
perish /ˈperɪʃ/ *v.* 死；毁灭	be destroyed; die	They said that this flower would not ***perish*** even when frost comes. 他们说这花即使在霜降时也不会死。
perpetrate /ˈpɜːpɪtreɪt/ *v.* 犯（罪）	do or commit (crime, fraud, trick or anything bad)	The police still don't know who ***perpetrated*** the murder of the housewife. 警方仍不知道是谁谋杀了那位家庭主妇。
perpetuate /pə(ɜː)ˈpetʃʊeɪt/ *v.* 使不朽	make perpetual; keep from being forgotten; preserve	This monument was built to ***perpetuate*** the memory of the national hero. 建造纪念碑使民族英雄永垂不朽。

WORD	MEANING	TYPICAL USE
personality /ˌpɜːsəˈnælɪtɪ/ *n.* 人格；个性	the quality that makes one person be different and act differently from another; character; disposition	Many psychologists are inclined to attribute the formation of ***personality*** entirely to the operation of the cultural and physical environment. 许多心理学家认为，人格的形成完全归因于文化与物质环境的作用。
personalty /ˈpɜːsənəltɪ/ *n.* 私人财产	personal property	That car is his ***personalty***; using it without his permission is illegal. 这辆车是他的私人财产，未经他允许而使用是非法的。
persecute /ˈpɜːsɪkjuːt/ *v.* 迫害	harass persistently; oppress; torment; wrong	Blessed are those who are ***persecuted*** for righteousness' sake. 那些因正直而受迫害的人有福了。
prosecute /ˈprɒsɪkjuːt/ *v.* 1. 对……提起公诉	1. try by law; bring a case before a law court	The engineer of the wrecked train was ***prosecuted*** for criminal negligence. 这辆撞坏火车的司机因过失伤害而被提起公诉。

WORD	MEANING	TYPICAL USE
2. 进行	2. carry out; follow up; pursue	He ***prosecuted*** an inquiry into reasons for the company's failure. 他对公司失败的原因进行调查。

EXERCISE 21.3 从第三部分中选出最恰当的单词,填入空格内:

1. Some countries have ______ forbidding the use of soft coal for heating.
   (A) ordinances　　(B) ordnances
2. A countless number of young soldiers ______ to win the war.
   (A) parished　　(B) perished
3. The country ______ in postage stamps the centenary of her political independence.
   (A) perpetrated　　(B) perpetuated
4. The job is very difficult; it requires a man of strong ______.
   (A) personality　　(B) personalty
5. The old man ______ the dog by whipping it cruelly whenever it came near.
   (A) persecuted　　(B) prosecuted

解答　1. A　2. B　3. B　4. A　5. A

第四部分

WORD	MEANING	TYPICAL USE
portable /ˈpɔːtəbl/ *adj.* 可携带的	capable of being carried or moved; easily carried	The author takes his ***portable*** typewriter wherever he goes. 作家随身携带他的手提打字机。
potable /ˈpəʊtəbl/ *adj.* 适于饮用的	fit for drinking; drinkable	They set up purifying systems in dozens of places where the water was not ***potable***. 他们在许多水不适于饮用的地方设置了净化系统。
prescribe /prɪsˈkraɪb/ *v.* 1. 命令	1. recommend a rule to be followed; order; direct	Good citizens always do what the laws ***prescribe***. 好公民总是遵守法律。
2. 开药方	2. order as a remedy or treatment	The doctor ***prescribed*** a new medicine for the pain in my joints. 医生为我的关节痛开了种新药。
proscribe /prəʊsˈkraɪb/ *v.* 禁止	forbid by law; prohibit as wrong; condemn	In earlier days, the church ***proscribed*** dancing and card playing. 早期的教会禁止跳舞和玩牌。

WORD	MEANING	TYPICAL USE
reality /rɪ(iː)ˈælɪtɪ/ *n.* 真实	the quality or state of being real; real existence; a real thing	Slaughter and destruction are terrible ***realities*** of war. 屠杀和破坏是战争的恐怖现实。
realty /ˈrɪəltɪ/ *n.* 不动产	real estate	His ***realty*** includes a big mansion. 他的不动产包括一栋大厦。
statue /ˈstætjuː/ *n.* 雕像	an image of a person or animal carved or cast in solid material; sculpture	Nearly every city in the United States has a ***statue*** of some famous man. 在美国,几乎每个城市都有名人的雕像。
stature /ˈstætʃə(r)/ *n.* 身材	the height of a person or thing; tallness	A man six feet tall is above average ***stature*** in this part of the world. 在这片地区,一个人身高六英尺是高于普通身材的。
vacation /vəˈkeɪʃən; veɪˈkeɪʃən/ *n.* 假期	a time of rest and freedom from work; holiday	My family is going to have a short ***vacation*** on the east coast. 我的家人将要去东海岸度个短假。

WORD	MEANING	TYPICAL USE
vocation /vəʊˈkeɪʃən/ *n.* 职业	a particular occupation; business; profession; trade	You will not make a good teacher, unless you feel teaching is your ***vocation***. 除非你觉得教书是你的职业,否则你不会成为一个好老师。

EXERCISE 21.4 从第四部分中选出最恰当的单词,填入空格内:

1. A ______ radio is popular because we can take it wherever we go.
   (A) portable (B) potable
2. What punishment does the law ______ for this kind of crime?
   (A) prescribe (B) proscribe
3. Her dream of marrying a prince became a ______.
   (A) reality (B) realty
4. I watched him for nearly an hour; he sat rigid and immovable, like a ______.
   (A) statue (B) stature
5. She chose teaching as her ______ because she thought she had a special fitness for it.
   (A) vacation (B) vocation

解答 1. A 2. A 3. A 4. A 5. B

效果检测

EXERCISE 21.5 从第二栏中选出第一栏各词的正确词意：

COLUMN Ⅰ	COLUMN Ⅱ
______ 1. draught	(A) raise a person to a higher rank
______ 2. drought	(B) easily carried
______ 3. exalt	(C) harass persistently
______ 4. exult	(D) lack of rain
______ 5. personality	(E) a rough written form of anything
______ 6. personalty	(F) rejoice greatly
______ 7. persecute	(G) character
______ 8. prosecute	(H) fit for drinking
______ 9. portable	(I) personal property
______ 10. potable	(J) try by law

解答 1. E　2. D　3. A　4. F　5. G
6. I　7. C　8. J　9. B　10. H

EXERCISE 21.6 读下面的句子，选出句中斜体词所代表的意义：

______ 1. The regiment assembled troops and *supplies* to prepare for the attack.

(A) material　　(B) materiel

______ 2. She is very short-tempered; she never *hides* her anger on any occasion.

(A) disassembles　　(B) dissembles

______ 3. Where are you planning to go for your *holiday* this summer?

(A) vacation　　(B) vocation

______ 4. The scientist *abandoned* his country and helped the enemy.

(A) deserted (B) desserted

______ 5. It is difficult to *forbid* a party without infringing on the right of the individual to dissent.

(A) prescribe (B) proscribe

解答 1. B 2. B 3. A 4. A 5. B

EXERCISE 21.7 找出与斜体词的意义最接近的答案:

______ 1. delicious *dessert*

(A) meal (B) sweet food

(C) smell (D) exotic music

______ 2. *eligible* bachelor

(A) qualified (B) handsome

(C) educated (D) engaged

______ 3. bronze *statue*

(A) metal (B) vase

(C) sculpture (D) era

______ 4. heavy *ordnance*

(A) punishment (B) artillery

(C) tax (D) rain

______ 5. *eminent* biologist

(A) mediocre (B) outstanding

(C) enthusiastic (D) diligent

______ 6. *zealous* for fame

(A) indifferent (B) envious

(C) ready (D) eager

______ 7. *ingenuous* report

(A) sincere (B) wise

(C) carefully written (D) short

______ 8. traffic *ordinance*

(A) violation (B) accident

(C) regulation (D) jam

______ 9. dress *material*

(A) fabric (B) style

(C) manual (D) supplier

______ 10. *portable* television

(A) automatic (B) capable of being carried

(C) easy to set up (D) educational

解答 1. B 2. A 3. C 4. B 5. B
6. D 7. A 8. C 9. A 10. B

EXERCISE 21.8 从下列单词中选出最恰当的词,填入空格内:

VOCABULARY LIST

prosecuted	jealous	reality	ingenious
perpetrated	illegible	potable	imminent
ordinance	perished	stature	morale

1. The girl was ______ when she discovered that the boy loved someone else.
2. My sister is so ______ that she will think of a way to do the work more easily.
3. The black clouds, thunder and lightning show that a storm is ______.
4. I doubted the ______ of what he had seen; I thought he must have dreamed it.
5. He started an inquiry into the causes of the fire, and ______ it for several weeks.

6. Hundreds of settlers ______ that year because of drought, famine and epidemic diseases.
7. Trapped in the cave by a fall of rock, the men kept up their ______ by singing together.
8. The boy's handwriting was so bad that his letter to his mother was ______.
9. It usually takes a year for a dog to grow to its full ______.
10. The two thieves ______ the robbery of the jewelry store, and stole jewelry worth 2 million dollars.

解答 1. jealous 2. ingenious 3. imminent 4. reality 5. prosecuted 6. perished 7. morale 8. illegible 9. stature 10. perpetrated

LESSON 22

预备测验

选出最恰当的答案：

1. ______ is an *alumna* of a small local college in Illinois.
   (A) He　　(B) She　　(C) It
2. The boy was so angry he *clenched* his ______.
   (A) room　　(B) anger　　(C) fists
3. The soldier gave ______ a *contemptuous* look.
   (A) his lovely daughter
   (B) the deserter
   (C) his pal
4. An *egoist* lives only for ______ pleasure.
   (A) his own　　(B) somebody else's　　(C) everyone's
5. It is *immoral* to ______ another man's property.
   (A) buy　　(B) protect　　(C) steal

答案 1. B 2. C 3. B 4. A 5. C

第一部分

WORD	MEANING	TYPICAL USE
alumna /əˈlʌmnə/ *n.* 女毕业生 *pl.* alumnae	a female graduate of a school	My wife is an ***alumna*** of Wuhan University. 我妻子是武汉大学的毕业生。

WORD	MEANING	TYPICAL USE
alumnus /əˈlʌmnəs/ *n.* 男毕业生 *pl.* alumni	a male graduate of a school	President Kennedy was an ***alumnus*** of Harvard University. 肯尼迪总统是哈佛大学的毕业生。
alumni(*pl.*) /əˈlʌmnaɪ/ *n.* 毕业生 (复数形式)	graduates of a school	My son and my daughter are both ***alumni*** of Ohio State University. 我的儿子和女儿都是俄亥俄州立大学的毕业生。
amoral /eɪˈmɒrəl/ *adj.* 非道德的	not subject to moral judgment; lacking a knowledge of right and wrong; non-moral	Cats are ***amoral***; they can't be censured for killing birds. 猫不受道德约束,它们杀死鸟儿也不会受到责难。
immoral /ɪˈmɒrəl/ *adj.* 不道德的	violating morality; sinful; wicked	Lying and stealing are considered ***immoral*** conducts in every human society. 在人类社会中,说谎和偷窃被视为不道德的行为。

WORD	MEANING	TYPICAL USE
unmoral /ˌʌnˈmɒrəl/ *adj.* 无关道德问题的	not pertaining to morality; neither moral nor immoral	Many scientists believe their research to be ***unmoral***, no matter what the results will be. 许多科学家认为他们的研究与道德无关,不论这些研究将有什么结果。
avocation /ˌævəʊˈkeɪʃən/ *n.* 嗜好	something that a person does besides his regular business; hobby	Stamp collecting as well as fishing is Mr. Evan's favorite ***avocation***. 和钓鱼一样,集邮也是埃文先生最喜爱的嗜好。
vocation /vəʊˈkeɪʃən/ *n.* 职业	main job; occupation; profession	Bookkeeping is Mr. Jones' ***vocation***, and photography is his avocation. 簿记是琼斯先生的职业,摄影是他的副业。
biannual /baɪˈænjʊəl/ *adj.* 一年两度的	occurring twicc a year	Our school doctor recommends a ***biannual*** visit to the dentist; I am going to the dentist's for the second time this year. 我们校医建议一年去看两次牙医。我要去看牙医,这是我今年第二次去。

WORD	MEANING	TYPICAL USE
biennial /baɪˈenɪəl/ *adj.* 两年一次的	occurring once every two years; living for two years	The sophomores and seniors are taking the ***biennial*** exam this afternoon. 今天下午二年级和四年级的学生正在进行两年一次的考试。

EXERCISE 22.1 从第一部分中选出最恰当的单词,填入空格内:

1. Do you and your wife belong to the same ______ association?

   (A) alumna (B) alumnus (C) alumni

2. You can't blame the baby for breaking the antique vase because he is ______.

   (A) amoral (B) immoral (C) unmoral

3. Golf is a hobby of many people, but it is the ______ of a professional golfer.

   (A) avocation (B) vocation

4. The ______ examinations for the college applicants will be given in May and October this year.

   (A) biannual (B) biennial

解答 1. C 2. A 3. B 4. A

第二部分

WORD	MEANING	TYPICAL USE
chord /kɔːd/ *n.* 琴弦	a string of a stringed musical instrument	He is replacing the broken ***chord*** of his violin. 他正在更换小提琴上的断弦。
cord /kɔːd/ *n.* 细绳	a thick string; a very thin rope	He had tied the package with a ***cord*** before he took it to the post office. 在去邮局之前，他用细绳把包裹系好。
clench /klentʃ/ *v.* 咬紧（牙关）；紧握（拳头）	close tightly together; grasp firmly	He ***clenched*** his teeth to endure the pain of the wound suffered from the accident. 他咬紧牙关，忍受车祸受伤所带来的疼痛。
clinch /klɪntʃ/ *v.* 敲弯（钉头等）；使钉牢	secure firmly by bending down a protruding point, as of a nail or slope	By ***clinching*** nails over the canvas they held the torn sail to the mast. 他们在帆布上到处钉钉子，把破帆弄回桅杆。

WORD	MEANING	TYPICAL USE
climate /ˈklaɪmɪt/ *n.* 气候	the weather conditions of a place over a period of years	For fifty years or more the ***climate*** of the Arctic has been warming up gradually. 五十年或五十多年以来，北极的气候逐渐暖和起来。
weather /ˈweðə(r)/ *n.* 天气	condition of the air with respect to temperature, moisture, cloudiness, etc. around a certain place	The ***weather*** will be very hot and humid in Chongqing today. 今天重庆的天气将会炎热又潮湿。
compare /kəmˈpɛə(r)/ *v.* 比较	point out how persons or things are alike and how they differ	We ***compared*** two books to see which one had the better illustrations. 我们比较这两本书，看看哪一本的插图更好。
contrast /kənˈtræst/ *v.* 对比	compare persons or things (of different kinds) to show their differences	She ***contrasted*** her present life of luxury with the poverty of her childhood. 她将现在的富裕生活和童年的穷苦日子做了个对比。

WORD	MEANING	TYPICAL USE
connotation /ˌkɒnəʊˈteɪʃən/ *n.* 含意	the added meaning that a word suggests or implies	The words "snake" and "red" have unpleasant ***connotations*** for many people. 许多人认为"蛇"和"红色"有着不好的含意。
denotation /ˌdiːnəʊˈteɪʃən/ *n.*（词句的）意义	the exact, literal meaning of a word	The ***denotation*** of the word "home" is "place where one lives", but it has many connotations. "家"的意义是"一个人的住所"，但是它还有许多含意。

EXERCISE 22.2 从第二部分中选出最恰当的单词，填入空格内：

1. The porter tied the bundle of clothes with a ______ to carry it easily.
   (A) chord　　(B) cord
2. The carpenter ______ the nails of the bookcase he was building.
   (A) clenched　　(B) clinched
3. We have to cancel our picnic because of bad ______.
   (A) climate　　(B) weather
4. Before you buy meat, you should ______ its price at several stores.
   (A) compare　　(B) contrast

5. The ______ of the word "snake" is a legless reptile with a long, thin body.

(A) connotation (B) denotation

解答 1. B 2. B 3. B 4. A 5. B

第三部分

WORD	MEANING	TYPICAL USE
contemptible /kən'temptəbl/ *adj.* 可鄙的	deserving contempt or scorn; mean; low; worthless	Cheating on a test is considered one of the most ***contemptible*** acts in the Military Academy. 在军事学院，考试作弊被视为最可鄙的行为之一。
contemptuous /kən'temptjʊəs/ *adj.* 藐视的	showing or feeling contempt; scornful; disdainful	The rich man is ***contemptuous*** of my humble home and poor surroundings. 那富人看不起我寒酸的家和穷苦的环境。
continual /kən'tɪnjʊəl/ *adj.* 连续的	over and over again; regular but interrupted; frequent	We experienced a ***continual*** series of hot spells last summer. 去年夏天我们经历了一连串持续的高温天气。

WORD	MEANING	TYPICAL USE
continuous /kən'tɪnjʊəs/ *adj.* 不断的	continuing without stopping; ceaseless; unbroken; incessant	On holidays, we can see a ***continuous*** line of cars on highways. 假日里我们可以看到公路上的车辆络绎不绝。
credible /'kredəbl/ *adj.* 可信的	deserving or worthy of belief; believable; trustworthy; reliable	It hardly seems ***credible*** that your son has grown so tall in one year. 你儿子在一年之中竟长得这么高了，简直令人难以置信。
credulous /'kredjʊləs/ *adj.* 轻信的	too much inclined to believe; easily deceived; gullible	Only a ***credulous*** person would fall for that old trick. 只有轻信的人才会上那老把戏的当。
disinterested /dɪs'ɪntrɪstɪd/ *adj.* 公正的	free from selfish motives; impartial; unbiased; fair	An umpire must be an entirely ***disinterested*** but keen observer. 裁判必须是个完全公正又敏锐的观察者。
uninterested /ˌʌn'ɪntrɪstɪd/ *adj.* 不感兴趣的	not interested; uncaring	The audience yawned and seemed ***uninterested*** in the politician's speech. 听众打着哈欠，似乎对政治家的演说并不感兴趣。

WORD	MEANING	TYPICAL USE
disorganized /dɪsˈɔːgənaɪzd/ *adj.* 杂乱无章的	thrown into confusion and disorder; disarranged	The office where everything had worked so smoothly became completely ***disorganized*** after Mr. Levine resigned. 在莱文先生辞职后，这个原本运作得很顺畅的公司变得杂乱无章。
unorganized /ˌʌnˈɔːgənaɪzd/ *adj.* 未加组织的	not formed into a systematized whole	Form a union, an ***unorganized*** mob can accomplish nothing but chaos. 要组成一个团体，未加组织的群众只会一片混乱而不能成事。

EXERCISE 22.3 从第三部分中选出最恰当的单词，填入空格内：

1. Every employer has a ______ attitude toward sloppy work.

   (A) contemptible (B) contemptuous

2. No one likes ______ interruptions while he is reading a book.

   (A) continual (B) continuous

3. What he had said about the fire, though unusual, is ______.

   (A) credible (B) credulous

4. His action cannot be considered to be ______ because he hoped to make money out of the affair.

   (A) disinterested (B) uninterested

5. It's better to be ______ than not organized at all.
(A) disorganized (B) unorganized

解答 1. B 2. A 3. A 4. A 5. A

第四部分

WORD	MEANING	TYPICAL USE
divers /ˈdaɪvəz/ *adj.* 种种的	more than one; several; different	A well-balanced diet is made up of ***divers*** foods. 均衡的饮食是由多种食物构成的。
diverse /daɪˈvɜːs/ *adj.* 不同的	various; unlike; varied	A great many ***diverse*** opinions were expressed at the meeting, but none was worthwhile. 大家在会议中提出了许多不同的意见，却没有一个值得采纳。
dual /ˈdjʊ(uː)əl/ *adj.* 二重的；两层的	composed or consisting of two parts; double; twofold	The training airplane has ***dual*** controls, one set for the learner and one for the teacher. 教练机有两套控制系统，一套为学生而设，另一套为教师而设。

WORD	MEANING	TYPICAL USE
duel /ˈdjʊ(uː)əl/ *n.* 决斗；相斗	a formal fight to settle a quarrel or avenge an insult	The opposing two lawyers fought a ***duel*** to settle their differences. 两个敌对律师为解决他们之间的分歧而争斗。
egoist /ˈiːgəʊɪst/ *n.* 利己主义者	a person who seeks the welfare of himself; a self-centered, selfish person	John is such an ***egoist*** that he only cares about himself. 约翰是一个利己主义者，他只关心自己。
egotist /ˈiːgətɪst/ *n.* 自大者	a person who boasts too much about himself; a conceited person	Marian is such an ***egotist*** that she talks about herself all the time. 玛丽安是个自大的人，她总是谈论着自己。
emerge /ɪˈmɜːdʒ/ *v.* 出现	come out; come up; come into view	After the shower, the sun ***emerged*** from behind the clouds. 阵雨过后，太阳破云而出。
immerge /ɪˈmɜːdʒ/ *v.* 浸入	put under water; dip; submerge; immerse	He ***immerged*** his aching feet in a bucket of hot water. 他将疼痛的双脚浸入热水中。

WORD	MEANING	TYPICAL USE
emigrant /ˈemɪɡrənt/ *n.* 自本国移居他国者	a person who leaves one country to move to another	It is expected that the total number of ***emigrants*** from this country will reach 20,000 this year. 从这个国家来的移民,今年预计会达到两万。
immigrant /ˈɪmɪɡrənt/ *n.* 自他国移入者	a person who enters one country from another	California has several thousand ***immigrants*** from other states. 加州有数千个来自其他州的移民。

EXERCISE 22.4 从第四部分中选出最恰当的单词,填入空格内:

1. A person of ______ interests can talk about many subjects.

   (A) divers (B) diverse

2. ______ are fought with guns or swords in the presence of witnesses called seconds.

   (A) Duals (B) Duels

3. Perhaps the most eminent ______ that appeared in the world was Montaigne; he wrote too much about himself.

   (A) egoist (B) egotist

4. A considerable number of new facts ______ as a result of the careful investigation.

   (A) emerged (B) immerged

5. Canada has many ______ from Europe and Asia.

(A) emigrants (B) immigrants

解答 1. B 2. B 3. B 4. A 5. B

效果检测

EXERCISE 22.5 从第二栏中选出第一栏各词的正确词意：

COLUMN I	COLUMN II
______ 1. immoral	(A) a self-centered, selfish person
______ 2. unmoral	(B) the added meaning that a word implies
______ 3. chord	(C) showing contempt
______ 4. cord	(D) deserving contempt
______ 5. denotation	(E) a person who boasts too much about himself
______ 6. connotation	(F) the exact, literal meaning of a word
______ 7. egoist	(G) a very thin rope
______ 8. egotist	(H) violating morality
______ 9. contemptible	(I) not pertaining to morality
______ 10. contemptuous	(J) a string of a musical instrument

解答 1. H 2. I 3. J 4. G 5. F
6. B 7. A 8. E 9. D 10. C

EXERCISE 22.6 读下面的句子，选出句中斜体词部分所代表的意义：

______ 1. The *people who enter the U. S.* from Europe used to get off the boat in New York.

(A) emigrants to the U. S. (B) immigrants to the U. S.

______ 2. Both my daughters are *graduates* of Pembroke Women's College in Rhode Island.

(A) alumnae (B) alumni

______ 3. After his latest scandal, he hardly seems *trustworthy* as a politician.

(A) credible (B) credulous

______ 4. It seems that most employees in that company do not consider their boss a *mean* person.

(A) contemptible (B) contemptuous

______ 5. The brain needs a *constant* and uninterrupted supply of blood to function properly.

(A) continual (B) continuous

解答 1. B 2. A 3. A 4. A 5. B

EXERCISE 22.7 找出与斜体词的意义最接近的答案：

______ 1. *biannual* publication

(A) once every two years (B) twice a year

(C) lasting for a year (D) lasting for two years

______ 2. tropical *climate*

(A) weather conditions (B) storm

(C) region (D) crops and fruit

______ 3. *continual* hammering

(A) perpetual (B) unbroken

(C) over and over again (D) violent

______ 4. *disinterested* umpire

(A) bored (B) impartial

(C) disguised (D) wise

______ 5. *dual* purposes

(A) fighting (B) wicked

(C) appropriate (D) double

______ 6. *clinched* nails

(A) secured firmly (B) broken apart

(C) put together (D) fixed loosely

______ 7. *immoral* acts

(A) wicked (B) non-moral

(C) delayed (D) impolite

______ 8. *contemptuous* look

(A) showing contempt (B) concealed

(C) mean (D) deserving contempt

______ 9. *credulous* person

(A) reliable (B) self-centered

(C) sincere (D) gullible

______ 10. *clenched* fists

(A) fixed firmly (B) closed tightly

(C) opened widely (D) trembled violently

解答 1. B 2. A 3. C 4. B 5. D
6. A 7. A 8. A 9. D 10. B

EXERCISE 22.8 从下列单词中选出最恰当的词，填入空格内：

VOCABULARY LIST

immerged	duel	emigrants	uninterested
contemptible	credulous	connotations	contrasts
avocation	clenched	biennial	compared

1. It is very difficult to entertain anyone so ______ in everything.
2. I ______ my answers with the teacher's and found that I had made a mistake.
3. She was so ______ that the other children could fool her easily.
4. The reporter ______ his pencil in his teeth while he was wiping his glasses.
5. The ______ art shows were held in our city in 1970, 1972, 1974 and 1976.
6. "Skinny" and "slim" are two words for the same denotation, but their ______ are different.
7. Mr. Brown is a lawyer, but writing stories for children is his ______.
8. She ______ her right foot into the pool to see how cold the water was.
9. To avenge the insult, the man proposed a(n) ______ with handguns to the colonel.
10. The strained language of his speeches ______ oddly with the ease and naturalness of his letters.

解答

1. uninterested 2. compared 3. credulous
4. clenched 5. biennial 6. connotations
7. avocation 8. immerged 9. duel
10. contrasts

LESSON 23

预备测验

选出最恰当的答案：

1. ______ people believe in *humane* treatment of prisoners.

   (A) Diligent　　(B) Civilized　　(C) Primitive

2. The ______ is an *imaginary* circle around the earth.

   (A) moon　　(B) sun　　(C) equator

3. Because he ______, he is *liable* to fail.

   (A) is getting along well

   (B) is doing his best

   (C) wasn't working hard

4. He sat alone after the battle, *mourning* over the ______ of his best friend.

   (A) loss　　(B) achievement　　(C) help

5. A ______ can help some people to understand their *subconscious* urges.

   (A) physician　　(B) psychiatrist　　(C) surgeon

答案 1. B 2. C 3. C 4. A 5. B

第一部分

WORD	MEANING	TYPICAL USE
farther /ˈfɑːðə(r)/ *adv.* 更远地	at a greater distance	He has to leave now, he lives ***farther*** from here than I do. 他不得不现在就走,因为他住得比我还远。
further /ˈfɜːðə(r)/ *adv.* 更进一步地;此外	to a greater extent; more; additional	All the members of the committee agreed to inquire ***further*** into the matter. 委员会所有成员都同意对这件事作进一步调查。
hanged /hæŋd/ *v.* (hang 的过去式和过去分词) 吊死;绞死	put to death by hanging	The man living next door ***hanged*** himself in sorrow after his wife died. 隔壁的男人在妻子死后,因伤心过度而自缢了。
hung /hʌŋ/ *v.* (hang 的过去式和过去分词) 悬挂	suspended or caused to be suspended from a wall, ceiling, etc.	We ***hung*** our reproduction of "Mona Liza" above the fireplace. 我们将《蒙娜丽莎》的复制品挂在壁炉上方。

WORD	MEANING	TYPICAL USE
historic /hɪsˈtɒrɪk/ *adj.* 历史上著名的	famous or important in history; noted; celebrated; renowned	Guilin is one of the ***historic*** spots that you should visit. 桂林是你应当游览的名胜之一。
historical /hisˈtɒrɪkəl/ *adj.* 有关历史的	concerned with history	Upon retiring from office, the President gave all the ***historical*** papers to the library. 总统一退职就把所有历史文件送进图书馆。
human /ˈhjuːmən/ *adj.* 人类的	of or concerning man	The philosopher claims that kindness is a ***human*** trait, but I don't believe it. 那个哲学家声称仁慈是人类的特征，但是我不相信。
humane /hjʊ(uː)ˈmeɪn/ *adj.* 慈悲的；仁爱的	kind; tender; compassionate; merciful	***Humane*** people are considerate of not only other people but also animals. 慈悲为怀的人不仅关心他人，还关心动物。
imaginary /ɪˈmædʒɪnərɪ/ *adj.* 虚构的	existing only in the imagination; not real	Some people do not believe that ghosts are not real but ***imaginary*** beings. 有些人相信鬼是真实存在而非虚构的。

WORD	MEANING	TYPICAL USE
imaginative /ɪˈmædʒɪnətɪv/ *adj.* 富于想象的	having a good imagination; inventive	The *imaginative* child always likes to make up fairy tales. 这个富于想象力的小孩总喜欢编神话故事。

EXERCISE 23.1 从第一部分中选出最恰当的单词,填入空格内:

1. The crew pushed the boat ______ into the water to make it float.
   (A) farther (B) further
2. Upon entering he took off his coat and ______ it on the hook.
   (A) hanged (B) hung
3. It is a ______ fact that George Washington was the first President of the United States.
   (A) historic (B) historical
4. No life that breathes with ______ breath has ever truly longed for death.
   (A) human (B) humane
5. The storytellers must have great ______ power.
   (A) imaginary (B) imaginative

解答 1. A 2. B 3. B 4. A 5. B

第二部分

WORD	MEANING	TYPICAL USE
incomparable /ɪnˈkɒmpərəbl/ *adj.* 举世无双的	without equal; matchless; unique	Bessie Smith was an ***incomparable*** singer in her days. 贝西·史密斯在她那个时代是举世无双的歌手。
uncomparable /ʌnˈkɒmpərəbl/ *adj.* 无法比较的	so different that comparison is impossible; not open to comparison	It is foolish to compare horses with airplanes; they are ***uncomparable***. 去比较马和飞机的差异是愚蠢的；它们没有可比性。
incredible /ɪnˈkredəbl/ *adj.* 难以置信的	hard to believe; unbelievable	Some old superstitions seem ***incredible*** to most educated people. 有些古老的迷信对于大部分受过教育的人来说是难以置信的。
incredulous /ɪnˈkredjʊləs/ *adj.* 不信的	not ready to believe; doubting; skeptical	People nowadays are ***incredulous*** about ghosts and witches. 现在的人们都不相信鬼和巫婆。

WORD	MEANING	TYPICAL USE
lay /leɪ/ *v.* 放置	put something down; place; put	The gentleman ***laid*** his hand on his son's shoulder. 那绅士将手放在他儿子的肩上。
lie /laɪ/ *v.* 躺	have one's body in a flat position along the ground or other surface; recline	The wounded soldier was ***lying*** on the battlefield. 受伤的士兵躺在战场上。
apt /æpt/ *adj.* 1. 易于的	1. having a natural or habitual tendency to do something; usually expected to	This kind of shoe is ***apt*** to slip on wet ground. 这种鞋很容易在湿地上滑倒。
2. 聪明的	2. quick to learn	Henry is an ***apt*** student of the practical science. 亨利在应用科学这方面是个优秀的学生。
liable /ˈlaɪəbl/ *adj.* 1. 易患的	1. in danger of having or doing	Childern under the age of 10 are all ***liable*** to diseases. 10 岁以下的小孩易患疾病。
2. 应负责的	2. responsible for the consequences	He declared that he was not ***liable*** for his wife's debts. 他宣称他对妻子的债务不应承担责任。

WORD	MEANING	TYPICAL USE
likely /ˈlaɪklɪ/ *adj.* 有可能的	probable; expected but not as a matter of course	The weather forecast says that it's ***likely*** to be hot tomorrow. 天气预报说明天可能会变热。
luxuriant /lʌgˈzjʊərɪənt/ *adj.* 繁茂的；多产的	growing thick and green; producing abundantly; abundant	The backyard of our house has a ***luxuriant*** growth of weeds. 我们家的后院长了一大堆杂草。
luxurious /lʌgˈzjʊərɪəs/ *adj.* 奢侈的	fond of luxury; selfindulgent; giving luxury	She is too proud, too ***luxurious***, to marry an average man like you. 她太骄傲也太奢侈了，所以不能嫁给像你这样的普通人。

EXERCISE 23.2 从第二部分中选出最恰当的单词，填入空格内：

1. According to *Iliad* written by Homer, Helen of Troy had ______ beauty.
   (A) incomparable (B) uncomparable
2. It is ______ that a perfect man like you could have made such a mistake.
   (A) incredible (B) incredulous
3. A skillful workman is able to ______ bricks very accurately and quickly.
   (A) lay (B) lie
4. Children are ______ to be noisy while they are playing.
   (A) apt (B) liable

5. The governor of the state lives in a ______ mansion.

(A) luxuriant (B) luxurious

解答 1. A 2. A 3. A 4. A 5. B

第三部分

WORD	MEANING	TYPICAL USE
moan /məʊn/ *n.* 呻吟	a long, low sound of suffering	From time to time, during the night, there was a ***moan*** of pain from the sick man. 夜里，这位病人有好几次疼得呻吟起来。
mourn /mɔːn/ *v.* 哀悼	feel or show sorrow over; grieve; lament	The whole nation ***mourned*** the death of the much-loved President. 全国为备受敬爱的总统的逝世而哀悼。
oral /ˈɔːrəl/ *adj.* 口头的	using speech; not written; spoken	The company will give only ***oral*** tests to the applicants. 公司只通过口试来考查应聘者。

WORD	MEANING	TYPICAL USE
verbal /ˈvɜːbəl/ *adj.* 言辞的	in or of words, as distinguished from other means of description	This written report contains both a ***verbal*** description and a sketch of the building. 这份书面报告包括了对这座建筑的文字描述及草图。
personal /ˈpɜːsənəl/ *adj.* 亲自的；私人的	of, for or belonging to a particular person; individual; private	The minister made a ***personal*** visit to the scene of the fighting. 部长亲临战场视察。
personnel /ˌpɜːsəˈnel/ *n.* 人员；员工	the people employed in any work, business or service	The general issued an order to capture the hill to all ***personnel***. 将军下令要全体人员攻占该山头。
respectably /rɪsˈpektəblɪ/ *adv.* 相当好地	in a worthy or proper manner; moderately; very well	The man seemed poor, but he was ***respectably*** dressed. 这人似乎贫穷，但是衣着体面。
respectfully /rɪsˈpektfʊlɪ/ *adv.* 有礼貌地	in a respectful or polite manner; politely	Children should speak ***respectfully*** to their elders. 小孩跟长辈说话要有礼貌。

WORD	MEANING	TYPICAL USE
respectively /rɪsˈpektɪvlɪ/ *adv.* 个别地;各自地	in a specified order	The first, second and third prizes went to Jack, George and Frank ***respectively***. 一等奖、二等奖和三等奖分别颁给杰克、乔治和弗兰克。
raise /reɪz/ *v.* 1. 举起	1. lift something	She ***raised*** her finger to her lips as a sign for silence. 她举起手指放在唇边以示安静。
2. 饲养	2. grow or breed something	The farmer ***raises*** cattle and crops. 农夫饲养牛群,种植谷物。
rise /raɪz/ *v.* 升起;矗立	get up; arise; stand	The sun will ***rise*** at 5:45 tomorrow morning. 明天早晨太阳将在 5 点 45 分升起。

EXERCISE 23.3 从第三部分中选出最恰当的单词,填入空格内:

1. The sick man made a ______ in his sleep during the night.
   (A) moan (B) mourn
2. A(n) ______ agreement is not enough; we must have a written promise.
   (A) oral (B) verbal

3. You must apply for a job in the company's ______ office.

(A) personal (B) personnel

4. The woman struggled to bring up her children ______.

(A) respectably (B) respectfully

5. When the snow melts, the river will ______ to its banks.

(A) raise (B) rise

解答 1. A 2. A 3. B 4. A 5. B

第四部分

WORD	MEANING	TYPICAL USE
register /ˈredʒɪstə(r)/ *v.* 1. 登记;注册	1. write in a list or record; write one's name in a list	We have to go to the government patent office to ***register*** the new trade-mark. 我们必须去专利局注册新的商标。
2. 挂号	2. have a letter recorded in a post office	It is safe to ***register*** the letter containing the check. 带有支票的信件用挂号邮寄比较安全。
registrar /ˌredʒɪsˈtrɑː(r)/ *n.* 登记员;(学校里的)注册主任	a keeper of official records; official recorder.	Go to the ***registrar*** of the university to know your grades. 找大学里的注册主任去查你的成绩。

WORD	MEANING	TYPICAL USE
sailer /ˈseɪlə(r)/ *n.* 帆船	a ship with reference to its sailing power; a sailing vessel	The boat we are on is the best ***sailer*** in the fleet. 我们乘的这条船是这个船队中最好的帆船。
sailor /ˈseɪlə(r)/ *n.* 水手	a person with a job on a ship, especially one who is not a ship's officer	The men in our navy are called ***sailors*** if they are not officers. 在海军中,不是军官的,我们称之为水手。
salon /səˈlɒn/ *n.* 客厅;(营业性质的)店、厅	a large room for receiving or entertaining guests; place where customers go to see a hairdresser, beauty consultant, etc.	A group of college professors were waiting in the main ***salon*** to see the Minister of Education. 一群大学教授正在大厅里等着谒见教育部长。
saloon /səˈluːn/ *n.* 酒吧;(轮船的)大厅	a place where alcoholic drinks are sold and drunk; tavern; bar	The ship's passengers have their dinners in the dining ***saloon***. 船上的乘客在大厅里享用晚餐。

WORD	MEANING	TYPICAL USE
subconscious /ˌsʌbˈkɒnʃəs/ *adj.* 潜意识的	present in the mind but not fully perceived; existing but not felt	It was certain that Oswald might have a ***subconscious*** desire to injure his father. 在奥斯瓦尔德的潜意识里肯定有伤害他父亲的意图。
unconscious /ʌnˈkɒnʃəs/ *adj.* 1. 失去知觉的	1. not conscious; being fainted	Edna was ***unconscious*** for two hours after the accident. 车祸后,埃德娜昏迷了两个小时。
2. 不觉察的	2. not aware	The general was ***unconscious*** of being followed by the spy. 将军不知道他被间谍跟踪了。
transcript /trænˈskrɪpt/ *n.* 副本;誊本	a written or typewritten copy; a copy	The club's secretary prepared several ***transcripts*** of minutes of the meeting. 俱乐部的秘书准备了很多份会议记录的副本。
transcription /trænˈskrɪpʃən/ *n.* 誊写	the act or process of transcribing; copying	The ***transcription*** of words into phonetic symbols requires special training. 把文字转写为语音符号需要专门的训练。

EXERCISE 23.4 从第四部分中选出最恰当的单词,填入空格内:

1. Write to the ______ of the university to get the application form.
   (A) register　　(B) registrar
2. He got a job as a ______ of the ship to travel around the world.
   (A) sailer　　(B) sailor
3. The majority of the citizens of this village are tired of the ______ and want it to be closed.
   (A) salon　　(B) saloon
4. He was knocked completely ______ for several hours when the car struck him.
   (A) subconscious　　(B) unconscious
5. The college wanted a ______ of the student's high-school record.
   (A) transcript　　(B) transcription

解答　1. B　2. B　3. B　4. B　5. A

效果检测

EXERCISE 23.5 从第二栏中选出第一栏各词的正确词义:

COLUMN Ⅰ	COLUMN Ⅱ
______ 1. incomparable	(A) totally unaware
______ 2. uncomparable	(B) spoken
______ 3. historic	(C) without equal; matchless
______ 4. historical	(D) in or of words
______ 5. liable	(E) not open to comparison
______ 6. likely	(F) important in history
______ 7. oral	(G) concerned with history

_____ 8. verbal (H) in danger of having or doing

_____ 9. subconscious (I) existing but not felt

_____ 10. unconscious (J) probable

解答 1. C 2. E 3. F 4. G 5. H
6. J 7. B 8. D 9. I 10. A

EXERCISE 23.6 阅读下面句子,选出句中斜体词所代表的意义:

_____ 1. As she came in, she *placed* the plate on the table.

(A) laid (B) lied

_____ 2. You should always treat older people *politely*.

(A) respectfully (B) respectively

_____ 3. Children in school usually *lift* their hands to answer a question.

(A) raise (B) rise

_____ 4. She told him to clean his room and said *more* than he must make his bed.

(A) father (B) further

_____ 5. The mind of a storyteller has great *creative* powers.

(A) imaginary (B) imaginative

解答 1. A 2. A 3. A 4. B 5. B

EXERCISE 23.7 找出与斜体词的意义最接近的答案:

_____ 1. *raise* cattle

(A) arise (B) lift

(C) grow (D) raze

______ 2. *oral* examination

(A) listening (B) spoken

(C) verbal (D) written

______ 3. *incomparable* beauty

(A) matchless (B) not comparable

(C) uncontrastive (D) equal

______ 4. *historic* occasion

(A) concerned with history (B) resultant

(C) important in history (D) subsequent

______ 5. *humane* treatment

(A) personal (B) human

(C) compassionate (D) cruel

______ 6. an *apt* pupil

(A) liable (B) appropriate

(C) responsible (D) clever

______ 7. *imaginative* story

(A) imagined (B) not real

(C) showing imagination (D) existing in mind

______ 8. school *registrar*

(A) official recorder (B) list of names

(C) registration (D) records

______ 9. *personal* matter

(A) of human being (B) private

(C) belonging to everyone (D) not individual

______ 10. beauty *salon*

(A) shop (B) place

(C) maker (D) tavern

解答 1. C 2. B 3. A 4. C 5. C

6. D 7. C 8. A 9. B 10. A

EXERCISE 23.8 从下列单词中选出最恰当的词,填入空格内:

VOCABULARY LIST

hanged	human	imaginary	incredible
imaginative	incredulous	moan	verbal
mourns	respectively	personnel	luxurious

1. All the characters in this book are ______ but not real.
2. The criminal was sentenced to be ______ by the neck until dead.
3. The ______ of the company are unhappy about the recent changes.
4. She gave a glass of beer to the man and a toy rabbit to the baby, ______.
5. His story of having seen a ghost seemed ______ to his family.
6. The lady couldn't bear this kind of humble life because she was accustomed to a ______ life.
7. I heard the ______ of the patient all night; it wasn't a cheerful sound.
8. The old woman still ______ for her son, 30 years after his death.
9. To know what will happen in the future is beyond ______ power.
10. I was ______ when I heard that you had made such a mistake.

解答 1. imaginary 2. hanged 3. personnel
4. respectively 5. incredible 6. luxurious
7. moan 8. mourns 9. human
10. incredulous

LESSON 24

预备测验

选出最恰当的答案：

1. The *altar* must be placed in the most ______ part of the church.

   (A) sacred　　(B) hidden　　(C) open

2. The officer argued that we had to use *cannons* against the ______.

   (A) pollution　　(B) crime　　(C) enemy

3. The ______ will not be in *session* again until after Christmas.

   (A) market

   (B) train

   (C) National Assembly

4. A *stationary* object is ______ to aim at than a moving object.

   (A) nearer　　(B) easier　　(C) more accurate

5. The sudden *ascent* of the elevator made most of the passengers ______.

   (A) dizzy　　(B) happy　　(C) sleepy

解答 1. A 2. C 3. C 4. B 5. A

第一部分

WORD	MEANING	TYPICAL USE
altar /ˈɔːltə(r)/ *n.* 神坛	a table or raised level surface on which things are offered to a god	The woman knelt before the ***altar*** to pray to God for her son's safe return. 那妇人跪在神坛前面，祈求上苍保佑她的儿子能平安归来。
alter /ˈɔːltə(r)/ *v.* 改变	change; make different; vary; modify	If it rains, we have to ***alter*** our plans to have a picnic on Sunday. 如果星期天下雨，我们就得改变野餐的计划了。
ascent /əˈsent/ *n.* 攀登；上升	an act of going up; a rising; a climbing	Chinese mountain climbers made a successful ***ascent*** of Mt. McKinley in North America. 中国的登山者成功地攀登了北美的麦金利山。
assent /əˈsent/ *n.* 同意	acceptance of a proposal; agreement	I won't give my ***assent*** to her plan because it is not well prepared. 我不会同意她的计划，因为该计划并未做充分的准备。

WORD	MEANING	TYPICAL USE
cannon /ˈkænən/ *n.* 大炮	a large gun, often mounted on wheels	There are several old ***cannons*** on the wall of the castle. 城堡的墙上有几座古老的大炮。
canon /ˈkænən/ *n.* 教规	a rule or law, especially of religious faith	This ***canon*** has been enacted by the church council very recently. 教会就在最近通过了这条教规。
canvas /ˈkænvəs/ *n.* 帆布	strong rough cloth used for tents, sails, bags, etc.; sailcloth; tarpaulin	The tops of my sneakers are made of ***canvas***. 我的运动鞋的鞋面是帆布做的。
canvass /ˈkænvəs/ *v.* 招徕(顾客);兜售	ask for political support or sales or one's goods, especially going from house to house	The salesman ***canvassed*** the whole city for subscriptions of the magazine. 推销员走遍了全城请人订阅该杂志。
cession /ˈseʃən/ *n.* 割让	a handing over to another; ceding; giving up	The ***cession*** of the territory could not be avoided because they lost the war. 因为他们输了这场战争，割让领土是无法避免的。

WORD	MEANING	TYPICAL USE
session /ˈseʃən/ *n.* (议会等的)会议;开庭	a formal meeting of a parliament, lawcourt for discussing or deciding something	Be seated! The court is now in ***session***. 请坐好!现在开庭。

EXERCISE 24.1 从第一部分中选出最恰当的单词,填入空格内:

1. If the coat is too large, a tailor can ______ it to fit you.

   (A) altar (B) alter

2. The teacher gave his ______ to the students' plan to have a dancing party.

   (A) ascent (B) assent

3. His behavior offends the ______ of good manners.

   (A) cannons (B) canons

4. The Labor Party ______ all of this town but it won't win the election.

   (A) canvased (B) canvassed

5. This year's ______ of the National Assembly has been unusually long.

   (A) cession (B) session

解答 1. B 2. B 3. B 4. B 5. B

第二部分

WORD	MEANING	TYPICAL USE
faint /feɪnt/ 1. *v.* 昏厥	1. lose conciousness briefly	The soldier ***fainted*** at the sight of his own blood. 那士兵一看到自己的血就昏倒了。
2. *adj.* 模糊的	2. not clear; plain; dim	The color became ***faint*** as the sun set. 太阳下山后,颜色变得模糊不清。
feint /feɪnt/ *v.* 佯攻	feign an attack; make a pretended blow	He ***feinted*** with his left hand and hit me with his right. 他用左手虚晃一招,之后用右手打我。
intension /ɪnˈtenʃən/ *n.* 激烈	increase in degree; intensification; augmentation	In recent years there has been an ***intension*** of the struggle for political power in the country. 最近几年来,这个国家中争夺政治势力的情形愈演愈烈。
intention /ɪnˈtenʃən/ *n.* 意图	a determination to act in a certain way; purpose; design; plan	She felt offended at my remarks, but it wasn't my ***intention*** to hurt her. 我的评论冒犯了她,但我无意伤害她。

WORD	MEANING	TYPICAL USE
pray /preɪ/ *v.* 祈祷	speak to God in worship; offer worship; ask earnestly	There is nothing that we can do now but ***pray*** God helps us in our troubles. 现在除了祈求上帝帮助我们度过难关外，别无他法了。
prey /preɪ/ *n.* 被捕食的动物	an animal that is hunted and eaten by another animal	The lion seized its ***prey*** and ate it. 狮子抓住并吃掉了它的猎物。
principal /ˈprɪnsəpəl/ 1. *adj.* 首要的	1. most important; chief; main	Chicago is the ***principal*** city in the Midwest of the United States. 芝加哥是美国中西部首要的城市。
2. *n.* 中小学校长	2. the head of an elementary or secondary school	The ***principal*** told the teachers to dismiss school during the heavy snow-storm. 校长告诉老师们，暴风雪时学校停课。
principle /ˈprɪnsəpl/ *n.* 基本信条；真谛	a general rule or truth that is a foundation for other truths	This country was founded on the ***principle*** of individual freedom for all. 这个国家以全民自由的原则立国。

WORD	MEANING	TYPICAL USE
stationary /ˈsteɪʃənərɪ/ *adj.* 固定的	in a fixed position; standing still; not moving	The population of France remained ***stationary*** almost for a century. 近一个世纪以来,法国的人口并无多少变化。
stationery /ˈsteɪʃənərɪ/ *n.* 文具	writing materials such as paper, cards, etc.	Herbert bought a notebook at the ***stationery*** store. 赫伯特在文具店买了一本笔记本。

EXERCISE 24.2 从第二部分中选出最恰当的单词,填入空格内:

1. Some girls often ______ at the sight of a mouse.
   (A) faint　　(B) feint
2. Her ______ to help us was good, but she was only in our way.
   (A) intension　　(B) intention
3. The entire congregation bowed their heads to ______ to God.
   (A) pray　　(B) prey
4. Carelessness is a ______ cause of highway accident.
   (A) principal　　(B) principle
5. The man gave his son a box of ______ for Christmas.
   (A) stationary　　(B) stationery

解答　1. A　2. B　3. A　4. A　5. B

第三部分

WORD	MEANING	TYPICAL USE
address /əˈdres, ˈædres/ 1. *n.* 地址	1. the place to which one's mail is directed	Please write your name and ***address*** on this paper. 请在纸上写下你的姓名和地址。
2. *v.* 发表演说	2. make a speech to	The President ***addressed*** the nation on the subject of war and peace. 总统以战争与和平为主题,对全国发表演说。
attribute 1. /ˈætrɪbjuːt/ *n.* 性质	1. a quality belonging to the nature of a person or thing; characteristic	Darkness is an ***attribute*** of night, as brightness is that of day. 黑暗是夜晚的本质,而白昼的本质是光明。
2. /əˈtrɪbjʊ(uː)t/ *v.* 归因	2. believe something to be the result of	We ***attribute*** Edison's success to intelligence and hard work. 我们将爱迪生的成功归因于天分与努力。
committee /kəˈmɪtɪ/ *n.* 1. 委员会	1. a group of people chosen to do a particular job	The teachers appointed a ***committee*** of five members to plan the class picnic. 教师指定由五人组成的委员会计划班级野餐。

WORD	MEANING	TYPICAL USE
2.(法院指定的)监护人或管财人	2. a person entrusted by a court with the care of a person or estate	The court appointed Mr. Lansing as the ***committee*** that would take care of the boy's property. 法院指定兰辛先生做那个男孩的监护人,管理他的财产。
concert /ˈkɒnsət/ 1. *n.* 音乐会	1. a musical performance in which several musicians take part	She likes music very much; she never misses a ***concert***. 她很喜欢音乐,从来不会错过任何一场音乐会。
2. /kənˈsɜːt/ *v.* 协同工作	2. arrange a matter or act by agreement with someone	We ***concerted*** on the most proper methods for speedily executing the manager's instructions. 我们以最好的方式合作,以便迅速地执行经理的指示。
content 1. /ˈkɒntent/ *n.* 内容	1. what is contained in anything; all things inside	I tried but couldn't understand the ***content*** of his speech. 我试着去理解他演讲的内容,但还是不懂。

WORD	MEANING	TYPICAL USE
2. /kən'tent/ *v.* 使满意	2. make a person satisfied or happy; gratify; appease	John ***contented*** himself with two glasses of beer even though he could have had more. 约翰在喝了两杯啤酒之后就满足了，尽管他还可以再喝。

EXERCISE 24.3 选出斜体词的正确音标：

______ 1. Above all, patience is the most important *attribute* of a good teacher.

(A) /'ætrɪbjuːt/ (B) /ə'trɪbjʊ(uː)t/

______ 2. The orchestra gave a *concert* that lasted two hours.

(A) /'kɒnsət/ (B) /kən'sɜːt/

______ 3. Will it *content* you if I let you have the candy tomorrow?

(A) /'kɒntent/ (B) /kən'tent/

解答 1. A 2. A 3. B

第四部分

WORD	MEANING	TYPICAL USE
converse 1. /ˈkɒnvɜːs/ *n.* 相反的事物	1. the opposite of something	"Honest but poor" is the ***converse*** of "poor but honest". "诚实而穷"是"穷而诚实"的反语。
2. /kənˈvɜːs/ *v.* 谈话	2. talk together in an informal way; chat	He ***conversed*** with his wife about the summer vacation. 他和妻子谈有关暑假的事情。
desert 1. /ˈdezət/ *n.* 沙漠	1. a sandy region with very little rain and few trees	The Sahara is a great ***desert*** in the northern part of Africa. 撒哈拉沙漠是位于北非的大沙漠。
2. /dɪˈzɜːt/ *v.* 舍弃	2. go away and leave; abandon	After the family ***deserted*** the farm, its buildings fell to ruin. 在这家人舍弃农场之后,里边的房屋都成了废墟。
digest 1. /ˈdaɪdʒest/ *n.* 摘要	1. a short, condensed account; summary	The publisher decided to publish a ***digest*** of international law. 出版商决定出版一本国际法摘要。

WORD	MEANING	TYPICAL USE
2. /dɪˈdʒest, daɪ-/ *v.* 消化	2. be changed into a form the body can absorb	I like milk very much, but I can't ***digest*** it very well. 我很喜欢喝牛奶，但却消化不好。
instinct 1. /ˈɪnstɪŋkt/ *n.* 本能	1. inborn tendency to act in a certain way	Most animals have an ***instinct*** to protect their young. 保护幼小动物是大部分动物的本能。
2. /ɪnˈstɪŋkt/ *adj.* 充满的	2. charged or filled (with something)	Her face was ***instinct*** with benevolence and kindness. 她的神情充满了仁慈。
intimate 1. /ˈɪntɪmɪt/ *adj.* 亲密的	1. very familiar; known very well; close and familiar	Although the governor knew many people, he had few ***intimate*** friends. 州长虽然认识很多人，却没有几个密友。
2. /ˈɪntɪmeɪt/ *v.* 暗示	2. suggest indirectly; hint; imply	He ***intimated*** that he was dissatisfied with his job. 他暗示他不满意自己的工作。

EXERCISE 24.4 选出斜体词的正确音标：

______ 1. I disagree with your opinion; in fact, I believe the *converse* to be true.

(A) /ˈkɒnvɜːs/　　(B) /kənˈvɜːs/

______2. The government would build dams to harness electrical power and irrigate the *desert*.

(A) /ˈdezət/ (B) /dɪˈzɜːt/

______3. It takes a long time to *digest* heavy food.

(A) /ˈdaɪdʒest/ (B) /dɪˈdʒest/

______4. The very essence of an *instinct* is that it is followed independently of reason.

(A) /ˈɪnstɪŋkt/ (B) /ɪnˈstɪŋkt/

______5. Her smile *intimated* that she was very pleased.

(A) /ˈɪntɪmɪtɪd/ (B) /ˈɪntɪmeɪtɪd/

解答 1. A 2. A 3. B 4. A 5. B

第五部分

WORD	MEANING	TYPICAL USE
minute 1. /ˈmɪnɪt/ *n.* 分	1. one sixtieth of an hour; sixty seconds	The train arrived at exactly four ***minutes*** past eight. 火车刚好8:04到达。
2. /maɪˈnjuːt/ *adj.* 微小的	2. very small in size or degree; tiny; diminutive	There has been a ***minute*** improvement in the working conditions of the factory. 工厂的工作条件已有了微小的改善。

WORD	MEANING	TYPICAL USE
object 1. /ˈɒbdʒɪkt, -dʒekt/ *n.* 物体	1. something that can be seen or felt; thing	A dark ***object*** moved between me and the door. 有一个黑色的物体在我和门之间移动。
2. /əbˈdʒekt/ *v.* 反对	2. give as a reason against something; purpose	Do you ***object*** to my smoking in this room? 你反对我在房间里吸烟吗?
refuse 1. /rɪˈfjuːz/ *v.* 拒绝	1. say no; decline to accept; reject	He asked her to marry him but she ***refused***. 他向她求婚,但她拒绝了。
2. /ˈrefjuːs/ *n.* 垃圾	2. useless stuff; waste; rubbish; trash	The street-cleaning department took away all ***refuse*** from the street. 清洁队收走街上所有的垃圾。
tear 1. /tɪə/ *n.* 泪	1. a drop of salty liquid that flows from the eye during pain or sadness	The little girl was in ***tears*** because she'd lost her mother. 小女孩因失去了母亲而哭了。
2. /tɛə/ *v.* 撕	2. pull apart or into pieces by force	Don't ***tear*** up paper; put it in the waste basket. 不要把纸撕碎,把它丢进垃圾桶吧。
used /juːzd/ *adj.* 1. 用旧了的	not new; secondhand	The janitor removed ***used*** towels from the rack. 工友把旧毛巾从架子上拿开。

WORD	MEANING	TYPICAL USE
2. /juːst/ 习惯于	accustomed; usual	It took long to get ***used*** to foreign food. 要习惯外国的食物需要一段很长的时间。

EXERCISE 24.5 选出斜体词的正确音标：

______ 1. His writing is so *minute* that it's difficult to read.

(A) /ˈmɪnɪt/ (B) /maɪˈnjuːt/

______ 2. The national museum in Seoul is full of interesting *objects*.

(A) /ˈɒbdʒɪkts/ (B) /əbˈdʒekts/

______ 3. She *refused* him when he asked her to marry him.

(A) /rɪˈfjuːzd/ (B) /ˈrefjuːst/

______ 4. Why did you *tear* the cloth when I'd advised you to cut it with scissors?

(A) /tɪə/ (B) /tɛə/

______ 5. John's uncle sells *used* cars at Chongro.

(A) /juːzd/ (B) /juːst/

解答 1. B 2. A 3. A 4. B 5. A

效果检测

EXERCISE 24.6 从第二栏中选出第一栏各词的正确词义：

COLUMN I	COLUMN II
______ 1. ascent	(A) a large gun

______ 2. assent (B) a formal meeting

______ 3. cannon (C) handing over to another

______ 4. canon (D) purpose

______ 5. cession (E) agreement

______ 6. session (F) intensity

______ 7. intension (G) a rule or law

______ 8. intention (H) climbing

______ 9. stationary (I) writing materials

______ 10. stationery (J) not moving

解答 1. H 2. E 3. A 4. G 5. C
6. B 7. F 8. D 9. J 10. I

EXERCISE 24.7 读下面的句子,选出句中斜体词所代表的意义:

______ 1. He had a chance to *address* a large audience for the first time in his life.

(A) deliver a speech (B) show his ability

______ 2. A responsible man never *deserts* his wife and family.

(A) forgets (B) abandons

______ 3. He *intimated* a wish to go by saying that it was late.

(A) implied (B) mentioned

______ 4. Mother *objected* that the weather was too bad to play outdoors.

(A) opposed (B) doubted

______ 5. The picture on the wall is *instinct* with life and beauty.

(A) lacking (B) filled

解答 1. A 2. B 3. A 4. A 5. B

EXERCISE 24.8 选出不是斜体词词义的答案：

______ 1. *attribute*

(A) trait (B) lead to

(C) believe to be the result of

______ 2. *content*

(A) fortune (B) gratify

(C) what is contained in anything

______ 3. *converse*

(A) chat (B) the opposite of something

(C) preserve

______ 4. *instinct*

(A) natural tendency (B) charged

(C) extinguished

______ 5. *intimate*

(A) threaten (B) familiar

(C) hint

______ 6. *object*

(A) thing (B) oppose

(C) obligation

______ 7. *refuse*

(A) diffuse (B) reject

(C) waste

______ 8. *used*

(A) not new (B) accustomed

(C) not working

解答 1. B 2. A 3. C 4. C
5. A 6. C 7. A 8. C

EXERCISE 24.9 从下列单词中选出最恰当的词,填入空格内:

VOCABULARY LIST

minutes'	attributed	principles	committee
ascent	address	pray	instinct
feinted	tears	alter	stationary

1. The success of the present project can be ______ to Mr. Johnson.
2. The ______ of Mount Everest requires superhuman strength and endurance.
3. The population of this town has been ______ for ten years at about 12,000 people.
4. If the coat is too large, a tailor can ______ it to fit you.
5. A single regiment ______ on the front of the fortress while the rest of the division prepared to attack from the rear.
6. One of the ______ of this book is that explanations of words should be in simple language.
7. Don't forget to write the return ______ on the parcel.
8. Birds do not learn to build nests but build them by ______.
9. My wife burst into ______ when she heard the bad news.
10. It's only a few ______ walk from here to the station.

解答 1. attributed 2. ascent 3. stationary 4. alter 5. feinted 6. principles 7. address 8. instinct 9. tears 10. minutes'

单词索引

A

B

C

D

E

F

G

H

I

J

K

L

S

T

U

V

W

Z

本书所用国际音标符号对照表

表1. 元音

1	ɪ	bit
2	e	bed
3	æ	cat
4	ə	China
5	ʌ	cut
6	ɒ	dog
7	ʊ	foot
8	iː	meet
9	ɑː	car
10	ɜː	bird
11	ɔː	door
12	uː	food
13	əʊ	boat
14	eɪ	take
15	aɪ	bike
16	ɔɪ	boy
17	aʊ	how
18	ɪə	near
19	ɛə	pair
20	ʊə	poor
21	jʊ	pure
22	juː	useful
23	aɪə	fire
24	aʊə	sour

表2. 辅音

1	p	pen
2	b	bad
3	t	tea
4	d	did
5	k	cat
6	ɡ	game
7	tʃ	chain
8	dʒ	Jane
9	f	fall
10	v	voice
11	θ	thin
12	ð	then
13	s	so
14	z	zoo
15	ʃ	ship
16	ʒ	measure
17	h	how
18	m	man
19	n	no
20	ŋ	long
21	l	leg
22	r	red
23	j	yes
24	w	wet